W9-BDR-135

THE HORNBOOK OF
VIRGINIA HISTORY

Devisal of arms of the Virginia Company of London, from
The Survey of London, 1633, by John Stow

The Hornbook of Virginia History

A Ready-Reference Guide to
the Old Dominion's
People, Places, and Past

FOURTH EDITION

Edited by
Emily J. Salmon and Edward D. C. Campbell, Jr.

The Library of Virginia
Richmond • 1994

Published by authority of The Library Board

Andrew M. Cole, *Chair*
Reston, Virginia

Carol B. Davidson
Manakin-Sabot, Virginia

Tyler C. Millner, *Vice Chair*
Axton, Virginia

Margaret P. Forehand
Chesapeake, Virginia

Patricia Wilson Berger
Alexandria, Virginia

Serafim L. Guerra
Midland, Virginia

Marjorie M. Clark
Richmond, Virginia

Bobbie B. Hudson
Danville, Virginia

Dorothy N. Cowling
Richmond, Virginia

Patricia N. Lawler
Kilmarnock, Virginia

Gwendolyn A. Cumming
Hampton, Virginia

Andrew H. McCutcheon
Richmond, Virginia

Kay A. Cutler
Charlottesville, Virginia

Robbie G. Tate
Norton, Virginia

James B. Walthall
Richmond, Virginia

Library of Congress Cataloging-in-Publication Data

The hornbook of Virginia history : a ready-reference guide to the Old Dominion's people, places, and past / edited by Emily J. Salmon and Edward D.C. Campbell, Jr. — 4th ed.
    p.   cm.
    Includes bibliographical references and index.
    ISBN 0–88490–177–7 (hardback) — ISBN 0–88490–178–5 (paper)
    1. Virginia—History—Handbooks, manuals, etc.
    2. Virginia—Politics—Handbooks, manuals, etc.
    I. Salmon, Emily J. II. Campbell, Edward D. C., 1946–
    III. Library of Virginia.
    F226.H8 1994   94–22784
    975.5—dc20   CIP

Standard Book Numbers: 0–88490–177–7 casebound
                        0–88490–178–5 paperback
©The Library of Virginia 1994.
All rights reserved. Fourth edition 1994. Second impression, July 1995.
The Library of Virginia, Richmond, Virginia.
Printed in the United States of America.

This book is printed on acid-free paper meeting the requirements of the American Standard for Permanence of Paper for Printed Library Materials.

Cover illustration: The church ruins at Jamestown, a nineteenth-century lithograph by F. B. Schell and H. S. Beckwith. (Courtesy of the Association for the Preservation of Virginia Antiquities)

Cover design: Douglas W. Price, Virginia Office of Graphic Communications

CONTENTS

LIST OF ILLUSTRATIONS

All illustrations are from the collections of
The Library of Virginia unless otherwise
credited in captions.

PREFACE

This is the fourth edition of the *Hornbook of Virginia History*. The first edition, published in 1949 by the History Division of the Virginia Department of Conservation and Economic Development, was prepared by J. R. V. Daniel and an advisory committee. The second edition, published in 1965 by the Historical Publications Division of the Virginia State Library, was edited by William H. Gaines, Jr. The third edition, generally a revision of the second, was edited by Emily J. Salmon and published by the State Library in 1983.

This expanded and retitled edition is primarily an update of the third. Statistical data have been brought up to date throughout the text. New information has been added to the chapters on educational institutions, emblems of the commonwealth, and Virginians in the nation's service. The sections covering historic houses, places of worship, and other sites have been expanded substantially to include a wider variety of Virginia's important structures and places. The bibliography of suggested readings on Virginia history has also been revised to reflect current scholarship. New sections have been added on Virginia's lieutenant governors and attorneys general and on state parks, forests, and other protected areas. All text and captions have been edited in accordance with the new guidelines found in the fourteenth edition of the *Chicago Manual of Style*.

The fourth edition has benefited from the advice of many colleagues. Within the Division of Publications and Cultural Affairs, we are especially indebted to Donald W. Gunter, John T. Kneebone, and Brent Tarter for assistance in updating the brief history of Virginia; to Stacy Gibbons Moore for assembling the many illustrations and writing the captions; to Patricia A. Kloke for clerical help; and to division director Sandra Gioia Treadway, who coordinated the overall editorial work and production of the book. Paris Ashton-Bressler and Douglas W. Price, of the Virginia Office of Graphic Communications, ably guided the completed work through the design and final production process. Appreciation is also extended to members of the library's public-service staffs, particularly picture librarian Carolyn S. Parsons, picture assistant Petie Bogen-Garrett, and reference librarians Sarah J. Huggins, William C. Luebke, Catherine T. Mishler, Mary K. Sine, and Phyllis M. Young, as well as Lyndon H. Hart III, of the Archives Processing Section. Also of help were James Christian Hill, Calder Loth, Margaret T. Peters, John S. Salmon, and E. Randolph Turner III, all of the Virginia Department of Historic Resources; Frances S. Pollard, senior librarian of the Virginia Historical Society; Robert G. Waugh, Jr., and Paul W. Wynkoop, of the Department of Conservation and Recreation; and Lorraine Bruehl, Thad Cherry, Carl C. Knuth, and Joseph A. Williams, of the Department of Game and Inland Fisheries.

Finally, we wish to recognize the many patrons of The Library of Virginia whose interests and research inquiries have made each edition a better one.

—Emily J. Salmon
—Edward D. C. Campbell, Jr.

A NOTE ON HORNBOOKS

The hornbook—printed text mounted on a board or tablet and covered with a protective coating of translucent animal horn—was originally devised as an educational tool for children. Since medieval times, these handheld "books," shaped much like paddles, were inscribed with the alphabet, numerals, the Lord's Prayer, or other rudimentary text. Less destructible certainly than paper or even bound volumes, the hornbook was conceived with the realization that "the innocent mischief resulting from damp and grubby paws" ruined many a lesson. The typical hornbook was constructed by laying the printed sheet on a wooden base over which a thin layer of horn was then placed. The three layers were held together with a frame of thin brass strips, or latten, tacked in place. Hornbooks were often leather bound or silver plated, and text could also be engraved directly on ivory, bone, or even stone. In time, a hornbook came to mean an instructional tablet or primer of any kind.

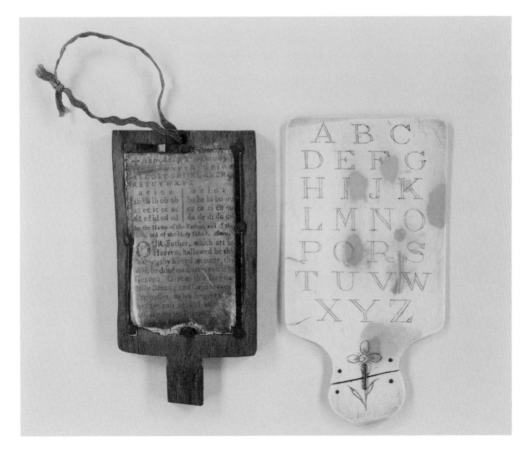

The mid-eighteenth-century English hornbook at left has a covering of isinglass, a gelatinous substance extracted from the glands of sturgeon (and a common cooking ingredient of the period), rather than horn. The one on the right is made of ivory. (*Library of Congress*)

THE HORNBOOK OF
VIRGINIA HISTORY

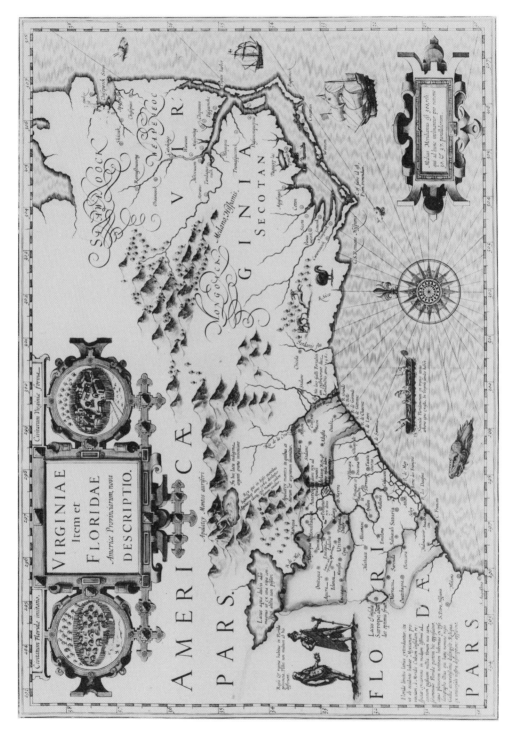

Virginiae Item et Floridae, drawn by Jodocus Hondius, was first published in the 1606 edition of *Mercator's Atlas*, named for geographer Gerhardus Mercator.

A SHORT HISTORY OF VIRGINIA

The Geographic Setting

As England's first permanent colony in North America, Virginia in 1607 claimed the greater part of the present United States and western Canada. With the settlement of Maryland in 1634 Virginia gave up the territory north of the Potomac River, and in 1665 the Crown assigned everything south of Currituck Inlet to the proprietors of Carolina. Throughout the eighteenth century, France and Spain ignored Virginia's claims to the lands west of the Mississippi River. At the end of the American Revolution, the 1783 Treaty of Paris fixed the western boundary of the United States, and of Virginia, at the Mississippi River.

Virginia's five major geographic regions are the tidewater, the piedmont, the Blue Ridge, the Valley of Virginia, and the Allegheny Mountains. The tidewater is Virginia's sandy coastal plain between the Atlantic Ocean and the fall line. This imaginary line runs from north to south and crosses the rivers of eastern Virginia at the points where they cease to be navigable. Their levels affected by tidal flow, the Potomac, Rappahannock, York, and James Rivers divide Virginia's northern tidewater into narrow peninsulas. The peninsula between the Potomac and the Rappahannock Rivers is called the Northern Neck. Today the name is generally applied only to the area comprising Lancaster, Northumberland, Richmond, and Westmoreland Counties, but in the colonial period the Northern Neck included all the land between the Potomac and Rappahannock Rivers from the Chesapeake Bay to their headwaters in the mountains. The Middle Peninsula, or Middle Neck, consists of the land between the Rappahannock and the York Rivers. The land between the York and James Rivers is often simply called the Peninsula. The Eastern Shore, that portion of Virginia and Maryland between the Chesapeake Bay and the Atlantic, is also considered to be part of the tidewater.

Piedmont is the name of the area of rolling hills between the fall line and the Blue Ridge Mountains. The word derives from a region of northern Italy and means "foot of the mountains." West of the piedmont, running from northeast to southwest, the Blue Ridge Mountains form the easternmost range of the Allegheny Mountains. Mount Rogers, the highest peak in Virginia, rises 5,729 feet above sea level in the southern part of this range.

Immediately west of the Blue Ridge lies a series of river valleys known collectively as the Valley of Virginia. The northernmost valley is that of the Shenandoah River, which flows north from Augusta County to its confluence with the Potomac at Harpers Ferry, West Virginia. The James and Roanoke Rivers and their tributaries drain the central portion of the Valley of Virginia, from northern Rockbridge County to Roanoke County. Rivers that flow westward into the Ohio River drain the southernmost part of the Valley of Virginia, southwest of the city of Roanoke: the New River flowing northwestward from North Carolina across Virginia to join the Kanawha in West Virginia, and the Clinch and Holston Rivers flowing southwestward into the drainage system of the Tennessee River. West of the Valley of Virginia, the

Allegheny Mountains, a part of the Appalachian system, lie along the Virginia–West Virginia border and in the extreme southwestern counties of Virginia.

In addition to these five regions, Virginians commonly speak of three other geographic areas for which precise boundaries are not as easily defined. The Southside is that area of tidewater and piedmont located between the James River and the Virginia–North Carolina line and east of the Blue Ridge Mountains. But the designation is often restricted to a smaller area, excluding the tidewater and upland counties, and sometimes also the northern counties of this region. Southwest Virginia is the region west of the Blue Ridge and south of Roanoke. Northern Virginia includes the Virginia cities and counties located within approximately thirty miles of the District of Columbia.

Virginia has a surface area of 40,598 square miles, including 1,000 square miles of inland waters but excluding the 1,728 square miles of coastal water within the commonwealth's jurisdiction. In 1990, the federal government owned 6 percent of the Old Dominion's land area. Ranked thirty-sixth in size among the fifty states, Virginia is bounded by the Atlantic Ocean, Maryland, West Virginia, Kentucky, Tennessee, and North Carolina. Virginia's southern border, from the Atlantic Ocean to Cumberland Gap, is 462 miles long; the distance from the northernmost corner of Frederick County to the North Carolina border is 201 miles. Virginia has 112 miles of Atlantic coastline, 230 miles of coastline on the Chesapeake Bay, and 3,315 miles of tidal shoreline. The state's geographical center, determined by the United States Geological Survey to be 78° 37′ 5″W, 37° 30′ 6″N, is in Buckingham County two miles south and one-half mile west of Mount Rush. Virginia's approximate mean altitude is 950 feet above sea level.

Native Americans and Virginia

Humans made their first marks on the Virginia landscape approximately eleven thousand years ago. The long process of discovery and adaptation in the vast North American continent had begun some forty thousand years earlier when America's first immigrants, ancestors of today's Native Americans, had migrated in periodic waves across the Beringia land bridge from Siberia to Alaska. While their nomadic descendants have often been characterized as hunters of the several larger North American animals that had survived the Ice Age—such as the hairy mammoth, mastodon, and bison—the earliest Indians migrating across stretches east of the Mississippi River tended to hunt smaller game. In what became Virginia, for example, bear, deer, elk, and moose were more common, although fossil remains of mastodon and mammoth have been found in the Saltville area of southwestern Virginia. Scientists, however, are thus far unable to confirm that either giant was habitually hunted by the area's peoples.

As early as about 9500 B.C., family groups of these accomplished hunters began frequenting what was to be Virginia. These early Native Americans established semipermanent base camps at several sites, including Flint Run, or Thunderbird, in Warren County, and the Williamson Site in Dinwiddie County. Indians hunted game near streams and marshes and also quarried jasper (a quartz) at Flint Run and chert in Dinwiddie for making tools and weapons. By 5000 B.C., these ancient people had also begun making axes using quartzite and basalt.

During the subsequent several thousand years, Native Americans found congenial shelter at many locations within the present boundaries of Virginia. Hunting, fish-

A weroan or great Lorde of Virginia (above) and *Their manner of careynge ther Children (below)*, engraved by Théodore de Bry after watercolors by John White and published in Thomas Harriot's sixteenth-century account, *A briefe and true report of the new found land of Virginia.*

The Town of Secota, from Harriot's *Briefe and true report*. The scene is representative of a tidewater Indian village at the time of English settlement.

ing, and foraging peoples moved and settled in families, built campsites on hilltops near streams, and exploited the rich supply of shellfish. By A.D. 900, the aboriginal population had adopted the bow and arrow as its primary hunting weapon in place of the *atlatl*, or spear thrower. Archaeologists have found partial remains of the earlier weapon at sites dating as far back as 6000 B.C. A shaft hooked at one end and weighted with polished stones fastened at midpoint for balance, the *atlatl* was held parallel to the spear and notched to its butt end. When drawn back and then thrown overhand, slinging or whipping the spear, it could double the force and distance of the hunter's otherwise simple weapon.

By the time they had developed the bow and arrow, early Indians had also turned to raising crops near semipermanent villages and begun to make elaborate pottery and ornaments of bone and shell. Long-distance trading along forest paths and rivers became common, with trade routes that extended from the Atlantic coastal areas far inland to the northwest and southwest. The Hopewell Burial Mound people of the Ohio River valley, for example, procured sheet mica from tribes living in the Appalachian Mountains, and for centuries before 1607 tidewater Virginia tribes traded for copper from the Great Lakes.

By the approximate time that Christopher Columbus was exploring the islands of the Caribbean, Indians of coastal Virginia were living in permanent villages and farming the rich tidewater lowlands from the James River north to the Potomac. Speaking an Algonquian language, these Powhatan tribes raised maize, beans, squash, sunflowers, and tobacco as well as gathered the abundant food resources of the tidewater region. By 1607, seasonal hunting, fishing, and foraging had enabled the Powhatans to develop a complex and unified society.

The era of the European incursion and the development of an Indian frontier in Virginia began with intermittent Indian-Spanish contacts in the 1560s. Increasingly interested in *Bahía de Santa María* (the Chesapeake Bay) and *Ajacan* (Virginia), Spain in 1570 attempted to establish a Jesuit mission on the south bank of the York River. Rejecting the priests' proselytizing, the tidewater tribes destroyed the mission in 1571. A year later, Spanish troops from Florida retaliated, killing many Indians and leaving the survivors with the vivid experience of European weaponry. About the same time as these Spanish contacts, Powhatan (or *Wahunsenacawh*) consolidated some thirty Algonquian groups to form a Powhatan chiefdom known as *Tsenacommaco* (Sen-a-kóm-ma-ka), perhaps translated as "densely inhabited land." More than thirteen thousand persons loyal to Powhatan lived in the six-thousand-square-mile chiefdom.

Although the Powhatans held various beliefs concerning the afterlife, the origins of their world, and their multiple gods, one anthropomorphic deity—"okeus," or *kwiokos*—served as the principal spiritual guardian of the chiefdom. Priests, clothed in special garb, maintained numerous temples erected in the deity's honor, as well as communicated with the other gods in behalf of the chiefdom and in time even contributed to councils of war. The chiefdom was also characterized by a male-initiation rite, known as the *huskanaw*, and by the leadership of a supreme chieftain, or *mamanatowick*, and lesser chiefs, or *weroances*. The *weroances* could be male or female (*weroansqua*) and merited considerable respect. They were, for example, the only individuals besides the priests accorded an afterlife. Moreover, male *weroances*, with their wealth, were able to take far more wives than ordinary men. The *mamanatowick* Powhatan eventually had more than one hundred wives. In addition to its bond of loyalty to its various leaders, the Powhatan chiefdom was unified by the threat of both native and

European enemies, by the strength of the Pamunkey tribe (whose tribal lands were near present-day West Point, Virginia), and by the religious beliefs surrounding the deity "okeus." The Powhatans were culturally similar to other Indians of the Atlantic coastal region.

Although early Jamestown colonists such as Captain John Smith and William Strachey recorded many of the basic features of Powhatan life, much less is known today about the several other Virginia Indian groups that Europeans encountered after disease and dislocation had already altered their aboriginal cultures. By 1675, Siouan-speaking tribes in the piedmont—the Saponi, Tutelo, Occaneechi, Monacan, and Manahoac—had abandoned many of their precontact ways. South of the James River, the Iroquoian-speaking Nottoways and Meherrins gave way to European settlers beginning about 1650.

During the two years immediately after Englishmen arrived in 1607, the Pamunkey tribe remained stronger than the newly arrived colonists, but, rather than resort to force, Powhatan at first chose to trade for copper with the English and to court them as allies against his rivals. Hostilities and warfare prevailed, however, between 1609 and 1614. The arrival of expert English military commanders and armor-clad musketeers after 1611 harbingered the decline of the tidewater tribes. Powhatan and the English negotiated a peace in 1614. Four years later, Powhatan died. Since the Powhatan chiefdom functioned as a matrilineal society—with authority passing in order of age not down from the male, but from the female to her sons, then to her daughters, and finally to the sons and then daughters of the eldest daughter—Powhatan was succeeded not by one of his children but by his brother, Opitchapam. An ineffective leader, he was in turn succeeded by his younger and far-more-capable brother, Opechancanough.

On 22 March 1622, Opechancanough attempted to annihilate the much-enlarged and rapidly expanding English population in what is now sometimes referred to as the English-Powhatan War of 1622. More than three hundred colonists—one-sixth of the English population—were killed in a series of well-planned and coordinated morning attacks at settlements from Henrico to the mouth of the James River. The attacks initiated a decade of sustained warfare between the English settlers and Native American tribes from Virginia. A tenuous peace was reestablished in 1632, but on 17 April 1644 Opechancanough once again tried to expel the English from Virginia. In his second, more desperate uprising, five hundred colonists in the more exposed settlements were slain, but the English settlers by then numbered eight thousand, and they soundly defeated Opechancanough's warriors. By 1646, the Powhatan chiefdom had ceased to exist. Its people—by then largely dependent on the English for their survival—lived within small, independent districts or tribes under lesser chiefs. By 1677, they lived primarily on reservation lands.

In 1676 the peace was shattered once again: that time by conflict between settlers in northern Virginia and the Maryland-based Susquehannocks and Doegs. Farther south, dissatisfied with Governor William Berkeley's inability to rid the colony of what they saw as an Indian menace, a newly arrived settler Nathaniel Bacon and his followers departed from the governor's carefully conceived policy and raided Occaneechi and Pamunkey villages in Virginia. A year and a rebellion later, on 29 May 1677, the colonists concluded a peace treaty with the remnants of the Meherrin, Monacan, Nottoway, Pamunkey, Powhatan, and Saponi tribes, all of which avowed allegiance to the queen of the Pamunkey and to the king of England.

Pamunkey chief George M. Cook presenting fresh fowl at the governor's mansion upon the visit of President William Howard Taft, 22 November 1910. The Pamunkey gift of local game to the governor has been an autumn tradition since the seventeenth century.

During the eighteenth and nineteenth centuries distinct tribal identities were increasingly difficult to sustain, as the number of Indians in Virginia declined. Today, some fifteen thousand descendants of five Powhatan tribes (the Chickahominy, Mattaponi, Nansemond, Pamunkey, and Rappahannock) as well as of several other Indian groups reside in Virginia, some of them on the Pamunkey and Mattaponi reservations in King William County. Although the land that became the commonwealth of Virginia was home to numerous Native American tribes, only eight since the early twentieth century have maintained active, formally organized tribal governments recognized by the Virginia General Assembly: the Chickahominy and the Chickahominy Eastern Division, the Mattaponi and Upper Mattaponi, the Monacan, Nansemond, and Pamunkey, and the United Rappahannock. While the Pamunkey, Mattaponi, and Upper Mattaponi live primarily in King William County, the Chickahominy and Chickahominy Eastern Division are in Charles City and New Kent Counties, respectively. The Monacans reside primarily in Amherst County, on or near Bear Mountain; the Nansemonds in Chesapeake, Norfolk, Suffolk, and Virginia Beach; and the United Rappahannock in an area between the Rappahannock and Mattaponi Rivers in Essex, King and Queen, and Caroline Counties.

English Virginians

After several unsuccessful English colonizing efforts at Roanoke Island during the 1580s, King James I in 1606 issued a charter authorizing a group of investors to form the Virginia Company of London and settle colonists in North America. A council appointed by the king was to direct the enterprise from England, with management of day-to-day affairs in the colony entrusted to a second council of settlers. The charter provided that these transplanted Englishmen should enjoy the same legal rights and privileges as those who remained at home. A year later, 104 English colonists aboard the *Susan Constant*, *Godspeed*, and *Discovery* reached the Virginia coast at Cape Henry after an eighteen-week ocean voyage. Sailing west into the river they named for their king, these men and boys stepped ashore on 14 May 1607 at the marshy, malarial peninsula now known as Jamestown. In time "James Cittie" survived and prospered where other colonies, such as Roanoke, had failed, but for several years its triangular fort, built of wooden palisades, remained only a tenuous foothold on the vast continent.

Virginia had been named to honor Elizabeth I, the Virgin Queen, during whose reign from 1558 to 1603 the English had made their first attempts to found colonies in North America. Culminating three decades of English experimentation, the Jamestown settlement was the first to realize the ideas of colonial promoters such as the Reverend Richard Hakluyt. An Elizabethan cleric and historian, Hakluyt epitomized the varied motives—piety and profit, Christianity and capitalism—that appealed to Englishmen of all backgrounds and that characterized Virginia's early history. The English hoped that Virginia could be a bulwark against Spanish expansion in America, a base for missionary activities among Indian peoples, and a source of gold, silver, and raw materials that England could not produce.

From 1607 to 1609 Jamestown was a struggling outpost with erratic direction and support from the Virginia Company of London. The first summer was disastrous. The marshy peninsula, surrounded by brackish water and infested with malaria-carrying mosquitoes, was safe from attack but unhealthy. Virginia's hot and humid summers dangerously enervated colonists accustomed to England's cooler climate. More than half those who landed in May died before the summer was over, and the contagion of gold fever blinded the colonists to the food resources of Virginia's lands and waters. Only one Englishman, the indomitable and knowledgeable Captain John Smith, possessed the insights of a leader. As both an adopted Powhatan Indian and president of the colony's Council, Smith provided the crucial link between the colonists' hunger and the Indians' corn, while also putting the colonists to work by enforcing his rule that "he that will not worke, shall not eate." When Smith departed the colony in October 1609, however, Virginia again became a battleground of factions.

By then, Englishmen in London had recognized that Virginia's vast promise was worth fighting for. In 1609 the directors of the Virginia Company of London had obtained from James I a new charter that provided for a military governor with absolute authority to manage the company's affairs in America more efficiently. The original grant of 1606 had given the company control of a small rectangular area extending fifty miles north and south of the point of settlement and running one hundred miles inland, but under the company's second charter, Virginia stretched for two hundred miles north and south of Point Comfort and for an indefinite distance inland. The new boundaries, in short, enclosed a large part of the area destined to become the United States.

The church ruins at Jamestown, a nineteenth-century lithograph by F. B. Schell and H. S. Beckwith *(Courtesy of the Association for the Preservation of Virginia Antiquities)*

Encouraged by the company's changes, English investors financed larger expeditions. Inspired by dreams of Indian conversions to Anglicanism and of rich returns on their investments, and prodded by company propaganda and salesmanship, English men and women from all walks of life pledged some £40,000 to the company in 1609–1610 alone. With these funds the Virginia Company dispatched Lieutenant Governor Thomas Gates and a shipload of additional colonists, who arrived in May 1610. At Jamestown, Gates met with horror the sixty-five colonists who had survived the desperate winter "Starving Time" of 1609–1610. Famine, disease, and Powhatan attacks had created an atmosphere of hopelessness much in contrast to the optimism of the London investors. On 10 June, Gates and the colonists abandoned the fort at Jamestown. They were sailing down the James en route to Newfoundland when the timely arrival of Governor Thomas West, baron De La Warr, with another shipload of colonists and needed supplies prevented Virginia from becoming a second lost colony.

Between 1610 and 1614 De La Warr and his subordinates, Gates and Sir Thomas Dale, military veterans of the English garrisons in the Low Countries, enforced martial law, stabilized Jamestown's government, waged war against the Powhatans, and instituted a new land policy. The colonists had been working company-owned land in common and drawing their rations from the company store, but Dale began to assign settlers small plots of ground on which they could grow crops for their own profit. Sprawling new settlements pushed many of the Indians west along the river toward Henrico, at the falls of the James River.

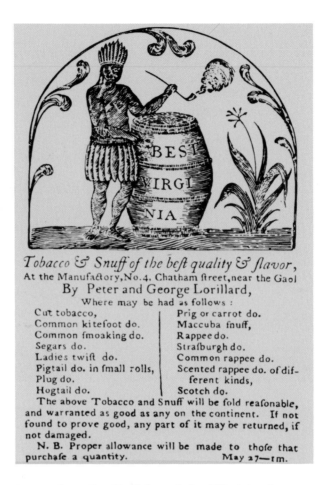

Among the earliest English symbols of Virginia tobacco
were the Indian, usually resplendent in headdress and
smoking a pipe, and the hogshead.

The turning point of Virginia's early history came in 1614. In that year of momentous events, one of the recurring Indian wars ended. Powhatan's daughter Pocahontas accepted Christianity, was baptized Lady Rebecca, and married colonist John Rolfe. That same year, as the result of his experiments with the West Indian plant *Nicotiana tabacum*, Rolfe shipped Virginia's first marketable tobacco to England. Reflecting the newfound optimism of the colonists, Deputy Governor Dale wrote that Virginia offered "enough to content them" whether they sought "God, or Mammon."

Between 1614 and 1622 the population of the colony grew rapidly. Virginia tobacco's popularity in England increased, and the company gave its colonists title to land that had been worked communally. Company efforts to get the colonists to produce commodities such as glass, iron, and silk failed, but Virginians eagerly devoted their labor to growing tobacco. In 1616 the colony exported twenty-three hundred pounds of tobacco to England; by 1618 the quantity had increased twentyfold. Land by then had real value, and the company subdivided James River frontage among its stockholders and issued charters for several dozen "particular plantations," large settlements that became prototypes for subsequent, self-sufficient tobacco plantations. Labor, the commodity most in demand between 1614 and 1622, was supplied by thousands of people who came to the colony as servants indentured to work for seven years to repay the cost of their passages. Tobacco made Jamestown a boomtown. The glint of unlimited wealth from tobacco production captured English imaginations on both sides of the Atlantic, and many also hoped for more successful missionary efforts in light of Pocahontas's conversion and marriage. In 1616, Pocahontas sailed for England, where early the next year she was presented to James I and Queen Anne. Unfortunately, just before returning to Virginia, she died and was buried in England. She was just twenty-two years of age.

The military regime in Virginia ended after the Virginia Company of London adopted reform measures embodied in the so-called Great Charter of 1618. Unable to show its investors a cash profit, the company gave one hundred acres to each settler with seven years' residence in Virginia and one hundred acres per share to the English investors who held company stock. The company also offered rights to fifty acres of land to any person who traveled to Virginia at his own expense or who paid another person's passage. This "headright" system, the foundation of the colony's land policy for the rest of the century, promoted immigration and settlement. By the Great Charter of 1618 the Virginia Company also authorized the popular election of representatives from eleven different areas of settlement to meet with Governor George Yeardley and the Council and suggest solutions for the problems of Virginia's rapidly developing society. The General Assembly of 1619, the first representative legislative body in the New World, met in the church at Jamestown from 30 July to 4 August.

That same summer a Dutch man-of-war landed at Point Comfort, downstream from Jamestown, carrying "20. and odd Negroes." Although the first persons of African descent recorded in Virginia were "bought" by Governor Yeardley and merchant Abraham Peirsey, it remains uncertain whether they were enslaved or held in a status akin to that of indentured servants, workers bound for a fixed term of service, usually in exchange for ship's passage and maintenance. Virginians at that time did not consistently distinguish between "buying" a person's services or "buying" the person outright. None of the Africans, of course, arrived with the papers of indenture that white servants usually brought, a situation that left them vulnerable to exploitation. Nonetheless, there were by the 1650s a number of free people of color in the colony, and there were no specific references to slavery in Virginia's laws until long after 1619. After 1660, however, landowners passed numerous laws to control the labor needed to work the colony, whether through temporary indentured servitude or permanent bondage. The institution of chattel racial slavery thus emerged gradually during the seventeenth century. Finally, in 1705, the General Assembly consolidated previous legislation to produce a systematic "slave code," the culmination of events that could hardly have been anticipated in 1619.

Early in 1620, the Virginia Company of London sent ninety unmarried Englishwomen to the colony, and the next year solicited private subscriptions to transport another fifty-seven single girls and widows. Their presence enabled the formation of families, while their culinary, sewing, and domestic-manufacturing skills improved the quality of life for those male settlers fortunate enough to find a mate among the new arrivals. In ensuing years, women increasingly crossed the Atlantic with their fathers and husbands, or followed soon after, though many more female immigrants in the first half of the seventeenth century came as indentured servants.

Pocahontas, oil portrait, 1891, by William Ludwell Sheppard.
Sheppard based his likeness on an earlier painting copied from a
engraving published in London before Pocahontas's death in 1617.

Whether bound out or free, each found that hard work was the norm for all but the
very elite, yet the colonists' New World offered women greater economic mobility and
slightly more freedom from the constraints of patriarchal society than would have
been possible in England at the time.

Although James I and many Englishmen thought tobacco was foul, unhealthy,
and immoral, within only six years the "sotweed" had transformed the Virginia
colony and given it a future. A 1620 pamphlet declared that "the Colony beginneth
now to have the face and fashion of an orderly State, and such as is likely to grow and
prosper." In recognition of the colony's development, the Virginia Company also started
a college at Henrico for the education of Indians and young colonists.

The expanding Christian colony was a threat to Powhatan culture.
Opechancanough's 1622 coordinated attack on the English settlements left more than
three hundred English settlers, one-sixth of Virginia's total white population, dead in
their fields or houses. According to colonist William Capps the attack "burst the
heart" of the survivors, hundreds of whom died in the following year from famine or
disease. A warning by a friendly Indian named Chanco saved Jamestown itself, but
once-thriving outlying plantations were destroyed. As many as four thousand
colonists perished between 1618 and 1623, and, in retrospect, it is obvious that immigration and settlement had proceeded too haphazardly in Virginia.

The Royal Colony

The colony's high mortality and the company's seeming mismanagement shocked
royal officials in London. On 24 May 1624 the Crown revoked the charter of the bank-

rupt and repeatedly discredited Virginia Company of London. Almost seventeen years to the day after the landing at Jamestown, Virginia became England's first royal colony.

King James died in 1625, and during the next decade his successor, Charles I, gave the colony little attention or support. Sir Francis Wyatt, the last company-appointed governor, continued in office as the royal governor until May 1626 and was succeeded by former governor Sir George Yeardley. They and their councillors dominated Virginia's government, economy, and society during the crisis-plagued 1620s, achieving stability and promoting growth by skillful management of land, labor, trade, and the militia. Even in wartime, the lure of wealth and status drew poor and rich alike, and Virginia's tobacco exports continued to increase.

By 1635, however, the leading members of the Council had tired of Governor Sir John Harvey's unwillingness to share political control and so thrust him from office. Thereafter, influential planters cooperated only with those royal officials who respected their political power, joined them in seeking high prices for tobacco, protected their landed estates, and defended their rights as Englishmen. Continued immigration swelled the population to more than ten thousand by 1640 and to approximately nineteen thousand by 1653, while territorial expansion necessitated the creation in 1634 of eight county governments. During the first quarter of the seventeenth century, English immigrants had demonstrated that they could succeed as well as survive in Virginia.

During the middle third of the seventeenth century, Virginians developed the basic form of government that they maintained until the American Revolution. At the top of the pyramid was the governor, who was appointed by the king. Sharing his

Official seals of the Virginia Company of London

A mid-eighteenth-century copperplate engraving, from one of the "Bodleian plates" discovered at Oxford University, illustrates the Williamsburg Capitol *(middle left)*, the Wren Building *(top center)*, and the Governor's Palace *(middle right)*. It represents the only detailed architectural drawings of each of the original buildings. *(Colonial Williamsburg Foundation)*

executive authority was the Council, composed of about a dozen prominent colonial planters appointed by Crown authority. The councillors also constituted colonial Virginia's highest judicial body, the General Court, and after 1643 the upper house of the General Assembly. Below the councillors were the burgesses, members of the General Assembly elected to represent the counties (and before 1660 the Anglican parishes as well) in the General Assembly. In 1643, when the burgesses began to meet separately from the councillors, the House of Burgesses began its slow growth toward mid-eighteenth-century political prominence.

Local Government

Towns, boroughs, or cities were rare in colonial Virginia. After the formation of Virginia's first eight shires in 1634, county courts served as the units of government immediate to the inhabitants of tidewater and piedmont farms and plantations. In each county, the justices of the peace who comprised the court met, usually once a month, to issue marriage licenses, settle estates, plan for roads or ferries, and try civil and criminal cases. Three other important county officials were the sheriff, whose duties included collecting the county levy, making arrests, serving summonses of the court, and enforcing laws; the clerk, who kept the county's legal records; and the county lieutenant, who commanded the militia. All of these officials held office by virtue of the royal governor's appointment.

The established, or official, church of the colony was the Church of England. In the absence of a resident bishop, the local units of ecclesiastical government, parishes and their vestries, dominated early Virginia's religious affairs more than was the case in England. Control of each parish rested in the hands of the vestry, a committee of laymen who administered the financial affairs of the local church and elected the minister. The vestries, like the county courts, were the domains of prominent local landholders, who after 1757 had exclusive power to appoint members to fill vacancies. Virginia's vestries and county courts were the first training grounds for the statesmen who came to prominence as members of the House of Burgesses and Council.

The Tobacco Economy

Despite disease and death, continued immigration rapidly increased Virginia's population from a total of about ten thousand people in 1640 to twenty-seven thousand in 1660 and forty-three thousand in 1680. Men outnumbered women in seventeenth-century Virginia, but women tended to live longer than men. Many of these

Virginia paper money with tobacco-leaf motif, printed in 1778 by Hall and Sellers of Philadelphia *(The Historical Society of Pennsylvania)*

A Tobacco Plantation, from *Tobacco: Its History and Associations* (1859). The cultivation of tobacco, Virginia's first successful economic base, quickly became dependent upon a large labor force of African slaves.

inhabitants were young men who worked their own small tracts of land. A large minority were indentured servants, most of whom acquired land after their periods of servitude ended. Some, such as Adam Thoroughgood, of Princess Anne County, achieved high offices in the colony. African Americans, many of them employed as indentured servants, constituted about 5 percent of Virginia's population in 1671, but a significant number of black Virginians, such as Anthony Johnson, of Northampton County, were successful farmers. Scholars remain uncertain about the precise origins of chattel slavery in Virginia, but not until 1705, when Virginia's first slave codes hardened race into caste, was slavery forced on generations of black Virginians.

Throughout the colonial period the Virginia Company of London, the Crown, and several royal governors tried to diversify Virginia's economy, but tobacco dominated Chesapeake agriculture. Readily available land, the demand for tobacco in England and Europe, and the profit for its producers kept the colony dependent on this one crop. Tobacco even served as Virginia's principal currency. Virginians used tobacco to purchase imported goods from England, to pay local tithes and taxes, and to acquire land and labor with which to grow more of it.

The middle third of the seventeenth century was a time of population growth and of general prosperity, but it had its moments of crisis. In 1644, Opechancanough, feeble but still implacably resistant to the English colonists' incursions, led what remained of the Powhatan chiefdom in a last desperate effort. Under the personal command of the new governor, Sir William Berkeley, the colonists retaliated decisively, captured the aged Opechancanough (who was treacherously murdered by his jailer), and imposed a treaty in 1646 that brought peace for a generation.

Virginia and the Commonwealth of England

In 1642, the year Sir William Berkeley arrived as governor of Virginia, armies of the Crown and of Parliament began fighting the English Civil War. Parliament's armies won in 1646. Three years later King Charles I was tried and beheaded and England was proclaimed a commonwealth. Governor Berkeley, an ardent royalist, and the General Assembly condemned these "traitorous proceedings" and declared allegiance to the fugitive Prince Charles. The colony was vulnerable to the Commonwealth's navy, and in 1652 Parliament sent a small fleet and three commissioners—two of them, Samuel Mathews and Richard Bennett, prominent Virginians—to secure the surrenders of Virginia and of Maryland to the authority of the "Commonwealth of England as it is now Established, without Kinge or howse of Lords." After hostile maneuvering on both sides, Governor Berkeley and the colonists recognized that sustained resistance was impossible and surrendered without bloodshed. The governor and General Assembly negotiated generous terms of capitulation: Berkeley retired to his plantation at Green Spring, royalists retained their property, the legal code remained in force with references to royal authority deleted, and use of the Anglican prayer book was permitted. Lacking any instructions from the Commonwealth of England, the General Assembly met in April and May 1652, continued Virginia's existing form of government, and elected Richard Bennett as governor. Virginians who had supported Parliament's commercial and religious policies, such as Governor Bennett, Secretary William Claiborne, and the colony's agent in England, Samuel Mathews Sr., held most of the colony's high offices during the Interregnum. During the 1640s Sir William Berkeley and the General Assembly had kept Virginia's tobacco trade open to Dutch merchants, but the submission of Virginia and Maryland to Parliament also brought the Chesapeake tobacco trade under the terms of the Navigation Act of 1651, which required that colonial produce be shipped to England in English ships.

Early in 1660, uncertain about affairs in England after the death of Lord Protector Oliver Cromwell and the abdication of his son and successor, Richard, and faced with the recent death of Governor Samuel Mathews Jr., the General Assembly asked Sir William Berkeley to resume the governorship. In March, after careful negotiations, Berkeley agreed to serve as governor "until such a command and commission come out of England as shall be by the Assembly adjudged lawfull." News of the restoration of Charles II in May 1660 reached Virginia by the autumn. Governor Berkeley received a new commission from the king, and when the General Assembly met the following October it affirmed the Restoration by putting references to the Crown back into the colony's legal code.

According to tradition, Charles II, touched by the colony's loyalty during his exile, gave Virginia the nickname "The Old Dominion." It is more likely, however, that the name refers to Virginia's status as England's oldest colony in America, and that it derives from Charles II's acknowledgment of a gift of silk from "our auntient Collonie of Virginia" in 1660. The phrase "most Ancient Colloney and Dominion" was used in official documents as early as 1699.

The renewal of Stuart government brought few benefits to Virginia. Charles II embraced the Commonwealth's mercantilist policy, and with the Navigation Act of 1660 restrictions on colonial commerce were continued. During the 1660s Governor Berkeley unsuccessfully attempted to reopen the tobacco trade with the Dutch merchants and to diversify Virginia's agriculture. Declining tobacco prices reached the bottom of a depression in 1666, recovered during the mid-1670s, and then slid again to a depressed level from 1680 to 1713. When the General Assembly passed laws to limit tobacco production, the Crown disallowed them.

Sir William Berkeley, portrait attributed to Sir Peter Lely *(Courtesy of the Virginia Historical Society, Richmond, Virginia)*

Explorations into the Interior

By the terms of the 1646 treaty ending Opechancanough's 1644 war against the English, Virginia's Indians relinquished their lands stretching south from the falls of the James River to Cape Henry. Just the year before, the General Assembly had ordered the construction of four forts along the fall line: Fort Royal on the Pamunkey, Fort James on the Chickahominy, Fort Charles on the James, and Fort Henry on the Appomattox River. With the prospects of war reduced, the string of frontier defense posts instead became the bases from which the colonists ventured into the unknown lands beyond. Having no idea of the continent's size, many believed that perhaps the narrow chain of mountains to the west might mark a midpoint, with the South Seas just beyond.

Fort Henry, built on the site of present-day Petersburg, was for thirty years the residence of Captain Abraham Wood, one of seventeenth-century Virginia's principal explorers and traders. Wood organized or accompanied several expeditions into the interior. On one, in 1650, Wood and Edward Bland led a small company from Fort Henry along the Blackwater River and south as far as present-day Weldon, North Carolina. Bland's descriptive journal of the expedition, *The Discovery of New Brittaine*, was published in London in 1651.

John Lederer, a German physician, undertook three expeditions to find a pass through the mountains to the East India Sea. On his second, in 1670, Lederer accompanied twenty-one Henrico County militiamen commanded by Major William Harris as far as present-day Buckingham County. From there, Lederer and a guide continued southward into North Carolina as far as the Cape Fear River. Later that same year, Lederer led an expedition of ten Englishmen and five Indians along the Rappahannock River, then west until they reached the "Apalataean-mountains," but again failed to find a pass through the Blue Ridge.

The first recorded discovery of the trans-Allegheny region was made the next year by Thomas Batte and Robert Hallom. By September 1671, the expedition, sent by Abraham Wood, had reached an area north of present-day Rocky Mount; the next day an Indian guide led the party through the Blue Ridge Mountains, probably at Adney Gap. After following the New River, the explorers crossed the Allegheny range at East River Mountain near present-day Narrows, Virginia, and descended into the Ohio River basin.

It was a dramatic moment in the history of the Virginia frontier. Near the present-day town of Matewan, on the West Virginia–Kentucky line, the Englishmen branded a tree with Governor Berkeley's initials and claimed the region for Charles II. Only three months before, at Sault Sainte Marie, between Lakes Huron and Superior, a party of French and Indians erected a wooden cross, thus establishing a rival claim to the vast region known as the Ohio Country.

In 1673, Abraham Wood commissioned yet another expedition, led by James Needham and Gabriel Arthur, charged with finding the still elusive South Seas. Their initial attempt made little progress, but a second foray reached as far as present-day Rome, Georgia. Needham journeyed back to Fort Henry for supplies, but died on the return trek. Arthur continued on and accompanied Indian raiding parties into West Florida, South Carolina, and then north as far as the Ohio River before returning to Virginia in 1674.

These disparate explorations gathered valuable information for future traders and settlers, providing accurate descriptions of the southwestern piedmont and irrefutable evidence that the continent was far more vast than previously imagined. And, despite France's claims, by 1700 English fur traders would reach the Ohio River valley, with settlers soon to follow. In the contest with France, England's—and Virginia's—claims to the Ohio Country would ultimately be decided by the French and Indian War.

Bacon's Rebellion and Its Aftermath

Bacon's Rebellion of 1676 erupted after a long period of unsettled politics, economic hardship, and a number of frightening incidents. On the Potomac River frontier in July 1675 a dispute arose between trader Thomas Mathew and a group of Doeg Indians who lived on the Maryland side of the river. Charging Mathew had cheated them in trade, the Doegs raided his plantation and stole some hogs. Mathew and a party of colonists gave chase and killed several Indians. The Doegs retaliated by killing Mathew's herdsman, and the situation deteriorated rapidly. Ignoring Governor Berkeley's demand for "a full and thorough inquisition" into the true causes of the several murders, the county militia officers broadened the conflict with a series of raids in which members and chieftains of the previously uninvolved Susquehannock tribe were killed. As news of King Philip's War reached the colony from New England, unreasoning fear swept Virginia's frontier settlements. By late spring 1676, Governor Berkeley's long-successful policy of protecting Virginia's peaceful, tributary Indian tribes had been broken by angry men for whom one Indian was as fair a target as the next.

The angry settlers found their leader in Nathaniel Bacon, a well-connected Henrico County planter who had come from England only two years before but who had already been appointed to a seat on the Council. In September 1675, while conflict had raged near the Potomac, Bacon had seized some friendly Appomattox Indians in a dispute over ownership of some corn, and Berkeley had rebuked him for this "rash heady action." Impatient with Berkeley, Bacon raised a troop of volunteers and requested a commission from the governor to lead his followers against the Indians. When Berkeley refused to endorse vigilante action, Bacon defiantly led his seventy men into battle. With the aid of the friendly Occaneechi Indians, Bacon routed a band of Susquehannocks near the Roanoke River. Then, becoming suspicious of his allies, he attacked and defeated them as well. Berkeley, meanwhile, in May 1676 proclaimed Bacon and his men to be in rebellion and arrested him when he returned to Jamestown in June. Thus began a series of charges and countercharges, attacks and counterattacks, that ended with the colony in civil strife and Bacon in open rebellion against the government.

By September 1676 the rebels had driven Berkeley and his followers across the Chesapeake to the Eastern Shore and Bacon's men had burned Jamestown. But when Bacon died of a fever in October, the revolt collapsed. By the end of the year Sir William Berkeley, now aged and embittered, had regained control of Virginia and begun to exact vengeance against those who had supported Bacon. A royal regiment—whose requirements of food, lodging, and salary caused problems for the colonial government—had arrived in Virginia too late to assist Berkeley.

Bacon's Rebellion interrupted the tobacco trade, severely reduced Charles II's customs revenue, and gave added weight to the designs of James, duke of York, for consolidating imperial control over the American colonies. Charles II sent a three-man commission to investigate the rebellion and a lieutenant governor to replace Berkeley.

After thirty-five years of loyal and generally effective service to the Crown and its Virginia subjects, Berkeley was recalled to England, where he died in July 1677. The Crown tightened its control over the American colonies, sending Virginia a succession of firm-handed governors who challenged the accumulated powers of the General Assembly. Further Stuart designs on Virginia's political institutions ended in 1688 when England's Glorious Revolution sent James II into exile and brought the Protestant Mary and her Dutch husband, William of Orange, to the throne.

In the decade of the 1690s the prosperous province of fifty-three thousand persons experienced three new beginnings. First, at Whitehall, near London, administration of England's colonial empire was placed in the hands of the new Commissioners of Trade and Plantations, or Board of Trade. Second, after fire destroyed the colony's third Jamestown statehouse on 21 October 1698, the decision was made to move the capital from its unhealthy island five miles inland to Middle Plantation, which was then renamed Williamsburg. And third, several years earlier, inspired by the bishop of London's representative, Commissary James Blair, Virginians raised more than £2,000 toward the establishment of a college, and English friends contributed even more. In 1693 the king and queen issued a royal charter to the College of William and Mary, making it the second institution of higher learning in British North America, Harvard having been founded in 1636. By 1700 the college's central hall (known today as the Wren Building) stood at Williamsburg.

Nathaniel Bacon and his Followers, by Howard Pyle, from *Harper's Monthly Magazine*, March 1901

Virginia's Second Century

The first half of the eighteenth century was a period of rapid increase in population. The number of Virginians quadrupled during the period, rising from about fifty-eight thousand in 1700 to more than two hundred thirty thousand at midcentury. Expanded tobacco production and the increasing reliance on enslaved, rather than indentured, laborers brought a dramatic increase in the proportion of blacks in Virginia's population during the eighteenth century. The new century also witnessed the expansion of settlement beyond the fall line into the rolling hills of the piedmont. Towns sprang up near the falls of Virginia's major rivers: Alexandria on the Potomac, Fredericksburg on the Rappahannock, Richmond on the James, and Petersburg on the Appomattox. Throughout the eighteenth century Virginia's westward movement had strategic importance in the imperial rivalry between Great Britain and France.

Alexander Spotswood and the Knights of the Golden Horseshoe
exploring territories west of the Blue Ridge in 1716

Immigration, soil depletion in many parts of the tidewater, land speculation, and the leadership of far-sighted governors like Alexander Spotswood promoted back-country growth. As settlement edged toward the Blue Ridge Mountains, the formation of new counties beyond the fall line extended tidewater institutions into the west. The piedmont frontier was developed less by poor farmers in search of opportunity than by the colony's leading families, such as the Randolphs, Carters, Pages, and Nicholases, who acquired the best acreage along the rivers. The piedmont became an area of immense tobacco estates, some as large as thirteen thousand acres. Much of the colony's land was granted in huge parcels to speculators, such as Robert ("King") Carter, William Byrd II, and William Beverley, but non-Virginians, such as Jacob Stover, of Pennsylvania, and Benjamin Borden, of New Jersey, acquired extensive landholdings in the Valley of Virginia, that fertile region between the Blue Ridge and the Alleghenies explored in 1716 by Governor Alexander Spotswood and his Knights of the Golden Horseshoe. One such speculator was James Patton, an Irish sea captain who, after numerous Atlantic crossings ferrying immigrants to Virginia, became an agent for William Beverley. Patton eventually acquired his own land grants on the James, Roanoke, New, and Holston Rivers, selling the tracts to settlers traveling through the Valley.

By midcentury, settlement in the Valley extended southward as far as the Roanoke area, which fast became a departure point toward the lands farther west. Although the Blue Ridge Mountains hindered emigration from eastern Virginia, southward travel from Pennsylvania was easy. German and Scotch-Irish settlers who moved south along the Great Wagon Road to grow wheat and other grains as their principal crops made the Virginia and North Carolina backcountry a land of small farms. During these same years, prominent Virginians were forming syndicates, such as the Ohio Company and the Loyal Company, to acquire extensive tracts of unexplored lands beyond the Alleghenies. These companies planned to hold their western lands until the region was opened to settlement and then sell small parcels to actual pioneers.

The Great War for the Empire

Along the waterway formed by the Saint Lawrence River, the Great Lakes, and the Mississippi River west and north of Britain's seaboard colonies sprawled the fur-trad-ing empire of New France. During the first half of the eighteenth-century the French extended their trade and their country's colonial claims into the Ohio River valley, an area that the British had claimed since 1609 by virtue of the First Charter of the Virginia Company of London. In 1754 Lieutenant Governor Robert Dinwiddie of Virginia sent George Washington and a small force of militiamen into the disputed ter-ritory. Strategic Fort Duquesne, which the French were building at the forks of the Ohio River, was Washington's objective, but the French repulsed Washington's militia-men. The British government then sent to America a force of regulars under Major General Edward Braddock. In May 1755 Braddock's army, augmented by colonial militiamen, marched west from the Potomac to assault Fort Duquesne again. On the morning of 9 July the French and their Indian allies attacked Braddock's command. Unprepared for their opponents' guerrilla tactics, the red-coated British fought in regi-mented battle order, suffered a disastrous defeat, and retreated in confusion. Braddock was mortally wounded. Washington, a member of his staff, escaped unhurt. After this catastrophe, residents on the Virginia frontier lived in constant fear of attack by Indians friendly to the French.

George Washington raising the British flag at Fort Duquesne

British fortunes ebbed during the next three years of the French and Indian War (the name given to the North American operations of the Seven Years' War). Then, in 1758, William Pitt formed a vigorous British administration and sent new armies to America. The army commanded by Brigadier General James Forbes, together with a force of militia under Washington, occupied Fort Duquesne on 25 November 1758. Virginia, whose titular governor, John Campbell, earl of Loudoun, commanded all British forces in North America, was now relatively safe from Indian attack. Quebec surrendered to General James Wolfe on 18 September 1759, and Admiral George Rodney conquered the French West Indies in 1762. By a treaty signed in 1762, France gave its ally, Spain, its territories west of the Mississippi, and by the Treaty of Paris, which ended the Great War for the Empire on 10 February 1763, France ceded to Great Britain all claims to Acadia, Canada, Cape Breton, and its territories east of the Mississippi.

Victory ended foreign challenges to Virginia's western claims, but the colonists were disappointed in their expectations of occupying the territory beyond the Alleghenies. Hoping to prevent clashes between settlers and Indians, the British government issued a proclamation in 1763 forbidding settlement west of the mountains. This action aroused great resentment in Virginia and in other colonies claiming western lands. In spite of the proclamation, Virginians began to cross the Alleghenies and settle along the Ohio in the area that became known as Kentucky. Unwittingly, the Crown had raised one of the divisive issues that started the colonists on the road to independence.

Independence

In 1763, at end of the Great War for the Empire, Britain had an unprecedented public debt. To pay it, Parliament imposed heavy taxes on the residents of Great Britain and tightened the administration of the trade and navigation acts. Colonial merchants, accustomed to lax enforcement and evasion of some duties, disliked the strict new customs regulations. In 1764 Parliament also decided to impose direct taxes upon the colonists with "certain Stamp Duties" that would be implemented in 1765. The Stamp Act established a system of excise taxes on numerous types of printed matter—affecting the price of broadsides, newspapers, most types of legal documents, even playing cards.

Virginians in the House of Burgesses objected that while Parliament had a constitutional right to legislate for the regulation of trade, it could not levy taxes for the express purpose of raising revenue; only the elected representatives of the colonists, in their colonial legislatures, could tax the people of England's American colonies. On 29 May 1765 the burgesses adopted strong resolutions of protest sponsored by Patrick Henry, a new member of the House who had earned a reputation as a powerful orator by defending the assembly's legislative power in the celebrated Parsons' Cause in 1763. Henry's resolutions put Virginia in the forefront of colonial resistance to Parliament, and they were endorsed by the legislatures of several other colonies.

In response to pressure from British and American merchants, Parliament repealed the Stamp Act in 1766 but at the same time imposed duties on certain imported articles and passed the Declaratory Act, which affirmed its presumed right to legislate over the colonies "in all cases whatsoever." The dispute simmered until December 1773, when patriots threw a cargo of British East India Company tea into Boston harbor rather than allow collection of the tax. Parliament responded with legislation designed to punish the city of Boston and coerce the colonies into obedience, but these Intolerable Acts only stiffened colonial resolve. Virginia again led the protests. In May 1774, the House of Burgesses ordered a day of fasting, humiliation, and prayer and adopted resolutions denouncing the coercive acts of Parliament. Governor John Murray, earl of Dunmore, promptly dissolved the assembly. As they had done before, the former burgesses left the Capitol and reconvened as private citizens in Williamsburg's largest available room, at the Raleigh Tavern. There they called upon the other colonies to send deputies to a congress in Philadelphia that September for the purpose of coordinating colonial policy.

When the First Continental Congress met, Peyton Randolph, Speaker of the Virginia House of Burgesses, was elected its president. The other members from Virginia were Richard Bland, Patrick Henry, Richard Henry Lee, Edmund Pendleton, George Washington, and Benjamin Harrison of Berkeley. Congress adopted a nonimportation association modeled on one developed by the Virginia Convention of 1774, in hopes that economic pressure on British merchants might inspire Parliament to soften its policies. By the next spring it was clear that the association had not worked. Parliament had given no evidence of retreat. In March 1775 Virginia's second revolutionary convention met in Richmond at Henrico Parish Church (renamed Saint John's fifty years later). Patrick Henry offered a resolution that the colony be put into a posture of defense. "Gentlemen may cry 'Peace! Peace!' but there is no peace," he thundered. "The war is actually begun!" Henry predicted that the next news from the north would bring word of clashing arms, and in fact British troops and

Massachusetts militiamen did begin the war near Lexington and Concord on 19 April 1775. That same month Governor Dunmore removed the public gunpowder from the magazine in Williamsburg lest it fall into patriot hands, an act that seemed to confirm fears that the British planned to subdue the colonies by force.

The time for resistance had come. "Give me liberty, or give me death" became the watchword of Virginia patriots. Meeting continuously in Philadelphia throughout 1775, Congress by December had moved inexorably toward independence from Great Britain. Governor Dunmore had fled Williamsburg with a small force and established military headquarters near Norfolk. Virginia's second and third revolutionary conventions had met, and the latter had created the Committee of Safety, with Edmund Pendleton as its president, to act as an executive body between conventions. Governor Dunmore nevertheless refused to abandon Virginia and throughout the summer of 1775 planned a pincerlike, coordinated attack along the colony's western and northern reaches in order to separate the Old Dominion from the northern colonies and force an early surrender. The capture of Dunmore's agent—charged with the initial planning for raising an army of Indian allies and loyalists—foiled that portion of the governor's plan.

John Murray, fourth earl of Dunmore (1732–1809), oil on canvas, 1929, by Charles X. Harris, from the original by Sir Joshua Reynolds. Dunmore was the last royal governor of Virginia. (*Virginia Historical Society, Richmond, Virginia*)

A prerestoration view of the Powder Magazine at Williamsburg

In September, open conflict erupted in the Norfolk area, where loyalist activity in support of Dunmore suggested that the move for independence was weakening. During October and November, Dunmore's forces fought engagements throughout the Hampton Roads area, losing an encounter at Hampton and winning at Kemp's Landing. After weeks of maneuvering, Dunmore's troops on 9 December 1775 lost a pitched battle at Great Bridge, abandoned Norfolk, and fled to the British ships off-shore.

On New Year's Day 1776, the British fired at Virginians assembled on the Norfolk docks and sent troops ashore to capture supplies and burn any buildings sheltering snipers. The destruction and fighting continued throughout the night and convinced the Virginia commanders that they faced the major British offensive they had nervously anticipated. The officers were mistaken but allowed their troops, like the British, to set fires in the town. Even though both sides participated in the devastation, the burning of Norfolk convinced many in the colonies, not just Virginians, that the war for independence must proceed. Considered with the British burning of Falmouth, now Portland, Maine, two and a half months earlier, these "flaming arguments" were probably more persuasive than even the publication later in January 1776 of Thomas Paine's famous polemic, *Common Sense*.

The last of Virginia's revolutionary conventions met in Williamsburg from 6 May through 5 July 1776. On 15 May the members voted unanimously to instruct the Virginia members of Congress to introduce a resolution calling for independence. On 7 June Richard Henry Lee moved in Congress that the colonies "were, and of right ought to be, free and independent states." After a month of deliberation, Congress passed Lee's motion on 2 July and two days later explained its action to the world in the Declaration of Independence, written by Thomas Jefferson.

George Wythe (1726–1806), miniature painted on ivory, ca. 1770, by Henry Benbridge *(Courtesy of the R. W. Norton Art Gallery, Shreveport, Louisiana)*

The Declaration of Rights and the Constitution of 1776

On 12 June the Virginia revolutionary convention adopted the Virginia Declaration of Rights, drafted by George Mason, which spelled out such fundamental liberties as freedom of religion, freedom of the press, and the right to a jury trial, in both civil and criminal cases. The Virginia Declaration of Rights was a model for other states and, in time, for the United States Bill of Rights and for the French Declaration of the Rights of Man and of the Citizen adopted in 1789. Virginia's first written constitution, which the convention adopted on 29 June 1776, created a republic, or commonwealth—a form of government in which ultimate authority is exercised by a sovereign people united for the common good, or common weal. To avoid recurrence of the perceived abuses of executive authority by George III and Governor Dunmore, the Constitution of 1776 severely restricted the powers of the executive branch of government; it gave the General Assembly authority not only to make laws but also to choose the governor, the eight members of the Council of State to advise the governor on the exercise of his limited powers, the attorney general, and all judges and other state officials. The convention named Patrick Henry as the first governor of the independent commonwealth of Virginia. Twice reelected, Henry served three one-year terms and was succeeded in 1779 by Thomas Jefferson, who was reelected once. Jefferson's successor was Thomas Nelson Jr., a general in the state militia who commanded Virginia troops at the siege of Yorktown.

Although the Convention of 1776 rejected a program of democratic reforms suggested by Thomas Jefferson, the General Assembly appointed a committee of

Jefferson, Thomas Ludwell Lee, George Mason, Edmund Pendleton, and George Wythe to draft a revision of Virginia's laws. Completed in 1779, Jefferson's committee report recommended eliminating capital punishment for most crimes, disestablishing the Anglican church, and abolishing both primogeniture (by which, in the absence of instructions otherwise, all inherited land passed to the eldest son) and entail (by which heirs were prevented from disposing of inherited land). During the 1780s the General Assembly adopted most of Jefferson's bills. The most famous is the Virginia Statute for Religious Freedom, which James Madison, a member of the House of Delegates from Orange County, skillfully guided through the legislature in 1786.

The Revolutionary War

During the first years of the war, Virginia regiments fought in South Carolina, New York, New Jersey, and Pennsylvania. With George Washington they suffered through the winter at Valley Forge. Other important Virginia generals during the Revolution were Daniel Morgan, whose riflemen participated in an invasion of Canada and fought in every theater of the war, George Rogers Clark, who conquered the territory west of the Allegheny Mountains, Andrew Lewis, Hugh Mercer, John Peter Gabriel Muhlenberg, Charles Scott, Adam Stephen, and William Woodford. Many other Virginia officers won fame during the war, and Henry ("Light-Horse Harry") Lee's cavalry performed ably in the southern states. The enemy did not attack Virginia until late in 1780, but by the next summer British armies under Generals

Surrender of Cornwallis at Yorktown, 1781, engraved from a painting by Armand Dumaresq

Design for the Washington Monument in Richmond's Capitol Square, by Edward B. White, of Charleston, South Carolina, dated November 1849. The proposal was eventually rejected in favor of a design submitted by New York–born sculptor Thomas Crawford.

Charles Cornwallis, William Phillips, and Benedict Arnold had twice swept through the tidewater, and Lieutenant Colonel Banastre Tarleton's raiders had struck as far inland as Charlottesville. Richmond, the new capital city, was burned. Military stores at Petersburg, Point of Fork, and Gosport were destroyed.

On the home front, Virginia women supported the war effort in a variety of ways. They wove homespun cloth as a substitute for boycotted English textiles, assisted with planting and harvesting crops in the absence of husbands-turned-soldiers, and provided food and horses to fill army requisitions. Some worked at the Westham Foundry in Richmond or the gunnery in Fredericksburg making ammunition for local militia, while others attached themselves to military units and performed essential services such as washing, cooking, sewing, and nursing. Only one woman is known to have participated in actual combat. Anna Maria Lane fought "in the garb, and with the courage of a soldier" with her husband's unit at the Battle of Germantown, Pennsylvania, in 1777 and later received a substantial pension from the Virginia General Assembly for her patriotism and service. In 1780, Martha Washington and Martha Wayles Jefferson inspired women from Alexandria to Williamsburg to raise thousands of dollars for the army through their churches and other community organizations. At least one Virginia woman expressed the hope that the principles of the Revolution might be applied to women as well as men in the new American nation. During the war, Hannah Lee Corbin asked her brother Richard Henry Lee to use his influence in Congress to give the vote to widows like herself who paid taxes but had no voice in how their money was spent. She was doomed to disappointment.

In the spring of 1781, Continental troops commanded by the Marquis de Lafayette forced Cornwallis toward the Chesapeake Bay, and in July the British took up defensive positions near Yorktown. When a French fleet commanded by Admiral François Joseph Paul de Grasse, comte de Grasse-Tilly, prevented the British navy from entering the bay, Washington and the Continental army, aided by the French troops of General Jean Baptiste Donatien de Vimeur, comte de Rochambeau, forced Cornwallis to surrender his army on 19 October 1781. The Peace of Paris between the United States, Great Britain, France, and Spain formally ended the war in 1783.

The thirteen newly independent states had united themselves under the Articles of Confederation, a constitution drafted in 1777 that delegated few powers to the Congress and left extensive powers to the states. Lacking strong claims to western lands, Maryland delayed ratifying the Articles of Confederation until 1781, after Virginia declared itself willing to treat the unsettled west as nationally owned territory. Virginia deeded its lands north of the Ohio River to the nation in 1784. In the Ordinance of 1785, drafted by Thomas Jefferson, Congress provided that the territory be surveyed into 640-acre sections, or townships. Two years later Congress passed the Northwest Ordinance of 1787, which provided for the administration of this western territory, established mechanisms for the formation of new states in the Northwest Territory, and prohibited the introduction of slavery there. The states of Illinois, Indiana, Michigan, Ohio, and Wisconsin (as well as part of Minnesota) were later formed from Virginia's so-called Old Northwest. In 1792 the Virginia counties south of the Ohio River formed the commonwealth of Kentucky. Later, in 1863, fifty counties in western Virginia became the state of West Virginia. As a result, one of Virginia's nicknames is Mother of States.

The Old Dominion and the New Nation

Virginia's agricultural economy recovered rapidly after the Revolutionary War, but the new nation had severe problems. It was too weak to force the British to evacuate posts in the Ohio River valley or to guarantee westerners' rights to navigate the Mississippi River. Renewed commerce with Britain was troubled by confusions about debts that many Americans, including a large number of Virginians, had contracted with British mercantile firms prior to the Revolution. The Peace of Paris of 1783, which ended the war, had recognized the validity of these debts, but Congress under the Articles of Confederation lacked sufficient authority to enforce its terms. And Congress had financial problems of its own: a national war debt, no authority to raise taxes, and states that either refused or were unable to contribute money to the support of the national government.

Virginians took the lead in the movement to strengthen the national government. In 1786, the General Assembly called for a conference in Annapolis to discuss commercial problems with neighboring Maryland. That gathering in turn recommended a constitutional convention to meet in Philadelphia in the summer of 1787. George Washington, who was elected president of the convention, headed Virginia's distinguished delegation, which included John Blair, James Madison, George Mason, George Wythe, and Edmund Randolph. Governor Randolph presented the Virginia Plan for a new central government, which, largely the work of James Madison, became the basis of the convention's debate and earned its author the sobriquet Father of the Constitution.

The stronger national government proposed to the states in 1787 awakened fears of centralization among many patriots of the revolutionary generation. Patrick Henry led Virginia's opposition to ratification of the Constitution. George Mason criticized the document, as he had in Philadelphia, in part because it lacked a bill of rights, and for months Governor Edmund Randolph favored a second convention to amend the proposed constitution before it was ratified. In the end, the Virginia Convention of 1788, which met in Richmond, searchingly examined the document during a month of debate and voted eighty-nine to seventy-nine to ratify it.

Elected to the First Congress, Madison drafted amendments in the form of a bill of rights to protect Americans from possible abuses of power by the national government. He modeled his amendments on the Virginia Declaration of Rights and included provisions suggested by the Virginia Convention of 1788. On 25 September 1789 Congress submitted the proposed amendments to the state legislatures for ratification, and during the next two years ten states approved them. The ratification of the Bill of Rights by the General Assembly of Virginia on 15 December 1791 put the handiwork of Virginia's statesmen into the Constitution of the United States.

George Washington served as the first president of the United States from 1789 to 1797. During the 1790s, Thomas Jefferson, the secretary of state, and James Madison formed the nation's first political party in opposition to the Federalist commercial and financial policies advocated by the secretary of the treasury, Alexander Hamilton. Virginia's Democratic-Republicans, as their party was known, led the nation's resistance to the Alien and Sedition Acts, which were passed by the Federalist congress in 1798 and restricted the liberties of American citizens. In 1799 the General Assembly adopted resolutions written by Madison against the acts, and the Kentucky legislature passed Jefferson's even stronger resolutions.

Jefferson won election as vice president of the United States in 1796, and in the presidential election of 1800 he narrowly defeated the incumbent, John Adams. Jefferson's inauguration on 4 March 1801 began a twenty-four-year period in which the nation chose Democratic-Republican presidents from Virginia—Jefferson (1801–1809), Madison (1809–1817), and James Monroe (1817–1825). These three presidents and Washington are sometimes called the Virginia Dynasty. Four other native Virginians served as president of the United States: William Henry Harrison was elected

GEN. WM. H. HARRISON.

William Henry Harrison's election to the presidency in 1840 relied heavily on emotional appeal. Campaign images depicted the general seated in front of a log cabin with a barrel of cider, emphasizing his status as a military hero and his role as a candidate of the people.

president in 1840, and was after his sudden death in office succeeded by John Tyler in 1841; Zachary Taylor was elected president in 1848; and in 1912 the nation elected Staunton-born Woodrow Wilson. Virginia is thus sometimes called the Mother of Presidents.

During Madison's administration the United States and Great Britain fought the War of 1812. In June 1813 the British attempted to capture Norfolk, but a small band of Virginia militia entrenched on Craney Island at the mouth of the Elizabeth River repulsed the invaders. British naval vessels raided Virginia towns and plantations on the Chesapeake Bay during the war, and in 1814 the British army burned the new capital city of Washington, D.C. Winfield Scott, of Petersburg, and William Henry Harrison, of Charles City County, won national prominence during the War of 1812. Harrison went on to become governor of Ohio and, for thirty days in 1841, president of the United States. Scott commanded American troops during the 1846 war with Mexico, ran for president on the Whig Party ticket in 1852, and briefly commanded the Union armies at the outbreak of the Civil War.

Most Virginians were Democratic-Republicans during the 1790s, and as the Federalist Party dwindled toward extinction after 1800, many Virginia Federalists either joined their former foes or retired from politics. John Marshall did neither. A Richmond lawyer of great skill, Marshall while serving as a special emissary to France during the Adams administration had become a national hero for his prudent conduct during a 1797–1798 rift in diplomatic relations known as the XYZ affair. Adams named him secretary of state in 1800 and, near the end of his term in 1801, appointed Marshall chief justice of the United States Supreme Court. Until his death in 1835 Marshall guided the Court with a firm hand, strengthening the national government and assuring that an independent federal judiciary was the final interpreter of the Constitution of the United States.

Letters, Learning, and Cultural Change

Presbyterians founded Hampden-Sydney Academy in Prince Edward County at the beginning of the American Revolution. Shortly thereafter, Liberty Hall Academy (later named Washington College and finally Washington and Lee University) introduced a collegiate curriculum and gave Virginia its third institution of higher learning. Thomas Jefferson proposed a three-tiered system of publicly supported county primary schools, regional preparatory schools, and a state university. He never persuaded the General Assembly to adopt the entire proposal, but in 1819 he did obtain a charter for the University of Virginia. Six years later, in buildings he designed, Jefferson's university opened its doors to students. In 1830 the Methodists founded Randolph-Macon College, and in 1839 the state created Virginia Military Institute, the nation's first state-supported military college.

For the daughters of Virginia's more prosperous families, hundreds of institutes and academies began offering challenging curricula. By the 1850s, several of the schools, such as the Female Collegiate Institute in Buckingham County, began referring to themselves as colleges, suggesting the advanced educational level to which they aspired. As female education became increasingly perceived as an essential part of a political society reliant upon mothers to raise virtuous sons and future citizens, schools also became available to impoverished youths in cities such as Alexandria, Fredericksburg, Petersburg, and Richmond. Women across Virginia also organized a wide variety of benevolent institutions to address other pressing community needs and to provide an outlet for their talents.

A view of the Female Collegiate Institute in Buckingham County, from the cover of the "Buckingham Polka," written by Arnaud Préot and copyrighted in 1852.

Virginia women gained some control over their property during the antebellum period. Although age-old laws still prohibited married women from owning land and goods in their own right, equity law increasingly allowed women to create separate estates prior to marriage and to challenge restrictive provisions in their husbands' wills. For a variety of reasons, a higher proportion of women than ever before—both white and free black—owned property in the first half of the nineteenth century and controlled its destiny through purchase, sale, gift, or bequest. The prevailing image of women as private creatures responsible exclusively for the happiness and moral virtue of their families did not change appreciably even as women participated in activities beyond their homes. Nonetheless, reality often belied the image, and throughout the period women continued to expand the boundaries of their public world.

Among Virginia's important writers during the first half of the nineteenth century was William Wirt. A lawyer who served nearly twelve years as attorney general of the United States, Wirt published searching commentaries on Virginia history and society. His books include *Letters of the British Spy* (1803), *The Old Bachelor* (1814), and a biography of Patrick Henry, which gained nationwide acclaim. Other influential writers included Virginia Randolph Cary, author of the widely read guide *Letters on Female Character*, published in 1828, and Mary Randolph, author of *The Virginia House-wife*, first printed in 1824 and by 1830 already in its fourth edition. The Irish immigrant John Daly Burk completed a three-volume *History of Virginia*. George Tucker wrote a biography of Thomas Jefferson, William Cabell Rives wrote a biography of James Madison, and John Marshall and Mason Locke Weems each wrote biographies of George Washington. Henry ("Light-Horse Harry") Lee compiled a history of the southern theater of the American Revolution. William A. Caruthers and Nathaniel Beverley Tucker wrote novels, and Tucker's father, St. George Tucker, a poet of considerable talent, published the first American edition of William Blackstone's *Commentaries on the Laws of England*.

The *Southern Literary Messenger*, a monthly magazine founded in 1834, was published in Richmond for more than twenty years. Its most distinguished editor was Boston-born Edgar Allan Poe, who published trenchant criticism and original poetry in the *Messenger* and elsewhere. Poe's successor was the poet John R. Thompson, who retained the post until the Civil War and became one of the most frequently quoted war correspondents in the South. Newspapers flourished during the first half of the nineteenth century, and every sizable Virginia town boasted at least one. Two Richmond papers had great influence in national politics: Thomas Ritchie's *Enquirer* was the South's most important Democratic newspaper, and John Hampden Pleasants took the opposing side with his *Richmond Whig*.

Virginians also made important contributions to science. Meriwether Lewis and William Clark explored the Louisiana territory purchased from France in 1803 and reported on the geography, Indians, flora, and fauna of the Great Plains, Rocky Mountains, and Pacific slope. In addition to their political tracts, John Taylor of Caroline and Edmund Ruffin published their experiments with scientific agriculture, particularly in the use of fertilizers and crop rotation. Thomas Jefferson designed a prizewinning plow, and his son-in-law Thomas Mann Randolph experimented with contour plowing. Cyrus McCormick, of Rockbridge County, developed a reaping machine for grain farmers that revolutionized American agriculture. Another Rockbridge County native, James Edward Allen Gibbs, perfected a sewing machine in

1855. Matthew Fontaine Maury, of Spotsylvania County, was an oceanographer of international renown whose studies of ocean currents earned him the nickname Pathfinder of the Seas.

Meriwether Lewis (1774–1809), tinted engraving, 1816

An Age of Improvement

In the decade before 1776, the General Assembly authorized several joint-stock companies formed for such projects as linking the James and York Rivers by a canal at Williamsburg, improving navigation on the James and Potomac Rivers, and connecting the Chesapeake Bay and Currituck Sound by a canal through the Dismal Swamp into North Carolina. The American Revolution disrupted these efforts, but in 1784 the assembly again authorized companies to construct canals and locks for "Improving the Navigation of James River" and "Opening and Extending the Navigation of Potowmack River." The commonwealth initially bought one-sixth of the James River Company stock and one-tenth of the stock of the Potomac River Company, of which George Washington was the first president.

In 1816 the General Assembly created the Board of Public Works to oversee the state's involvement in such enterprises. With its new Internal Improvement Fund, the commonwealth purchased 40 percent of each company's stock, using money generated by public bonds that, in turn, were retired out of annual tax receipts. In the 1830s railroads supplanted canals and turnpikes as Virginia's most important internal improvements, and the commonwealth became a major proprietor of railroad stock as well. Even after several midwestern states defaulted on their bonds during the depression that followed the economic panic of 1837, Virginia issued bonds to purchase stock

The James River and Kanawha Canal upon completion in 1851 traveled 197 miles up the James River from Richmond to Buchanan. It was sold less than thirty years later to the Richmond and Alleghany Railroad, which laid its tracks on the canal's towpath.

Plans for the Virginia State Penitentiary, 1797, by architect Benjamin Henry Latrobe

in corporations devoted to internal improvements. During the antebellum period, the state government invested approximately $37 million in internal improvements of all kinds and $18.5 million in railroad stocks alone. Almost half of this total investment occurred during the 1850s. With the improvements on the James and Potomac Rivers, agricultural produce moved cheaply to market downstream, but planned linkages of the Potomac and Ohio Rivers and the James and Kanawha Rivers were never completed. Virginia, therefore, did not benefit as greatly from its canals as New York did from the Erie Canal. Before railroads supplanted canals, the eastern counties of Virginia profited from these public works much more than the western.

Virginia in 1773 had been the first British colony to establish a medical institution (now Eastern State Hospital) devoted exclusively to the treatment of mental illness. The hospital accepted both whites and, in segregated facilities, free blacks as well; in 1846 the General Assembly passed legislation admitting slaves. Another such facility (now Western State Hospital) opened in Staunton in 1828. The state's early prison system also reflected a progressive impulse. With a design adapted by Benjamin Henry Latrobe and opened in March 1800, the penitentiary was an attempt to mix productive work with correction. Charles Stephen Morgan, superintendent from 1832 until his death in 1859, instituted rehabilitation programs, such as a shoe manufactory, to teach prisoners marketable manual skills.

Politics and the Constitutions of 1830 and 1851

Between 1800 and 1820 all of Virginia's presidential electors voted for Virginians Thomas Jefferson, James Madison, and James Monroe. From 1824 through 1856 the presidential candidates of the Democratic Party always carried Virginia, but Virginia-born Whig candidates William Henry Harrison and Zachary Taylor narrowed the state's Democratic margins of victory in 1840 and in 1848. Antebellum Virginia was hardly a one-party state. The Whigs were strong, and John Randolph of Roanoke led a formidably independent Democratic faction. Moreover, a group of men sometimes called the Richmond Junto exerted varying degrees of influence in national Democratic Party affairs. They included Wilson Cary Nicholas and his brother Philip Norborne Nicholas, Peter V. Daniel, John Brockenbrough and his brother William Brockenbrough, Andrew Stevenson, Richard E. Parker, William Foushee, and Thomas Ritchie. Closely allied by family and business connections, they were fervent Jacksonians during the 1820s and 1830s. None, though, shared Jackson's animus toward banks. Many of them, in fact, were among the most powerful bankers in Virginia: John Brockenbrough was affiliated with the Bank of Virginia, Wilson Cary Nicholas with the Richmond branch of the Second Bank of the United States, and Philip Norborne Nicholas with the Farmers Bank of Virginia. Although they could not always win all of Virginia's congressional seats or control the state legislature, in national elections they worked to carry the state for the Democrats, and Ritchie's *Richmond Enquirer* was a strong political voice in support of the party of Andrew Jackson and Martin Van Buren. Their support for internal improvements put the Virginia Democratic Party squarely behind the railway companies founded in the state during the 1840s and 1850s.

Twice between the American Revolution and the Civil War pressure from western counties for more proportionate strength in the General Assembly led to the calling of conventions to revise the state constitution. Under the Constitution of 1776 each county, regardless of its size, wealth, or population, was entitled to elect two members to the House of Delegates; groups of adjacent counties returned one senator each. Westerners wished to alter the constitution to obtain greater representation for the state's western reaches and to break the control that the small eastern counties held over legislation. The westerners also wanted governors elected by popular vote (rather than by the General Assembly) and popular elections of local officials (rather than the self-perpetuating system by which justices of the peace exerted so much influence in filling county court vacancies).

The Convention of 1829–1830 brought a remarkable group of statesmen to Richmond for what has been called "the last of the great constituent assemblies in American history." The delegates included former presidents James Madison and James Monroe, Chief Justice John Marshall, John Randolph of Roanoke, and future president John Tyler. The conservative eastern delegates prevailed, and the Constitution of 1830 differed little from that of 1776. The western counties won a slightly larger proportion of legislative seats, but the eastern counties continued to send the larger number of legislators to Richmond and to control public policy.

Twenty years later, the persistent sectional differences within Virginia also brought the Convention of 1850 into existence. At midcentury, although the number of Virginians living west of the Blue Ridge surpassed the number to the east, the eastern counties still maintained a majority in the legislature. The eastern majority not only instituted internal improvements and banking policies that the westerners opposed, but also blocked measures to create a public school system and reform local government. The Constitution of 1851 did, though, include provisions for the popular election of the governor, the removal of property qualifications for voting, and the electorate's right to choose local officials. The new constitution also granted more legislative seats to the western counties, reformed the judicial system, and abolished the Council of State. The slaveholding eastern counties in turn obtained restrictions affecting the freeing, or manumission, of slaves. In 1851 Joseph Johnson, of Harrison County (now in West Virginia), became Virginia's first popularly elected governor and the state's first governor from west of the Blue Ridge.

The Convention of 1829–30, oil on panel, by George Catlin (1796–1872). The artist, whose scene has been described as a "parliament of gnomes with huge heads and warped dwarf bodies," worked from individual life studies to create an accurate representation of facial features and expressions. *(Virginia Historical Society, Richmond, Virginia)*

Virginia and the Antebellum South

In August 1831 a group of Southampton County slaves under the leadership of Nat Turner, a preacher and slave, revolted. Nearly sixty people died in the violence that followed. After the local militia put down the rebellion, Turner and the other leaders were tried and hanged. The uprising provoked an extensive debate about slavery in the General Assembly session of 1831–1832. Some thirty years earlier, two aborted slave insurrections known as Gabriel's Rebellion and the Easter Plot had threatened Richmond and the surrounding counties. They, too, had engendered much debate. Thus by the 1830s, many white Virginians had grown increasingly uncomfortable with the "peculiar institution," and some had joined the American Colonization Society, which advocated transporting blacks to Africa or colonies in Central America and the Caribbean. During the 1831–1832 debates, Thomas Jefferson Randolph, grandson of Thomas Jefferson, and Thomas Marshall, son of the chief justice of the U.S. Supreme Court, introduced a plan for such colonization and for the gradual abolition of the institution of slavery. A prominent opponent of their plan was William Henry Roane, grandson of Patrick Henry. Only after a prolonged and shifting debate did the Virginia General Assembly embrace harsher racial attitudes in the aftermath of the Southampton Insurrection and reject any plan for emancipation.

As northern abolitionists grew more numerous and vocal during the 1830s and 1840s, southern defenders of slavery became more strident. Debate in Congress over the Wilmot Proviso, which proposed excluding slavery from territories acquired during the Mexican War (1846–1848), brought slavery to the center of American political debate. By the 1850s relations between free and slave states were strained; violence erupted in Kansas when slave owners sought to bring slaves into the western territories. As congressional debates over the issue intensified, the 1852 publication of Harriet Beecher Stowe's melodramatic novel, *Uncle Tom's Cabin*, and the Supreme Court's 1857 decision in the *Dred Scott* case reaffirming existing slavery laws, inflamed northern public opinion.

Although the living conditions of enslaved men and women in Virginia were somewhat less horrible than in the states of the cotton belt, the financial panics of 1819 and 1837 forced some white Virginians to sell their slaves, while others moved with their slaves to the harsher labors of the Deep South and West. During the second quar-

The auctioning of slaves in Christiansburg, ca. 1853, sketch by Lewis Miller *(Abby Aldrich Rockefeller Folk Art Center, Williamsburg, Va.)*

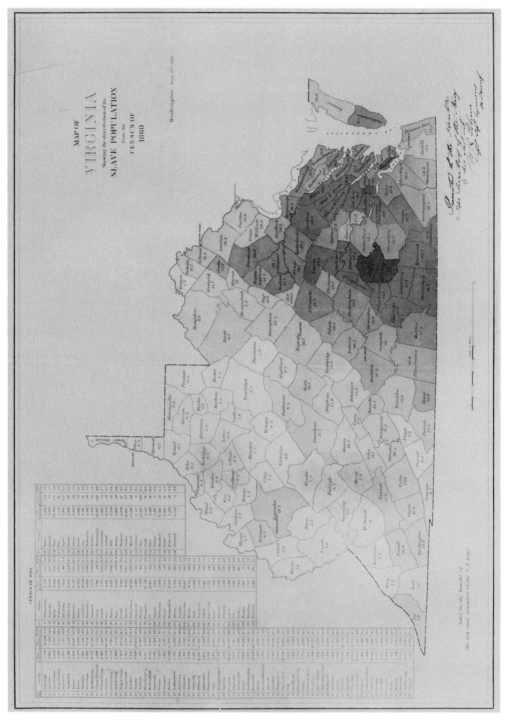

Map of Virginia Showing the distribution of its Slave Population from the Census of 1860. According to the map, on the eve of the Civil War, the Southside counties of Nottoway and Amelia held the largest percentage of slaves, 74 and 72.6, respectively.

ter of the nineteenth century, many black Virginians were sold in the markets of Memphis and New Orleans to the plantation owners of the Gulf states. In 1860, approximately four hundred ninety thousand Virginians, almost 40 percent of the entire population, were slaves; about four hundred thirty thousand of them lived east of the Blue Ridge. Slaves comprised as much as 60 percent of the population in several rural tidewater Virginia counties, 70 percent in the Southside. Urban industries such as the Tredegar Iron Works in Richmond also employed slaves and free blacks in their mills, and hundreds of slaves worked in tobacco factories in Danville, Lynchburg, Petersburg, and Richmond.

Although the politicians of the Cotton Kingdom most fully developed an intellectual defense for slavery (first as an unavoidable burden, then as a necessary evil, and finally by the 1850s as a positive good), Thomas R. Dew, of the College of William and Mary, also contributed to the formulation of the arguments. The writings and teachings of such ardent Virginia leaders as Edmund Ruffin and Nathaniel Beverley Tucker prepared other white Virginians for the possibility that the slave states might have to fight to preserve the institution of slavery.

Then, on the night of 16 October 1859, John Brown and eighteen followers crossed the Potomac River from Maryland at Harpers Ferry. They seized the United States arsenal on the seventeenth, intending to arm local blacks and begin a war to free the slaves. Governor Henry A. Wise dispatched state militiamen to the scene, and on the eighteenth, after a brief skirmish, United States Army colonel Robert E. Lee, his aide Lieutenant J. E. B. Stuart, and a company of marines captured Brown and his men. Convicted of treason against the commonwealth of Virginia, Brown was hanged on 2 December 1859. Rekindling among white Virginians the fears that surfaced after the Southampton Insurrection of 1831, Brown's raid seemed to support the Southern extremists' charge that all Northern abolitionists were intent on the violent destruction of Southern society.

Secession

A decade of inflammatory rhetoric had intensified the atmosphere in which Americans voted during the presidential election of 1860. The Republican Party nominated Abraham Lincoln, of Illinois, who was known to dislike slavery. The Democratic Party split into Northern and Southern factions that nominated, respectively, Senator Stephen A. Douglas, of Illinois, and Vice President John C. Breckinridge, of Kentucky. A new party, calling itself the Constitutional Union Party and devoting its platform solely to the preservation of the Union, nominated John Bell, of Tennessee. Lincoln won the Northern states and the election. Breckinridge carried most of the Southern states. Douglas ran a strong second in many areas of the country, and Bell won the border states, including Virginia, where Breckinridge finished a close second. The election of Lincoln provoked South Carolina to secede from the Union on 20 December 1860. Mississippi, Alabama, Florida, Georgia, Louisiana, and Texas followed. On 4 February 1861, representatives of the seven states met at Montgomery, Alabama, created the Confederate States of America, and formed a provisional government with Jefferson Davis as president.

Summoned by Governor John Letcher, the General Assembly of Virginia convened in special session on 7 January 1861. On 19 January the assembly called for the election on 4 February of delegates to a state convention, which met on 13 February.

Because a majority of the delegates wished to preserve the Union, the convention delayed its action while former U.S. president John Tyler chaired a peace conference in Washington, D.C., that sought to resolve the sectional crisis. The failure of that conference, together with a generally unfavorable reaction to Lincoln's inaugural address on 4 March, weakened the opponents of secession in the Virginia convention, but on 4 April the convention defeated by eighty-eight to forty-five a motion to recommend secession to the voters.

Then came the 12 April firing on Fort Sumter and Lincoln's 15 April call for seventy-five thousand volunteers to put down the rebellion. On 17 April the Virginia convention voted eighty-eight to fifty-five to secede and submitted the Ordinance of Secession to the voters for ratification. Delegates from Virginia's tidewater, piedmont, and Southside counties voted for secession along with several from the Valley of Virginia and a few from the far western counties. Delegates from the mountain counties, and most of those from the far western counties, cast the majority of the negative votes. On 23 May, the voters ratified the Ordinance of Secession. Virginia joined the Confederacy, and Richmond was named capital of the new nation.

The customhouse in Wheeling, from *Frank Leslie's Pictorial History of the War of 1861*

The Formation of West Virginia

The delegates from western Virginia who had opposed secession had left Richmond soon after the convention's fateful ballot on 17 April, and several were among the 436 men who met at Wheeling, in Ohio County, from 13 to 15 May to discuss the future of Virginia's pro-Union western counties. The people of the western counties voted overwhelmingly against secession in the May referendum. On 11 June, a second convention assembled at Wheeling, declared Virginia's state offices vacant, and named a slate of new officers with Francis H. Pierpont as governor. President Lincoln promptly recognized Pierpont's appointment, and from the summer of 1861 until the spring of 1865 Pierpont served as chief executive of such Virginia counties as were controlled by the Union army. In 1863 Pierpont moved the seat of his Restored government, as Virginia's pro-Union government-in-exile was known, from Wheeling to Alexandria. From there, it functioned in as many respects as possible as the state's one and rightful government, even sending representatives to the United States Congress.

Delegates from fifty western Virginia counties, meanwhile, met in a constitutional convention to create the state of West Virginia, which Congress admitted to the Union on 20 June 1863. Pierpont's General Assembly in Alexandria endorsed the formation of the new state, thus satisfying the provision in the Constitution of the United States that prevents the creation of a new state from the territory of an old state without the approval of the latter. As part of its constitution, the state of West Virginia agreed to assume a reasonable proportion of the public debt incurred prior to Virginia's secession from the Union.

The Civil War

Three days after it voted to remove Virginia from the Union, the Convention of 1861 created a three-member advisory council to assist Governor Letcher in preparing the state's defenses. Letcher named Francis Henney Smith, John James Allen, and Matthew Fontaine Maury to the council, and they were joined by Thomas Sherwood Haymond and Robert Latané Montague in May. The first important action of the council was to recommend that Letcher offer command of the state's defense forces to then U.S. Army colonel Robert E. Lee, who had also received an offer of command from his mentor and fellow Virginian, Union general Winfield Scott. Lee accepted the Virginia appointment and became commander of the state's forces on 23 April 1861. The overall Union strategy was to split the Confederacy by taking the Mississippi River and to disrupt the eastern states by blockading the coast and capturing Richmond. Eastern and northern Virginia thus became a primary battleground of the Civil War.

In twenty-six major battles and more than four hundred smaller engagements, more men fought and died in Virginia than in any other state. For almost four years, Lee and such capable field commanders as Thomas J. ("Stonewall") Jackson, J. E. B. Stuart, and Jubal A. Early repelled Union attempts to take Richmond and envelop Virginia. Although the Confederate strategy was essentially defensive, Lee carried the war into the Northern states when he advanced to Antietam, Maryland, in 1862 and to Gettysburg, Pennsylvania, in 1863. Both of Lee's invasions were turned back on

Stampede of Slaves from Hampton to Fortress Monroe, from *Harper's Weekly*, 17 August 1861. The scene illustrates the evacuation of slaves and Union soldiers from Hampton in fear of attack by Confederate forces.

bloody battlefields, but time and again he repulsed Union advances into Virginia. The first serious fighting in Virginia occurred in July 1861 near Manassas Junction, when Confederate generals P. G. T. Beauregard and Joseph E. Johnston defeated Irvin McDowell's Union troops at the First Battle of Manassas, also known as the First Battle of Bull Run. In 1862 Union forces commanded by General George B. McClellan attempted to reach Richmond by marching up the James River from a base camp near Yorktown. They reached the outskirts of the Confederate capital but were thrown back in the running battle known as the Seven Days, during which Lee assumed full command of what became known as the Army of Northern Virginia. Later in that year, after Lee's defeat at Antietam, Union forces advanced on Fredericksburg from the north and were again stalled.

On the home front, Virginians waged war of another sort. By late 1861, inflation was already rampant. Within a year, the prices of basic foodstuffs had doubled, even quadrupled. A barrel of flour cost three hundred dollars by 1863, twelve hundred dollars by 1865. Everything it seemed was in short supply. Without sufficient sources of medicine, for example, both the army and the civilian population were nearly helpless in the face of repeated outbreaks of pneumonia, scarlet fever, and smallpox. Cities throughout the Old Dominion filled to overflowing. Conditions were so severe that a large crowd of frustrated citizens on 2 April 1863 erupted in what became known as the Richmond Bread Riot. Distrustful of one another, Governor Letcher and the General Assembly could do little to alleviate the crises. "How I loath the word *war!*," wrote a Lexington woman in April 1862. "Our schools are closed, stores shut up, goods not to be bought, and so exorbitant we must do without."

The war affected society in other ways as well. With so many men in military service, Virginia women entered jobs and accepted roles previously closed to them, especially as hospital orderlies, government clerks, teachers, even munitions workers. Forty female workers died when a Richmond ammunition factory exploded in March 1863. Within weeks the plant reopened, with a full complement of other women ready to take their place. Although some of Virginia's half-million African Americans willingly worked in a variety of tasks, many thousands more were impressed into Confederate military service as laborers and drovers. Some toiled in skilled trades, assigned, for example, to work as blacksmiths, shoemakers, and coal miners. An "almost stampede," one Union officer called it, made their way to Federal lines and freedom. At least 5,723 black Virginians, and probably far more, joined the Union army.

The Army of Northern Virginia continued to hold off the Union's Army of the Potomac, at Second Manassas in August 1862, at Chancellorsville in May 1863, and again near Fredericksburg during the winter of 1863–1864. Not until 1864, when Ulysses S. Grant assumed command of Union forces, did the tide of battle move against the South. Backed by the North's greater population and industrial and agricultural resources, Grant began hammering the Army of Northern Virginia at the Battle of the Wilderness, west of Fredericksburg, in May, and unlike his predecessors pressed south in a relentless series of vicious clashes that brought the Union forces to the James River near Richmond in the middle of June. When Grant threw his army across the river to besiege Petersburg, Lee fortified the city with all the troops he could spare from the defensive lines at Richmond.

In the 1862 Peninsula campaign in Virginia, Union general George B. McClellan had locomotives shipped from Boston to White House, Virginia. There they were placed upon the Richmond and York River Railroad, which ran from Richmond to West Point.

On 2 April 1865, having determined that he could no longer hold Petersburg against Grant's assaults, Lee withdrew to the west along the valley of the Appomattox River, while Jefferson Davis and the Confederate government abandoned Richmond and retreated to Danville. Union troops entered the Confederate capital on 3 April to find that fires set to destroy Confederate supplies in the city had burned out of control and reduced much of Richmond's business district to rubble. Grant's army rushed to pursue Lee's retreating Confederates. On 9 April Lee surrendered his army to Grant at Appomattox Court House, bringing to an end the bloodiest war in American history.

The Effect of the Rebellion on the Homes of Virginia, from *Harper's Weekly,* 1864

Reconstruction

With the war over, Virginia faced the enormous task of reconstruction. The Old Dominion's once-formidable industrial base had been destroyed. Its railroads, too, were in ruins. Little survived of Fredericksburg but a few charred remains; much of Petersburg was utterly destroyed. Many of the state's other cities and towns—Bristol, Winchester, and Wytheville, to name only a few—had fared little better. The state's agrarian economy was so devastated that one northern observer commented that he could find "no sign of human industry, save here and there a sickly, half-cultivated corn field." Economic and social disruption was so severe that even six months after the war had ended, some twenty-five thousand Virginians survived only on the rations distributed by the Union army. Hundreds of thousands of others—African

Occupying Federal troops posing before a shell-damaged residence on Petersburg's
Bolingbroke Street just after the fall of the city on 2 April 1865

Americans, returning soldiers, and refugees—were without employment or shelter.
Worse, perhaps as many as thirty thousand Virginians had died in the war.

Amid all that, on 9 May 1865, precisely a month after the surrender at
Appomattox, President Andrew Johnson recognized Francis H. Pierpont as provisional
governor of Virginia. The new state government, based in Alexandria since 1863, faced
a formidable task. After moving his administration to Richmond, Pierpont, who
hoped for a swift reconciliation, adopted a policy of leniency toward the former
Confederates. His fellow Republicans, however, expressed increasing dismay with the
plan. Virginia's African Americans, who were especially eager to exercise their newfound rights, added a strong protest as well. Elections for local offices in July 1865 and

The Freedman's Village, Hampton, Virginia, from *Harper's Weekly,* 30 September 1865

for the General Assembly and the United States Congress that October resulted, however, in victories for numerous former Confederates. These fruits of President Johnson's conciliatory policies of Reconstruction hardly suited the factional Radical Republicans, who had sufficient strength in Congress to prevent Virginia's representatives from taking their seats.

The following summer Congress passed the Fourteenth Amendment to the Constitution, guaranteeing the rights of freedmen, repudiating war debts incurred by the Confederate states, and barring former Confederate officials from public office. When Virginia and other southern states balked at ratifying the amendment, Congress refused to seat any of the representatives and senators elected from the South. Then, in the spring of 1867, Congress enacted the first of a series of Radical Reconstruction acts and placed the South under military rule. The commonwealth of Virginia became Military District Number One, commanded by Major General John M. Schofield from 13 March 1867 until 2 June 1868, by Major General George Stoneman from 2 June 1868 to 31 March 1869, by Brigadier General Alexander S. Webb from 2 to 19 April 1869, and by Brigadier General E. R. S. Canby from 20 April 1869 until military rule ended on 26 January 1870.

In the autumn of 1867, complying with federal Reconstruction legislation, General Schofield had called for the election of delegates to a state constitutional convention that met in Richmond from 3 December 1867 to 16 April 1868. The delegates, elected in racially polarized voting, included seventy-three Radicals (among whom were twenty-four black Virginians and thirty-three white men of northern or foreign birth) and thirty-two members of a newly formed Conservative Party, most of them young Confederate veterans without prewar political experience. The majority elected as president of the convention John C. Underwood, a federal judge and native New Yorker who had lived in Virginia since the 1850s. After four and a half months of work, the convention delegates presented a document that departed significantly from previous practice by providing for universal manhood suffrage, establishing a statewide system of publicly supported schools, and democratizing the government of Virginia in several other respects. The Underwood Constitution, as it became generally known, also disfranchised many former Confederates and replaced Virginia's ancient system of county government controlled by justices of the peace with a township system patterned after the New England states.

General Schofield, who disliked the disfranchisement of so many former Confederates as well as the revamped format for local governance, refused to permit the required referendum on the new constitution to take place. Earlier, on 4 April 1868, he had appointed the moderate Republican Henry H. Wells as governor to replace Pierpont, but, because Schofield's successor General Stoneman also postponed elections, a year of political drift in Virginia followed. Meanwhile, Virginians sought to rebuild from the war's destruction, often seeking northern capital to do so. At the same time, Virginia's African Americans continued to struggle to make their newly won freedom a reality. Labor contracts negotiated by freedmen in 1866 and 1867, for example, were far more favorable than those negotiated at the war's end in 1865, in part because black leaders, often working through semisecret organizations such as the Union League, had acquired the power and skills to voice their community's own interests. The prominence of blacks, men of northern origins, and native-born political outsiders in the leadership of the Republican Party, however, only reinforced the determination of white Conservatives to gain control of state government.

Governor Wells proved to be a poor politician, managing to offend all factions of the Republican Party and even driving some of the moderate Republicans to make common cause with the Conservatives. In an attempt to break the political impasse, a nine-member committee, led by the Conservative Alexander H. H. Stuart, negotiated a compromise among the state's Conservative leaders, key members of Congress, and President Ulysses S. Grant. The Conservatives offered to accept the proposed state constitution, including its provisions granting freedmen the right to vote, provided that the sections regarding the treatment of former Confederates and the reform of local government be put separately before the electorate for ratification. On 6 July 1869 Virginians overwhelmingly approved the Underwood Constitution and rejected the provisions concerning former Confederates. More important, the Conservatives endorsed the ticket of a moderate Republican faction, the self-styled True Republicans, and its candidate, Gilbert C. Walker, a New Yorker who had settled in Norfolk in 1864 and become a banker and manufacturer. Walker easily defeated Governor Wells, and the Conservatives gained a majority in the General Assembly. On 8 October, to comply with a further condition for readmission to the Union, the General Assembly met to ratify the Fourteenth and Fifteenth Amendments. The latter prohibited states from denying the vote to any man on account of race. Congress thereafter accepted the election results and on 26 January 1870 President U. S. Grant signed the act readmitting Virginia's representatives to the national legislature. Reconstruction was over. During their short time in power, Virginia's Republicans had failed to establish a viable party. They had, though, brought blacks into the state's political life, and they had written a constitution that would serve the state well for more than thirty years.

Virginia and the New South

The late nineteenth century was a time of economic adjustment for the southern states. The abolition of slavery had destroyed the invested wealth of the slaveholder class, and the devastation of war had impoverished many southern farmers. The region lacked capital, and many of its leaders realized that recovery would be more rapid if northern capitalists were persuaded to invest in the South. Rebuilding the railroads required especially large amounts of money, a fact that soon brought many important southern railways under the control of northern financiers. Others, some of them initially reorganized and consolidated by southerners, were bought out by northern syndicates during the recession after the fiscal panic of 1873. Among the modern South's important railways formed during these years were the Norfolk and Western, the Southern, and the Chesapeake and Ohio, all of which traced their beginnings to antebellum Virginia.

The railroads were important to more than farmers. When the Norfolk and Western rails were laid west from Radford in 1883 they opened up the Pocahontas coalfields on the Virginia–West Virginia border and made it possible for coal mining companies to ship their product directly to the port of Norfolk. The parallel extension of Chesapeake and Ohio lines north of the James promoted the rapid growth of Newport News at the eastern terminus. Many communities along these routes prospered, but none more so than Big Lick. Renamed Roanoke in 1882, the city became an important railroad center and by the end of the century had the South's largest locomotive manufacturing plant.

Chesapeake and Ohio Railroad piers, Newport News, ca. 1900

Miners at the Pocahontas coalfields, ca. 1940

New industries developed in several regions of Virginia. Richmond, long a center for the manufacture and sale of tobacco products, became a national leader in the production of cigarettes after 1876. Danville developed a flourishing textile industry, drawing upon the cotton and wool sent from the Southeast. Economic growth fostered recovery in other elements of society, too. In 1872, the Virginia Agricultural and Mechanical College was founded at Blacksburg as the state's principal land-grant college. Randolph-Macon Woman's College (1891) in Lynchburg, the Virginia Normal and Collegiate Institute (1882) at Petersburg, and the Hampton Normal and Agricultural Institute (1868) were also established during this period.

Virginia's cultural leaders included the talented artists John Elder, William Ludwell Sheppard, and Conrad Wise Chapman, all Confederate veterans. John Banister Tabb wrote popular verse, and humorist George W. Bagby's stories of Virginia before and after the war combined social comment with gentle humor. Thomas Nelson Page, writing nostalgic tales of plantation life, and John Esten Cooke, writing novels about southern soldiers, found a ready market for romanticized tales of the Old South and the Civil War. Usually printed by northern publishers or in northern periodicals and read by a national audience, southern literature that glorified the Confederacy's Lost Cause provided the citizens of the New South, and the United States, with a mythic past seemingly free from any responsibility for slavery and the Civil War. The New South envisioned by men like Cooke and Page and the southern entrepreneurs was to be markedly different from the Old South and would foster business and industry as well as agriculture.

Several women also emerged as significant writers in the postwar period. Mary Virginia Hawes Terhune, writing under the pen name Marion Harland, was the most prolific. Publishing her first novel at age twenty-four, Harland eventually wrote twenty-five novels, an equal number of books on household advice, and numerous biographies, travel books, and magazine articles. Also popular were essayist, novelist, and short-story writer Constance Cary Harrison, perhaps best known for her *Recollections Grave and Gay* (1912), and Amélie Rives (later Troubetzkoy), whose controversial first novel, *The Quick or the Dead?* (1888), propelled her to instant fame. Virginian Elizabeth Keckley may have been the first African American to publish a best-seller. *Behind the Scenes: Thirty Years as a Slave and Four Years in the White House* (1868) described Keckley's experiences during the Civil War as a dressmaker and confidante to Mary Todd Lincoln. Many less-famous women also wrote for publication to support themselves or to supplement their family income, when few other employment opportunities existed.

Carpentry shop at Hampton Institute, ca. 1939. The school was established in 1868 as the Hampton Normal and Agricultural Institute.

Funders and Readjusters

The 1870 restoration of civilian government in Virginia did not transform the stormy decade of war and Reconstruction into an era of political calm. Governor Gilbert C. Walker and the Conservative majority in the General Assembly faced many problems, but the most vexing was the public debt. Virginia had entered the war with an accumulated debt of just over $37 million for turnpikes, canals, and railroads. No payments on the principal had been made during the conflict, and an 1866 attempt to fund two-thirds of the interest had failed. West Virginia, despite its earlier consent, would not agree to pay the share of the debt (about one-third) that Virginia thought it should assume, and negotiations between the two states broke down in 1866 and again in 1870. By 1 January 1871 the state debt, principal and interest, totaled

$47,287,141, and the creditors, most of whom were northerners and Europeans, were demanding payment.

The Fourteenth Amendment to the Constitution of the United States had invalidated the debts the Confederate states contracted during the Civil War, and several southern states repudiated some or all of their antebellum debts as well. But Governor Walker and the Conservatives announced in 1870 that Virginia would honor all its prewar obligations rather than risk alienating potential northern and foreign investors. The next year Virginia sold its canal stock and most of its valuable railroad stock, and Walker signed the Funding Act of 1871, designed to pay off Virginia's two-thirds of the debt by retiring old state bonds and certificates of indebtedness in exchange for new bonds that paid 6 percent interest and matured on 1 July 1905. (Other certificates were issued for West Virginia's unconceded third of the debt.) To ensure a prompt transition from the old bonds to the new, the state stopped paying interest on the earlier bonds and agreed that coupons from the new ones could be used to pay state taxes.

Described as "the most disastrous piece of economic legislation in Virginia history," the Funding Act of 1871 pledged the state to pay off a large debt at high interest. When citizens started paying taxes with the coupons instead of with cash, tax revenues fell to less than half the sum required to maintain state services and pay the state's creditors, and the pre-1871 balance in the state treasury suddenly became a staggering deficit. Faced with the dismal prospect of substantially increased taxes and reduced appropriations for such services as the new public school system, Virginians repeatedly attempted both to repeal the clause permitting payment of taxes with coupons and to refinance the debt at a lower interest rate. These efforts were denied by Conservative governors, adverse rulings by the state's Supreme Court of Appeals, and unenthusiastic investors.

An alternative to full payment of the state debt, which seemed an impossible task, was a partial repudiation of the debt and a good-faith effort to pay the balance. Advocates of this course came to be called Readjusters, and adherents to the policy adopted in 1871 were called Funders. For fifteen years the two factions battled each

Members of the House of Delegates Committee of Asylums and Prisons for the 1871–1872 and 1872–1873 sessions, a period of significant change in Virginia politics

other on the campaign trails and in the General Assembly. Dissatisfaction with the Funders mounted as public services deteriorated, taxes increased, and Virginians suffered during the depression that followed the financial panic of 1873. The leader of the Readjusters was Petersburg's William Mahone, a slightly built, bearded man of inexhaustible energy and ambition who had commanded Confederate forces at the Battle of the Crater and later had become a railroad tycoon. Mahone forged a coalition of Republicans from the mountain counties of Virginia, small businessmen, blacks who felt abandoned by the Republican Party and who opposed the reduction of school appropriations, and others disenchanted with the policies of the Funders. His organizing skills produced victories at the polls. In 1879 the Readjusters gained control of the General Assembly; in 1880 they sent Mahone to the United States Senate; and in 1881 the Readjuster William E. Cameron, of Petersburg, defeated the Funder John Warwick Daniel, a Democrat from Lynchburg, for governor.

The Readjusters immediately passed the Riddleberger Act of 1882, named for state senator Harrison Holt Riddleberger, which replaced the existing 6 percent bonds with new fifty-year bonds that paid 3 percent interest. The total face value of the new bonds was approximately one-third less than the 1871 bonds, and the new bonds' coupons could not be used to pay taxes. By appointing auditors who enforced the tax laws strictly, the Readjusters collected hundreds of thousands of dollars in delinquent taxes. They also reduced taxes on farms and small businesses and raised taxes on corporations and corporate property. By the simple reform of providing state assessors to determine the taxable value of railroad properties—rather than permitting railroad company officials to make these appraisals—the Readjusters greatly increased tax revenues. Measures such as these relieved the heavily burdened taxpayers and enriched

The nomination of William E. Cameron at the 1881 Readjuster state convention in Richmond

the state treasury. Within two years the Funders' deficit had been replaced by a $1.5 million surplus. Although the political debate about the state debts ended after federal courts upheld the Readjuster legislation, bondholders who failed to exchange old bonds for new ones and litigation over the payment of taxes with old bond coupons delayed final settlement of the debt question until 1892, when the General Assembly passed the Olcott Act, which satisfied creditors by issuing new one-hundred-year bonds (at 2 percent interest for the first decade and 3 percent thereafter) that paid off nearly 70 percent of that portion of the debt repudiated by the Riddleberger Act of 1882. Only the question of West Virginia's share remained, and it was settled in 1915 by the Supreme Court of the United States in *Virginia* v. *West Virginia*. West Virginia's share of the 1861 principal was set at 23.5 percent, less credits for the western counties' prewar contributions to Virginia's educational and other tax-supported funds. With accrued interest as of 1 July 1915, West Virginia owed Virginia $12,393,929.50, and between 1919 and 1939 paid the amount in full.

Readjusters and Democrats

The Readjusters' program included more than just the state debt. In addition to their strong support for the new public school system, the Readjusters attempted to improve the faculties and curricula of the Medical College of Virginia and the University of Virginia and replaced members of the governing boards of both schools. They established the Petersburg teacher training school for blacks that became Virginia State University. Although their attempts to regulate the state's railroads were largely unsuccessful, they had better luck with their efforts to stimulate Virginia's business economy by attracting capital from other states and countries. The Readjuster ascendancy in Virginia politics was as short as it was dramatic. Once the party had accomplished the main task for which it was founded, it fell apart. The conspicuous place of blacks in Mahone's organization and in the General Assembly provoked a white backlash, even among Mahone's own followers. When Mahone entered the United States Senate he joined the Republican Party, which alienated many Democrats who had helped bring his Readjusters to power. His use of federal patronage antagonized supporters who received less than they wished and gave him a reputation as an unscrupulous political boss. By the end of William E. Cameron's term as governor, warring factions split the Readjuster Party. In 1885 the Readjuster candidate, John S. Wise, lost a lopsided race for governor against the Democrat Fitzhugh Lee.

Mahone and his Republican allies remained important in Virginia politics, but the rejuvenated Democratic Party soon gained the ascendancy. Rebuilt by railroad executive John Warwick Daniel, a politician as skillful as Mahone, the Democratic Party attracted Whigs and Democrats, Confederates and Unionists, Funders and Readjusters, and many of the state's leading bankers, lawyers, and railroad executives. In an age of increasing racial prejudice, it was a white man's party unified by the occasional efforts of Republicans in Congress to assist southern blacks and by reminders of the important role blacks had played in Mahone's machine. Fitzhugh Lee's victory in 1885 began a Democratic Party domination of Virginia politics that lasted longer than three-quarters of a century. The next year Daniel replaced Mahone in the Senate, and in 1894 Daniel's principal lieutenant, Thomas Staples Martin, a lawyer and railroad lobbyist from Scottsville, won Virginia's other Senate seat.

John Mercer Langston was elected in 1888 and seated in
1890 as Virginia's first African American member of Congress.

Using finesse and flexibility to hold the coalition together, Daniel and Martin created a Democratic organization that contained few reformers. Martin, the able political manager, was the organization's leader from the time he entered the Senate until his death in 1919. Challenged by the Populists and the Progressives, Martin's organization did not always get its way in Richmond or Washington, D.C., but Martin was majority leader of the United States Senate in 1911–1913 and again in 1917–1919. The hard times that afflicted southern farmers in the late nineteenth century sparked occasional political revolts—the Grange movement in the 1870s, the Greenbackers in the 1880s, and the Populists in the 1890s—demanding reform of banking and railroad practices and an inflation of the currency. Although the Populist Party was not strong in Virginia, its proposals appealed to many Virginia farmers and to some of the politicians in Martin's organization. Daniel advocated the free coinage of silver in the 1890s and supported presidential candidate William Jennings Bryan in 1896, and many western Virginians objected to the railroads' practice of charging higher rates for short shipments. It cost farmers as much to ship a barrel of flour from Staunton to Richmond as from Memphis to Richmond. Readjuster legislation had not dealt with such matters, and many of Martin's followers sought to regulate the powerful corporations. Although the Populists strained the organization, Martin's wing of the state Democratic Party withstood most of the pressures for change, tolerating any dissident voices that it could not silence.

More far-reaching than the Populist proposals were the reforms advocated by the Progressives between 1900 and World War I. The inspiration for much of the period's legislation came from women who sought the help of state and local governments in redressing the many social and economic problems they had discovered through their work in community organizations. A coalition of Richmond churchwomen, for example, in 1901 had raised money for the Instructive Visiting Nurses' Association—an association of dedicated professional nurses attempting to provide basic health care for the city's poor. They were soon horrified by the depth of substandard housing and disease-ridden conditions that existed in Richmond's impoverished neighborhoods. Through the IVNA, they became vocal advocates of public health reform and regulation. In other instances, prominent clubwomen such as Lila Meade Valentine and Mary Munford, who founded the Richmond Education Association in 1900, quickly realized that poor classroom facilities, budget shortages, inadequate teacher salaries, and outdated curricula were not confined to Richmond's school system alone. They led the movement to organize the Cooperative Education Association, a statewide citizens' action group, launched a successful fund-raising effort known as the May Campaign of 1905, and inspired a network of fifty local education associations, most headed by women, that worked tirelessly to improve Virginia's public schools. Women from a wide variety of community organizations also formed partnerships with concerned male reformers to promote the major Progressive issues of the period: an eight-hour workday, prohibition of child labor, community sanitation ordinances, public health regulations, financial support for public education, stricter regulation of business and industry, consumer protection laws, the direct election of United States

The Late Campaign in Virginia—Democrats in Accomack Co. Entertaining Black Voters at an Oyster-Bake, **from** *Frank Leslie's Illustrated Newspaper,* 16 November 1889

senators, a federal income tax, and modernization of state and municipal governments.

This Progressive impulse carried Andrew Jackson Montague into the Virginia
governor's office in 1902 against the wishes of Senator Martin. Montague's accom-
plishments were modest compared with the records of Progressive governors in other
states, but his administration enacted some proposals that citizens' groups and individual leaders in Martin's organization favored, most notably in the area of public
education. Montague and his successors, Claude Augustus Swanson and William
Hodges Mann, increased appropriations for the schools while bridging the gap
between old-line and reform-minded Democrats. An able politician and the most progressive of Martin's loyal followers, Swanson joined Martin in the U.S. Senate after
Daniel died in 1910 and took the reins of the Democratic organization after Martin
died in 1919.

Church groups, like this one from the Norfolk area, ca. 1905, provided an important vehicle for
women helping to shape Virginia's social life around the turn of the century.

Virginia Confederate veterans' reunion, ca. 1900. The Constitution of 1902 in effect limited the vote to war veterans and their adult sons and to white male property owners. (*Courtesy of the Clarke County Historical Association*)

The Constitution of 1902

At the close of the nineteenth century, Virginia's Democrat-controlled General Assembly called for a convention to revise the Underwood Constitution, and the voters of Virginia approved the call in a spring 1900 referendum. The political forces that led to the Convention of 1901–1902 were many. Recent hard-fought campaigns had been expensive, and occasionally violent or corrupt, and many Virginians recognized the need for electoral reform. Some Democrats also wanted to streamline the state's judicial system, others agitated for Progressive reforms such as primary elections to nominate candidates for the United States Senate, and western Democrats still wanted to regulate the politically powerful railroads. At the same time, Democratic Party leaders from the eastern and southern portions of the state sought to deny the vote to blacks, whose allegiance to the Republican Party made it a formidable political factor. With public support for disfranchisement growing, the voters elected twelve Republican and eighty-eight Democratic delegates to the convention that met in two sessions between 12 June 1901 and 26 June 1902.

The convention adopted suffrage restrictions prepared by Carter Glass, of Lynchburg, similar to those introduced in several other southern states, in order to deny the vote to black Virginians without appearing to violate the letter of the Fifteenth Amendment to the Constitution of the United States. The Constitution of 1902 limited the vote to war veterans and their adult sons and to property owners who had paid at least $1 in property taxes during the previous year or who could give "a reasonable explanation" of any portion of the new state constitution. After 1 January 1904, any twenty-one-year-old male meeting the residency requirement could register to vote if he had paid a $1.50 poll tax for each of the preceding three years, completed the registration application in his own handwriting, and satisfactorily answered "any and all questions" asked by the registrar concerning "his qualifications as an elector." Other provisions of the Constitution of 1902 and the new election laws gave the Democratic majority in the General Assembly the power to appoint and supervise most of the registrars and polling-place officers, who often arranged for the Democratic Party to pay the poll taxes of poor Democrats but who found that few blacks or white Republicans gave acceptable answers to questions about the constitution or their qualifications. In this way, the suffrage provisions of the new constitution reduced the number of Virginia's voters by more than half and cut the number of black voters from about one hundred forty-seven thousand to fewer than ten thousand by 1904.

The Constitution of 1902 kept the reins of government in the General Assembly, where they had traditionally been, and for the first time a Virginia constitution expressly prohibited the education of "white and colored children" in the same schools. The constitution's Progressive features were restricted to primary elections to nominate candidates for the United States Senate, a reformed county court system, and the creation of the State Corporation Commission, which soon forced railroads to abandon the difference in freight rates for long and short shipments. Rather than submit its work to the voters, many of whom might not have voted to ratify a constitution designed to deny their future participation in politics, the Convention of 1901–1902 proclaimed that the new constitution would take effect on 10 July 1902. This unorthodox procedure surprised many Virginians but was approved by the governor and the General Assembly as well as by the state Supreme Court of Appeals in its *Taylor* v. *Commonwealth* decision of 1903.

Although Senator Martin's organization had reluctantly supported the call for the convention only in the face of Progressive pressure, he and his faction embraced the new constitution and used the altered suffrage provisions to their advantage. The Virginia electorate was thereby rendered small and relatively manageable for many years to come, and, except in some of the mountain counties, the Republicans were no longer an effective opposition party. The number of Virginia voters did, however, increase after the Nineteenth Amendment to the Constitution of the United States extended the franchise to women in 1920, but until the 1950s the poll tax, complicated registration procedures, and activities of local officials kept the proportion of Virginia voters lower than any other state's. Not until the federal Voting Rights Act of 1965 and the *Harper* v. *Virginia State Board of Elections* decision by the U.S. Supreme Court the following year—invalidating poll taxes as requirements for voter registration—was the work of the Convention of 1901–1902 undone.

Woman Suffrage

The first attempt to organize Virginia women in a campaign for the right to vote occurred in May 1870, when Richmonder Anna Whitehead Bodeker invited several men and women sympathetic to the cause to a meeting that launched the first Virginia State Woman Suffrage Association. Between 1870 and 1872, Bodeker, as president of the new association, tried to win public support for woman suffrage by writing articles for the local press and inviting many prominent national suffrage leaders to lecture before Richmond audiences. She also attempted unsuccessfully to vote in the municipal election in November 1871, asserting her qualifications under the new Fourteenth and Fifteenth Amendments to the U.S. Constitution. Despite Anna Bodeker's energetic efforts, the movement did not gain many followers and soon faded from public consciousness. Virginia women faced tremendous pressure in the post–Civil War period to conform to traditional ways, and conservative politicians were unwilling to consider seriously an issue linked in their minds with the much-hated politics of Radical Reconstruction.

Orra Gray Langhorne, of Lynchburg, attempted to revive the Virginia suffrage issue during the 1890s, but the association she founded and led was also short-lived. Finally, in 1909, a dedicated group that included writers Ellen Glasgow, Mary Johnston, and Kate Langley Bosher, artist Adèle Clark, and reformer Lila Meade Valentine came together in Richmond to form the Equal Suffrage League of Virginia. Within its first few months, the league, under the able direction of Lila Valentine, joined with the National American Woman Suffrage Association and began a public campaign to educate Virginia citizens on the issue. Virginia's suffragists argued that, as taxpayers and citizens, women deserved and wanted the vote and that their influence in politics would improve the quality of government at all levels. Public opinion responded slowly to the league's message, but membership in the organization climbed steadily and spread to other areas of the state. In 1914, the Equal Suffrage League reported 45 local chapters; by 1916 that number had grown to 115. Antisuffragists formed a counter organization to refute the league's arguments, claiming that most Virginia women had no interest in voting and that woman suffrage

A 1915 suffrage rally on the steps of the Virginia Capitol led by Lila Meade Valentine, president of the Equal Suffrage League of Virginia (*Valentine Museum, Richmond, Virginia*)

would open the door for black women to vote, thus violating the spirit behind Virginia's 1902 constitution.

The Equal Suffrage League's strategy focused on winning support in the General Assembly for a voting-rights amendment to the state constitution. Some suffragists grew impatient with the painstaking approach and broke ranks, joining the more militant Congressional Union (later the National Woman's Party), then pressuring Congress and President Woodrow Wilson to enact a federal suffrage amendment. The National Woman's Party demonstrated in Washington, D.C., during World War I, while mainstream suffragists instead directed their energies to the war effort. Pauline Adams, president of the Norfolk branch of the National Woman's Party, was among the protestors arrested and sent to federal prison in Lorton, Virginia.

Virginia suffragists succeeded in bringing the issue to the floor of the General Assembly three times between 1912 and 1916, but not once did the vote come close to passage. Although they took heart in 1918 when Great Britain gave women the vote, and celebrated the following year when Virginia-born Nancy Astor became Britain's first woman member of Parliament, disappointment marked their efforts to convert Virginia's political establishment. When Congress passed the Nineteenth Amendment in June 1919, the Equal Suffrage League fought hard for ratification but Virginia politicians did not relent. Virginia women at last won the right to vote in August 1920, when the Nineteenth Amendment became law, but the General Assembly stubbornly withheld its ratification until 1952.

The Equal Suffrage League gave way to the nonpartisan League of Women Voters, which sponsored registration drives, voter education programs, and lobbying efforts on behalf of social welfare issues. In January 1924, Sarah Lee Fain and Helen Timmons Henderson became the first Virginia women elected to serve in the House of Delegates.

Sarah Lee Fain (left) and Helen Timmons Henderson (right), the first Virginia women to serve in the House of Delegates. Both were elected in 1924.

Governor Harry Flood Byrd at the launching of the USS *Houston* at Newport News shipyards, 7 September 1929

The Byrd Organization

Within two years of Thomas Martin's death in 1919, the demise of several other Democratic Party leaders created vacancies in the organization that were filled by conservative young men. Foremost among the rising generation was Harry Flood Byrd, of Winchester, whose father Richard E. Byrd and uncle Henry D. Flood had been key figures in Martin's organization. Byrd became state Democratic Party chairman in 1922 and was elected governor in 1925. During his four-year term, Byrd reorganized the executive branch of state government, lessening the number of state agencies, consolidating departments, and cutting operating expenses. He successfully campaigned for constitutional amendments to reduce the number of elected state officials, empowering the governor to appoint and dismiss most of the state agency heads, and for the first time giving the governor of Virginia control of the administration of state government.

Byrd also strengthened his personal influence in the Democratic Party. During the 1920s, with Senator Claude Swanson increasingly engrossed in national politics, Harry Byrd cultivated a personal following throughout the state, installing loyal men in county and city offices and in key positions in Richmond, most notably Everett Randolph Combs as state comptroller. Deploying the powers of his office with great skill, Governor Byrd built a powerful base from which he intended to challenge Swanson's primacy within the Democratic Party organization. When President Franklin D. Roosevelt appointed him secretary of the navy in 1933, Swanson broke his ties with state politics. Succeeding Swanson in the U.S. Senate, Byrd remained until his resignation in 1965 the dominant figure in Virginia politics.

Harry F. Byrd Sr. committed the state Democratic Party to low taxes, the poll tax, and (under the banner "Pay as You Go") steadfast opposition to public debt for any purpose. Becoming critical of the New Deal early in Roosevelt's first administration, Senator Byrd spent his years in Washington fighting to reduce the size and expenditures of the federal government. Byrd reluctantly endorsed Roosevelt in the presidential election of 1936 but never thereafter supported a Democratic Party presidential nominee. Roosevelt nevertheless carried Virginia in 1936, 1940, and 1944, and Harry S. Truman won the state in 1948 by a narrow margin provided by black voters in the Norfolk and Hampton precincts. After 1952—as the Byrd organization's commitment to conservative principles supplanted its historic affiliation with the Democratic Party—Republican presidential candidates carried Virginia in every election, except when the state supported fellow southerner Lyndon B. Johnson in 1964.

The Great Depression

The economic collapse that followed the stock market crash of 1929 crippled Virginia. The Old Dominion's farmers had faced hard times throughout the 1920s, but by the inauguration of President Franklin D. Roosevelt in March 1933 nearly every Virginian had been affected by the Great Depression. The federal government responded to the crisis with a wide variety of assistance agencies. One of the largest of the New Deal programs, the Public Works Administration (PWA), invested approximately $117.3 million toward 740 federal projects in Virginia as well as another 350 local ones scattered across the state. Within a three-year period, for example, Virginia schools received $11.8 million in PWA funds, of which $1.75 million was for the state's predominantly rural African American school districts. The PWA financed a wide variety of other programs, including a housing project in Altavista, a waste-treatment plant in Staunton, harbor improvements in Newport News, and additions to the Veterans Administration Hospital in Roanoke. The Blue Ridge, Colonial, and Skyline Drive Parkways were also PWA projects. Colleges benefited as well: several buildings at the College of William and Mary, Mary Washington College, and Virginia Polytechnic Institute were constructed with PWA funds. Both the Virginia State Library and the Alderman Library at the University of Virginia were also built with substantial federal assistance.

The popular Civilian Conservation Corps (CCC), founded in March 1933, opened its first camp in the nation in April 1933 within the George Washington National Forest, near Luray. Between 1933 and 1942, the CCC spent $109 million in the Old Dominion, employing 107,210 men in more than eighty Virginia camps. The workers, all between the ages of eighteen and twenty-five, built 986 bridges, strung 2,128 miles of telephone line, stocked waterways with 1.3 million fish, planted 15.2 million trees, and developed Virginia's first state park system.

In June 1933, the Virginia Emergency Relief Administration began directing additional federal aid to the more than eighty thousand Virginians still on relief. Under the direction of William A. Smith, a Petersburg engineer, the agency employed approximately forty-five thousand of them on more than twenty-five hundred work-relief projects. One such program, the Women's Work Division, under the direction of Richmonder Ella Agnew, found tasks for even the most unskilled. Some found work

Depression-era photograph of local residents at the Nethers Post Office, Madison County

as cooks, others were assigned to cleaning duties in government offices, and some staffed child-care centers. In Portsmouth and Norfolk, for example, women joined rat-catching patrols to reduce the chance of epidemic disease.

The federal Works Progress Administration (WPA), created in 1935, funded locally sponsored projects and was especially intended to provide a "security wage" for those still in search of work. The WPA in 1938, for instance, hired unemployed farm workers from the tidewater area: within a year they created the Norfolk Botanical Gardens from what had been an overgrown 120-acre tract. Virginia's WPA wage ranged from twenty-one to seventy-five dollars per month and, unlike many other federal programs, could be used to assist the many unemployed white-collar workers. One WPA relief program, the Virginia Writers' Project, begun in November 1935, produced two noteworthy books in 1940: *Virginia: A Guide to the Old Dominion*, a volume in the American Guide series, and *The Negro in Virginia*, sponsored by Hampton Institute. The WPA in eight years employed as many as ninety-five thousand Virginians and paid approximately $66 million in wages. By 1943, with the rush of wartime economic activity in Virginia and elsewhere, the WPA as well as the New Deal's other programs came to an end.

Unemployed farm workers from the Norfolk area hired in 1938 by the Works Progress Administration to create a public garden in a 120-acre tract of woodland. The Norfolk Botanical Gardens opened a year later. *(From the collection of the Norfolk Public Library)*

Desegregation

World War II, with its stirring rhetoric of national unity and its threatening example of Nazi racism, reinvigorated the long struggle for civil rights for African Americans. Immediately before the war, Norfolk teacher Melvin O. Alston had won a ruling in the federal courts that local school boards had to offer equal pay to black and white teachers. Teachers across the state subsequently began pressing for parity in their salaries. Returning black veterans were especially determined to obtain their rights, and campaigns to register black voters sprang up in several places during the late 1940s. Moreover, for the first time since 1900, African American candidates made serious runs for local elective offices. One such candidate, attorney Oliver W. Hill, won election to the Richmond City Council in 1948.

Meanwhile, a series of decisions by the United States Supreme Court increasingly undermined the legal basis for racial segregation. In *Morgan* v. *Commonwealth of Virginia*, for example, the Court in 1946 addressed the issue of segregation in interstate commerce and ruled against the long-standing practice. It was, though, in its 17 May 1954 landmark decision, *Brown* v. *Board of Public Education of Topeka, Kansas*, that the Court dealt its most crippling blow to separatism. The Court ruled that the racial segregation of public schools was unconstitutional. In 1952, a federal district court in the case of *Davis* v. *County School Board of Prince Edward County, Va.*, had agreed that a local black high school had received unequal resources, but the lower court had nevertheless upheld the education system's policy of segregation. It was the Supreme Court in the *Brown* case two years later that firmly declared that separate schools for blacks and whites were inherently unequal and in violation of the Fourteenth Amendment's guarantee of "equal protection of the laws."

By the mid-1950s, postwar Virginia had entered a period of swift change, particularly as its urban population expanded and manufacturing began to drive the economy. Public education thus played an especially important role both for parents and for those who sought to entice business and industry to the state. The Byrd organization, with its voting strength based in rural Virginia, had nonetheless successfully fought off challenges from moderate Republicans and even from reformers within its own Democratic Party who sought a more modern and responsive state government.

At first stunned into silence by the 1954 Supreme Court decision, the Byrd organization soon responded to the ruling with a plan of opposition formulated by Senator Byrd and James J. Kilpatrick, then editor of the *Richmond News Leader*. Rather than abandon segregation, resisters prepared to deny state aid to any public school that placed white and black pupils in the same classroom. Initially, what became known as the Massive Resistance movement was popular among many white Virginians, but its consequences soon became apparent. In September 1958 the public schools in Front Royal closed. Those in Charlottesville, Norfolk, and Prince Edward County followed,

A group gathered for the "Story Hour" at the Robert Robinson Library, a "Negro Branch," in Alexandria, ca. 1945

and closings in Richmond and northern Virginia appeared imminent. After one last defiant speech, Governor J. Lindsay Almond Jr. broke with the Byrd organization, called the General Assembly into special session in January 1959, and by a one-vote margin in the Senate managed to repeal the state's Massive Resistance legislation. In its place, many of Virginia's white leaders embraced what one historian has called "passive resistance," accepting token desegregation while seeking to delay and limit any further change. Public schools reopened everywhere except in Prince Edward County, where for years white children attended segregated private schools. In contrast, black children faced a public school system that remained closed until 1964: some ceased schooling altogether; others attended makeshift classes in their neighborhood churches; still others simply left the county.

Most of the Byrd organization's leaders continued to fight against the federal enforcement of desegregation. Byrd and Congressman Howard W. Smith, of Alexandria, delayed, but were unable to prevent, passage of the federal Civil Rights Act of 1964 and the Voting Rights Act of 1965. The enforcement of these statutes gradually eroded rigid segregation in housing, education, employment, and public services and enabled black Virginians once again to exert some measure of influence in the traditionally all-white domain of state politics.

Despite the court rulings and federal legislation, school desegregation still proceeded slowly in Virginia, as elsewhere in the South. In 1968, however, with the Supreme Court's ruling in *Green* v. *County School Board of New Kent County*, localities were required to demonstrate actual progress in desegregation. The pace of change then quickened. School systems in Richmond and other cities, for example, began busing students to school in an effort to overcome the effects of residential segregation. Busing, though, proved unpopular with white parents and only reinforced the movement of whites away from the cities and into the suburbs, in effect resegregating the city schools they left behind. A plan to bus students from adjacent counties to Richmond's city schools and thereby lessen the impact of changing demographics was, however, rejected by the Supreme Court in 1973 and the resegregation of urban schools continued. Despite many positive changes, the complete promise of desegregation remains unfulfilled.

Contemporary Virginia

Both world wars significantly affected Virginia. The state, in turn, contributed much to the conflicts' outcome. The shipyards at Newport News as well as the many military bases that were scattered about both the lower James River basin and northern Virginia attracted huge numbers of civilian workers from rural Virginia, North Carolina, and other states, forever altering the demographics of the Old Dominion. Along the James River, in Prince George County near Petersburg, for example, a World War I munitions plant fostered the growth of a new city, Hopewell, and the evolution of a massive postwar chemical industry based there and in Richmond. Downriver, the Hampton Roads shipyards by 1918 had launched more naval tonnage than all the other navy yards in the country combined. During World War II, the munitions plant at Radford, along the New River in Montgomery County, employed as many as twenty thousand workers. In Newport News, shipyard workers by 1945 had built more than four hundred ships—totaling approximately three and a half mil-

Virginians in the 80th Division, France, 1918 (*U.S. Army Signal Corps*)

lion tons—for the war effort. By 1945, too, nearly 1.7 million men and women had passed through the sprawling Hampton Roads Port of Embarkation.

The depression-era and wartime growth of both the military and the federal government rapidly increased the population of many Virginia cities and counties, especially in the southeastern and northern portions of the state, while growth in state government similarly boosted the population of Richmond and its surrounding counties. Between 1900 and 1990, for example, Virginia's population more than tripled, from 1,854,184 to 6,187,358—representing 2.5 percent of the nation's total population, and ranking twelfth among the states. In 1900, only 18 percent of the Old Dominion's citizens lived in communities of more than twenty-five thousand persons. By 1990, however, nearly 80 percent of all Virginians lived within the state's 41 independent cities and 188 incorporated towns. More than 72 percent of all Virginians lived in eight metropolitan areas: including 1,732,437 in northern Virginia; 1,443,244 in the Norfolk, Virginia Beach, and Newport News corridor; 865,640 in the greater Petersburg and Richmond areas combined; with another 224,477 in Roanoke, 193,928 in Lynchburg, 131,107 in Charlottesville, 108,711 in Danville, and 87,517 Virginians in the Bristol area. By the same year, Chesterfield, Fairfax, Henrico, and Prince William ranked among the state's most populous counties. According to the 1990 federal census, Virginia's Native American population numbered 15,282, while 77.4 percent of the commonwealth's other citizens—4,791,739 people—were Caucasian (of whom 160,288, just over 3 percent, were of Hispanic heritage). African Americans comprised 18.8 percent of the population (1,162,994); 2.6 percent (159,053) were of Asian or

World's largest wind tunnel, Langley Field, ca. 1940 *(NASA, Langley Research Center)*

Polynesian ancestry, with another 2.6 percent represented by other races. The 1990 census returns also reflected the recent immigration of large numbers of Koreans, Vietnamese, and other Asians, often displaced by economic, military, or political conflicts in their homelands.

By 1991, approximately 3.3 million of these Virginians were included in the civilian work force. Federal, state, and local governments remained Virginia's largest employers, providing jobs in 1991 for nearly 19 percent of the Old Dominion's employed population. The remainder of the state's work force was engaged in a wide variety of economic activities: of the state's 3,113,000 nonmilitary employees, approximately 411,200 (13.2 percent) worked in the manufacturing sector, with another 2,419,300 Virginians (77.7 percent) in nonmanufacturing enterprises ranging from mining, contract construction, and transportation to wholesale and retail trade, finance and insurance, service industries, and government agencies. Some 282,500 Virginians (9.1 percent) were employed within the agricultural economy. While 193,000 Virginians were listed as unemployed in 1991 (5.8 percent of the state's civilian labor pool), the commonwealth has long benefited from one of the nation's lowest unemployment rates. The diversity of the Old Dominion's economy has during the twentieth century often cushioned the state from the more severe degrees of job displacement so common to many other areas of the country. For example, despite the significant economic downturn of recent years, Virginians in 1990 earned more than $122 billion in personal income, a 5.8 percent increase over 1989. By 1990, too, the state had a per capita income of $19,671, highest among the southeastern states and above the national average of $18,691.

Much of the commonwealth's economic investment and governmental attention has been directed toward education. Public school enrollment reached a peak of 1,142,998 pupils during the 1975–1976 academic year, requiring a combined federal, state, and local expenditure of nearly $2 billion for the year. In contrast, while there were fewer students (1,029,949) enrolled in the state's more than 1,750 public schools during the 1992–1993 year, annual expenditures for public elementary, junior, and high school education had leapt to nearly $6.2 billion. Virginia also includes five junior and two-year colleges, twenty-three community colleges, and forty-four senior colleges, universities, and postgraduate institutions.

In the arts, Virginia in the early 1900s fostered the efforts of several noted sculptors, including Frederick William Sievers, who completed statues for the Gettysburg battlefield and for Richmond's Monument Avenue, as well as Edward Virginius Valentine and the expatriate Moses Jacob Ezekiel. By the 1930s and 1940s several Virginia artists—most of them painters—such as Edmund Minor Archer, Julien Binford, Nell Blaine, Adèle Clark, Nora Houston, Marion Junkin, Theresa Pollak, and Adèle Williams, as well as African American artists Leslie G. Bolling and George H. Ben Johnson, for example, had also gained a measure of recognition. Photographer Frances Benjamin Johnston during the same period earned fame by specializing in architectural and garden views. The work of the nationally admired editorial cartoonist Fred O. Seibel graced the pages of the *Richmond Times-Dispatch* from 1926 to 1968, and Jeff MacNelly won two Pulitzer Prizes while working as editorial cartoonist for the *Richmond News Leader* during the 1970s.

In the performing arts, internationally known pianist and composer John Powell in the 1930s, along with several other researchers, began collecting and recording hundreds of examples of the Old Dominion's rich heritage of folk and gospel music. Between 1927 and 1943 Virginia's Carter Family contributed perhaps as much to preserving the culture of country music through its performances and recordings, a tradition sustained between 1952 and 1963 by Winchester native Patsy Cline and in more recent years by the Statler Brothers from Staunton. In classical music, the venerable Feldman Chamber Music Society in Norfolk in the 1980s received national recogni-

Photographer Frances Benjamin Johnston (1864–1952)

tion, while symphony orchestras grew in quality and size in northern Virginia and in Norfolk, Richmond, and Roanoke. Also by the early 1980s, the Virginia Opera Company and the Richmond Ballet had inaugurated annual series of major productions. As for the dramatic arts, the Barter Theatre in Abingdon, in Washington County, has since its founding by Robert Porterfield in 1933 made important contributions to the American stage; in the 1950s the Barksdale Theatre in Hanover County was among the first stage companies to foster the concept of the dinner-theater.

In Virginia belles lettres, James Branch Cabell in the early 1900s won considerable fame and notoriety as an experimental novelist; his *Jurgen: A Comedy of Justice*, published in 1919, was later the object of a sensational obscenity trial. Mary Johnston wrote more than a dozen highly popular historical novels during the first quarter of the century. The state's most accomplished writer, however, was Richmond novelist Ellen Glasgow, who won the Pulitzer Prize for literature in 1942 for her novel *In This Our Life*. Prominent recent Virginia writers include novelist William Styron, a native of Southampton County; essayist and novelist Tom Wolfe, of Richmond, who won a National Book Award in 1981; and poet and essayist Annie Dillard, who received a Pulitzer Prize in 1975 for *Pilgrim at Tinker Creek*, a reflection on life and on the surrounding Roanoke River valley. Other significant contemporary writers, to cite but several, include the late V. C. Andrews, Anne Beatty, Patricia Cornwell, Rita Dove, Florence King, Dave Smith, Lee Smith, and Dabney Stuart. Douglas Southall Freeman, editor of the *Richmond News Leader* for thirty-five years, won a Pulitzer Prize in 1935 for his four-volume biography of Robert E. Lee and had nearly completed his seven-volume biography of George Washington when he died in 1953. Equally prolific as a historian and social critic, Carter G. Woodson in 1915 formed the Association for the Study of Negro Life and History and until 1950 edited the national organization's journal; one of Woodson's books, *The Negro in Our History*, first published in 1922, has remained a landmark study through ten subsequent editions. Dumas Malone, editor

Richmond novelist Ellen Glasgow (1873–1945)
(Virginia Historical Society, Richmond, Virginia)

Carter G. Woodson (1875–1950), founder of the
Association for the Study of Negro Life and History

of the magisterial *Dictionary of American Biography* from 1929 to 1936 and later biographer-in-residence at the University of Virginia, received a Pulitzer Prize for the first five books of his six-volume life of Thomas Jefferson, completed in 1981. In 1992, Lewis B. Puller Jr. also won a Pulitzer citation: for his cathartic memoir of the Vietnam War, *Fortunate Son*. In journalism, besides Freeman, other noted Virginia editors included the retired writer Sherwood Anderson, who between 1927 and 1930 owned and edited the *Marion Democrat* and the *Smyth County News*; Virginius Dabney, of the *Richmond Times-Dispatch*; and Pulitzer Prize–winning editors Louis I. Jaffé and Lenoir Chambers, both of the *Norfolk Virginian-Pilot*. P. Bernard Young, owner and editor of the *Norfolk Journal and Guide* for almost forty years, and John Mitchell Jr., editor and publisher of the *Richmond Planet* for forty-five years, created two of the South's most influential African American newspapers.

The preservation and reconstruction of Virginia's eighteenth-century capital, begun by John D. Rockefeller Jr. and William Archer Rutherfoord Goodwin in the 1930s, made Williamsburg the inspiration for outdoor historical museums throughout the world. On a more local scale, the work in Richmond of preservationists Elizabeth Scott Bocock, Louise F. Catterall, and Mary Wingfield Scott, especially between 1930 and 1960, contributed much to the evolving concept of adaptive use of historic buildings and continued the work of the pioneering Association for the Preservation of Virginia Antiquities, organized in 1889.

Virginia in Transition

In 1965, Senator Harry F. Byrd retired from politics, and Mills E. Godwin Jr., an independent-minded conservative and one-time leader of the Massive Resistance movement, was elected governor. Godwin's administration marked the end of the Byrd organization as an institution and as the dominant faction in Virginia politics. In his first message to the General Assembly, Godwin broke sharply with the past by advocating a sales tax to support increased spending for public schools and other state programs. Also at Godwin's urging, the General Assembly established a commission under the chairmanship of former governor Albertis S. Harrison to revise the Constitution of 1902. Legislators completed the revision during special assembly ses-

Governor Mills E. Godwin arriving in Spain for trade negotiations, 30 March 1967

Governor John N. Dalton addressing the opening session of the 1981 Virginia General Assembly

sions in 1969 and 1970. Approved by a 72 percent majority of the voters on 3 November 1970, the constitution became effective on 1 January 1971. It permitted the issuance of general obligation bonds if authorized by voter referendum, increased the legislature's discretionary powers, enhanced the governor's authority to direct the programs of state agencies, and explicitly guaranteed every Virginia child the right to a quality public education. In 1972, the General Assembly established the state's first formal cabinet system, placing state agencies and programs under the administrative control of six cabinet secretaries appointed by and responsible to the governor.

Godwin's break with the pay-as-you-go orthodoxy of the Byrd organization occurred at the same time that other important changes were taking place in Virginia. The state's Republican Party experienced a resurgence, as many Democrats, unhappy with their party's presidential nominees, increasingly voted for Republican candidates. In 1970, for example, A. Linwood Holton became the first Republican governor in nearly a century. Holton, in turn, was succeeded by two more Republicans: Godwin, who left the Democratic Party and defeated Henry E. Howell in the 1973 gubernatorial election, and John N. Dalton, who defeated Howell in 1977. The Republican Party also won nine of the state's ten seats in the House of Representatives and one seat in the United States Senate, gained seats in the General Assembly, and won unprecedented numbers of local offices. Although the Democratic Party consistently won statewide elections during the 1980s, with the exception of a single Senate race, the Republican Party continued to gain strength in the General Assembly. Virginia by the 1970s and 1980s had re-emerged as a two-party state.

Although the pace was often slow, Virginia since World War II had changed in many other ways as well. In 1953, Kathryn H. Stone won election to the House of Delegates—the first woman elected to the General Assembly since the 1930s. Following her victory, numerous women of both parties sought election to public office. In 1979, Eva F. Scott became the first woman to win election to the Virginia Senate. By the early 1990s there were three women among the forty members of the Senate and twelve among the hundred members of the House of Delegates. In 1961, Hazel K. Barger, of Roanoke, was the Republican candidate for lieutenant governor, the first woman in Virginia nominated by a major party for statewide office. In another first, Edythe C. Harrison, of Norfolk, was the Democratic Party nominee for the United States Senate in 1984. Neither Barger nor Harrison won, but in 1985 Delegate Mary Sue Terry, of Henry County, did win election as attorney general of Virginia. The first woman to succeed in a statewide election, Terry won again in 1989 but failed in her bid for the governorship in 1993.

African Americans also gained a measure of political participation during the 1980s. By the end of the decade, blacks had won mayoral elections in most of Virginia's major cities. By 1990 also, blacks had served as city managers in several cities, including Petersburg and Richmond, and as school superintendents in numerous urban and county school systems. The first African American member of a governor's cabinet, and also the first woman cabinet officer in Virginia, was Dr. Jean L. Harris, secretary of Human Resources from 1978 to 1981. Thereafter, every governor's cabinet has included both blacks and women. African Americans also increased their membership in the General Assembly. In 1967 William Ferguson Reid, of Richmond, had won election to the House of Delegates, while two years later Lawrence Douglas Wilder, also of Richmond, won election to the Virginia Senate. They were the first blacks elected to their respective legislative houses in the twentieth century. Although in 1991 there were only two black men and one black woman in the Virginia Senate and only five black men and two black women in the House of Delegates, the reapportionment of the General Assembly's districts following the 1990 federal census seemed to promise that even more Virginians of African American descent would serve in later legislatures. The 1990 census also awarded the Old Dominion an eleventh seat in the House of Representatives. In 1992, following a radical realignment of the state's congressional districts, state senator Robert Cortez ("Bobby") Scott, of Newport News, was elected to the House of Representatives—only the second African American congressman from Virginia, and the first in the twentieth century (John Mercer Langston, born in Louisa County, won election in 1888 and was seated in 1890 as Virginia's first black member of Congress). In the same 1992 election, Delegate Leslie Byrne, of Falls Church, was also elected to the House of Representatives, the first woman member of Congress from Virginia. Most notable of all, Lawrence Douglas Wilder was elected lieutenant governor in 1985 and in 1989 became the first African American in the United States elected governor. Wilder took the oath of office as chief executive of the commonwealth of Virginia on 13 January 1990, a significant signal of change as the Old Dominion approached the end of its fourth century of recorded history.

The January 1990 inauguration of Lawrence Douglas Wilder, the nation's first elected African American governor

Inspector for the State Commission of Fisheries, Walter W. Rowell, examines a cluster of oysters in Wachapreague, Accomack County, ca. 1940. In 1974 the oyster became the state shell.

EMBLEMS OF THE COMMONWEALTH

The Seal

At the Convention of 1776, George Mason, spokesman for the committee that included Richard Henry Lee, George Wythe, and Robert Carter Nicholas, proposed the design for the great seal of the commonwealth on 5 July 1776. *Sic Semper Tyrannis* (Latin for Thus Always to Tyrants) was the state motto chosen for the obverse, or front, of the seal. The design approved by the Convention of 1776 remained unaltered until 1779, when the General Assembly passed a law drafted by Mason to change the motto on the reverse of the seal to its present wording, *Perseverando* (Latin for By Persevering). In all other respects, the present seal of the commonwealth has the design adopted in 1776. Artistic renderings of the convention's description varied, however, during the first century and a half of the seal's use. By 1930 more than a dozen variants of the seal of the commonwealth were being used by various state agencies. After the General Assembly appointed a committee to determine "the correct form and type of the State seal as adopted by the Constitutional Convention of seventeen hundred and seventy-six," it approved the following "accurate and faithful description of the great seal of this Commonwealth, as it was intended to be by Mason and Wythe and their associates":

> The great seal of the Commonwealth of Virginia shall consist of two metallic discs, two inches and one-fourth in diameter, with an ornamental border one-fourth of an inch wide, with such words and figures engraved thereon as will, when used, produce impressions to be described as follows: On the obverse, Virtus, the genius of the Commonwealth, dressed as an Amazon, resting on a spear in her right hand, point downward, touching the earth; and holding in her left hand, a sheathed sword, or parazonium, pointing upward; her head erect and face upturned; her left foot on the form of Tyranny represented by the prostrate body of a man, with his head to her left, his fallen crown near by, a broken chain in his left hand, and a scourge in his right. Above the group and within the border conforming therewith, shall be the word "Virginia," and, in the space below, in a curved line, shall be the motto, "Sic Semper Tyrannis." On the reverse, shall be placed a group consisting of Libertas, holding a wand and pileus in her right hand; on her right, Aeternitas, with a globe and phoenix in her right hand; on the left of Libertas, Ceres, with a cornucopia in her left hand, and an ear of wheat in her right; over this device in a curved line, the word "Perseverando."

While artists were preparing the current depiction of the great seal of the commonwealth in accord with the 1930 act of assembly, it was also decided that leaves of Virginia creeper be used in the prescribed "ornamental border."

The design as originally proposed by George Mason and his fellow committee members closely followed generally accepted elements in its depiction of the various figures. For example, the Roman deity Virtus, as described in *Bell's New Pantheon; or, Historical Directory of the Gods, Demi-Gods, Heroes, and Fabulous Personages of Antiquity,* published in London in 1790, was traditionally depicted "dressed like a woman, or rather like an Amazon, for she is generally represented as a military lady." Her attire in particular was meant to show "her character of readiness for action, and her look a firmness and resolution not to be conquered by any difficulties or dangers that may meet her in her way."

Seal of the commonwealth of Virginia

On the seal's reverse, the design of the three standing figures also closely followed accepted form. Libertas, a Roman deity of liberty, was most often pictured clothed in white and holding "the *rudis*, or wand, and in her right hand the cap of freedom," both of which "refer to the customs of the Romans in setting their slaves free." Ceres, the daughter of Saturn and Vesta, "blessed man with the art of cultivating the earth, having not only taught them to plow and to sow, but also to reap, harvest, and thresh out their grain," and, in a practical vein, had taught mankind to "fix limits or boundaries to ascertain their possessions." Aeternitas was the deity of eternity, usually depicted as a woman, and traditionally accompanied by "a bird, supposed to be a phoenix," as a symbol of immortality. She was also generally pictured holding a small globe, as a sign of her "sovereignty over all." Those who designed the seal did not, however, follow form in every instance. As she signified eternity, Aeternitas ordinarily wore "a covering on her head, because we can never find her beginning," and raiment that bared her legs "because we can see only those parts of her that are actually running on." The latter symbolic element was incorporated. The former, though, was not. Perhaps with good cause. In the case of the Old Dominion, the committee may have decided the beginning was indeed known: 1607.

The great seal of the commonwealth is affixed to documents signed by the governor and intended for use before tribunals and for purposes outside the jurisdiction of Virginia. A smaller version of the obverse of the great seal—one and nine-sixteenths inches in diameter—is used as the lesser seal of the commonwealth on other documents issued by authority of the governor as well as to authenticate the official signature of the secretary of the commonwealth.

The Flag

Virginia had no official state flag until the Virginia State Convention of 1861 passed an ordinance establishing a design virtually identical to that in current use. This flag, by act of assembly, has a deep blue field with a circular white center upon which is "painted or embroidered, to show on both sides alike, the obverse of the great seal of the Commonwealth." A white silk fringe adorns the edge farthest from the flagstaff.

In March 1954 the General Assembly adopted an official salute to the flag of Virginia, House Joint Resolution Number 52, which states: "I salute the flag of Virginia, with reverence and patriotic devotion to the 'Mother of States and Statesmen,' which it represents—the 'Old Dominion,' where liberty and independence were born."

Other Emblems

The state flower is the American dogwood (*Cornus florida*), selected by the General Assembly in 1918 to "foster a feeling of pride in our State and stimulate an interest in the history and traditions of the Commonwealth."

In 1940 the General Assembly adopted James A. Bland's "Carry Me Back to Old Virginia" as the state song to "develop and foster among our citizens and particularly among the children of our schools a feeling of pride in and affection for our

The American foxhound, shown here at a Middleburg dog show, was adopted as the state dog in 1966.

Commonwealth." Bland, an African American songwriter, composed the song in 1875 and copyrighted it in 1878 with its original title, "Carry Me Back to Old Virginny."

The General Assembly chose the Northern Cardinal (*Cardinalis cardinalis*) as the state bird in 1950 because of "its bright plumage and cheerful song." In eighteenth-century England the cardinal was called the "Virginia nightingale."

In 1956 the General Assembly adopted the dogwood (*Cornus florida*), since 1918 the state flower, as the state tree as well, since the dogwood "is well distributed throughout the Commonwealth and its beauty is symbolic of the many attractive features of this State."

In 1966 the General Assembly adopted the American foxhound as the state dog because "George Washington . . . imported fox hounds into this State for hunting purposes and all fox hounds are descendants of these dogs," and because "the American Fox Hound is one of four breeds of American origin, the other three originating in other states."

In 1974 the General Assembly adopted the oyster (*Crassostraea virginica*) as the state shell.

In 1982 the General Assembly adopted milk as the state beverage.

In 1986 the General Assembly designated the Blue Ridge Institute in Ferrum as the State Center for Blue Ridge Folklore.

In 1988 the General Assembly adopted the Chesapeake Bay deadrise as the official boat of the commonwealth.

The Chesapeake Bay deadrise, with its sharp bow, tiny cabin, and long cockpit, operates nearly everywhere on the bay for crabbing, oystering, and fishing. It was named as the state boat in 1988.

Easily identified by its yellow tiger-striped wings and dark tail, the tiger swallowtail butterfly (*Papilio glaucus linne*), is Virginia's state insect. It is one of the most common and conspicuous butterflies of the eastern United States. (*Photograph by Mark Fagerburg*)

In 1991 the General Assembly adopted the tiger swallowtail butterfly (*Papilio glaucus linne*) as the state insect.

In 1991 the General Assembly also adopted "square dancing, the American folk dance which traces its ancestry to the English Country Dance and the French Ballroom Dance, and which is called, cued, or prompted to the dancers, and includes squares, rounds, clogging, contra, line, the Virginia Reel, and heritage dances," as the state folk dance.

In 1993 the General Assembly adopted the brook trout (*Salvelinus fontinalis*) as the state fish.

In 1993 the General Assembly also adopted the *Chesapecten jeffersonius* as the state fossil. "This fossil was the first discovered in North America, being described in 1687 by the naturalist Martin Lister. It was named by malacologist Thomas Say to honor Thomas Jefferson for his interest in natural history. The fossil also celebrates the Chesapeake Bay, the largest estuary in the world."

The Brook Trout, of the salmon family, from *The American Angler's Book: The Natural History of Sporting Fish, and the Art of Taking Them*, by Thaddeus Norris, 1865. The brook trout *(Salvelinus fontinalis)*, surviving only in clear, cold water, populates the mountain rivers and streams of Virginia.

Nicknames

The most popular and enduring of Virginia's many nicknames is the Old Dominion. While this name clearly refers to Virginia's status as England's oldest colony in the Americas, it is impossible to trace the origin of the term with precision. Captain John Smith referred to the Jamestown colony as Old Virginia, a designation later used to distinguish the Chesapeake settlements from those in Massachusetts, which were collectively called New Virginia (and eventually, New England). A 1629 letter from Lord Baltimore to England's King Charles I mentioned the king's dominion of Virginia. In 1660 Charles II acknowledged a gift of silk from "our auntient dominion of Virginia." In 1663 Virginia's new seal bore the motto *En Dat Virginia Quintum* (Behold, Virginia Gives the Fifth), recognizing the colony's status alongside the king's four other dominions of England, Scotland, France, and Ireland. As early as 1699, the phrase "most Ancient Colloney and Dominion" appeared in official state documents.

Virginia is known, too, as the commonwealth of Virginia. A commonwealth is "a state in which the supreme power is vested in the people." The term as an official designation was first used in Virginia during the Interregnum (1649–1660), the period between the reigns of Charles I and Charles II during which Parliament's Oliver Cromwell as Lord Protector established a republican government known as the Commonwealth of England. Virginia became a royal colony again in 1660, and the word commonwealth was dropped from the governor's full title. When Virginia adopted its first constitution in 1776, the term commonwealth was reintroduced, most likely to emphasize that Virginia's new government was based upon the sovereignty of the people united for the common good, or common weal. The designation commonwealth of Virginia has been used in official records ever since. Three states besides Virginia adopted the appellation commonwealth: Kentucky, Massachusetts, and Pennsylvania.

Among the many other nicknames that have been applied to Virginia are Mother of Presidents, Mother of Statesmen, and Mother of States. Virginia is also known as the Cavalier State: the Cavaliers were those who supported the monarchy against Parliament and Cromwell during the English Civil Wars.

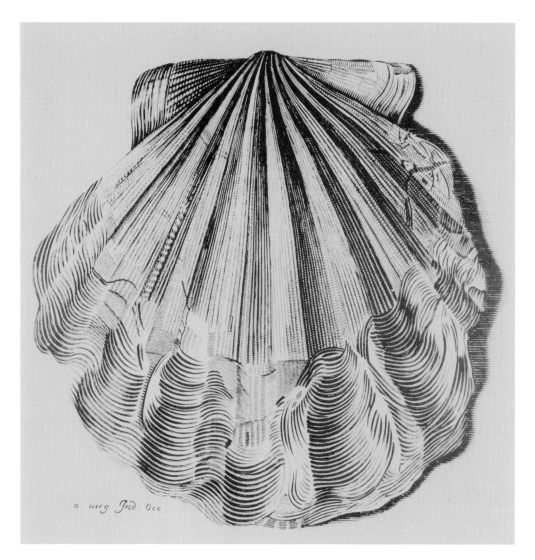

Reportedly the earliest depicted and described fossil from America, *Chesapecten jeffersonius*, a bivalve mollusk of millions of years ago, occurs in the Miocene and Pliocene deposits of the Atlantic Coastal Plain.

Depression-era Farm Security Administration photograph of spinach harvesting in Isle of Wight County. In 1940 nearly two-thirds of Virginia's population was rural.

POPULATION, 1610–1990

In June 1992 the United States Bureau of the Census reported that the 1990 population of Virginia was 6,187,358. In population size, Virginia ranked twelfth in the nation. Virginia's three most populous cities were Virginia Beach with 393,069 residents, Norfolk with 261,229, and Richmond with 203,056. The state's three most populous counties were Fairfax with a population of 818,584, Henrico with 217,881, and Prince William with 215,686. The following table shows the changes in Virginia's population from earliest settlement to the present. The figures for the period before 1790 (when the first federal census was taken) are approximate; figures for the years between 1790 and 1860 include those counties now in West Virginia.

Richmond's Broad Street, 1935

SOURCES: United States Bureau of the Census, *Historical Statistics of the United States: Colonial Times to 1970* (Washington, D.C., 1975), 1:36–37, 2:1168, for the years 1610 through 1780; U.S. Bureau of the Census, *Statistical Abstract of the United States: 1954* (Washington, D.C., 1954), for the years 1790 through 1950; U.S. Bureau of the Census, *County and City Data Book, 1962: A Statistical Abstract Supplement* (Washington, D.C., 1962), for the year 1960; U.S. Bureau of the Census, *1970 Census of Population: General Population Characteristics, Virginia.* U.S. Department of Commerce final report PC(1)–B48, October 1971, for the year 1970; U.S. Bureau of the Census, *1980 Census of Population: General Population Characteristics, Virginia.* Vol. 1, chap. B, pt. 48. U.S. Department of Commerce report PC80–1–B48, August 1982, for the year 1980; and U.S. Bureau of the Census, *1990 Census of Population: General Population Characteristics, Virginia.* U.S. Department of Commerce report CP–1–48, June 1992, for the year 1990; see also Edmund S. Morgan, "Population Growth in Seventeenth-Century Virginia," in *American Slavery—American Freedom: The Ordeal of Colonial Virginia* (New York, 1975), 395–405, for the years 1630 through 1700; and *Population Abstract of the United States: 1993 Edition* (McLean, Va.: Documents Index, 1993), for the years 1790 through 1990.

Population Growth

Year	Population	Rank among the colonies or states
1610	350	1st
1620	2,200	1st
1630	2,500	1st
1640	10,442	1st
1650	18,731	1st
1660	27,020	1st
1670	35,309	1st
1680	43,596	1st
1690	53,046	1st
1700	58,560	1st
1710	78,281	1st
1720	87,757	1st
1730	114,000	1st
1740	180,440	1st
1750	231,033	1st
1760	339,726	1st
1770	447,016	1st
1780	538,004	1st
1790	747,610	1st
1800	886,149	1st
1810	983,152	1st
1820	1,075,069	2d
1830	1,220,978	3d
1840	1,249,764	4th
1850	1,421,661	4th
1860	1,596,318	5th
1870	1,225,163	10th
1880	1,512,565	14th
1890	1,655,980	15th
1900	1,854,184	17th
1910	2,061,612	20th
1920	2,309,187	20th
1930	2,421,851	20th
1940	2,677,773	19th
1950	3,318,680	15th
1960	3,966,949	14th
1970	4,648,494	14th
1980	5,346,818	14th
1990	6,187,358	12th

The primary class of 1921–1922, Witten Mills High School, Tazewell County. More than 80 percent of primary-school-age children in Tazewell attended school in 1921.

In the Old Raleigh Tavern by Howard Pyle, from *Harper's New Monthly Magazine*, May 1896, depicts Thomas Jefferson, Richard Henry Lee, Patrick Henry, and Francis Lightfoot Lee drafting a proposal for the First Continental Congress.

HISTORIC DOCUMENTS

THE FIRST CHARTER OF THE VIRGINIA COMPANY OF LONDON, issued on 10 April 1606 by James I, established companies to found colonies in the New World.

THE SECOND CHARTER OF THE VIRGINIA COMPANY OF LONDON, issued on 23 May 1609, envisaged two colonies: the settlement at Jamestown under "one *able* and *absolute* governor" and another colony to the north.

THE THIRD CHARTER OF THE VIRGINIA COMPANY OF LONDON, issued on 12 March 1612, provided that company affairs be managed both by the treasurer and Council and by majority vote at quarterly meetings of the stockholders. The Third Charter remained in force until 24 May 1624 when, upon the dissolution of the Virginia Company, Virginia became a royal colony.

THE ORDINANCE AND CONSTITUTION OF **1621** was a commission from the Virginia Company of London issued to Sir Francis Wyatt on 24 July 1621 confirming the provisions of a document brought to Virginia in April 1619 by Sir George Yeardley. The original 1619 document, which led to the establishment of the first representative legislature in the New World, has been lost.

THE PROCEEDINGS OF THE VIRGINIA ASSEMBLY was the official journal of the assembly that met, at the call of Governor George Yeardley, at Jamestown from 30 July to 4 August 1619. The assembly included representatives from each of the colony's major subdivisions and plantations. This body, which developed into the present General Assembly of Virginia, was the first representative legislature in the New World.

THE DECLARATION OF THE PEOPLE was the proclamation issued on 3 August 1676 by Nathaniel Bacon Jr. at the height of his rebellion against the colonial government headed by Governor William Berkeley. In this declaration, Bacon claimed justification for his actions and recited the rebels' grievances against the governor.

THE CHARTER OF THE COLLEGE OF WILLIAM AND MARY IN VIRGINIA was granted on 19 February 1693 by the Crown in response to a 20 May 1691 petition from the General Assembly of Virginia asking for a "place of Universal Study, or perpetual College of Divinity, Philosophy, Languages, and other good arts and sciences."

THE STAMP ACT RESOLUTIONS were offered in the House of Burgesses by Patrick Henry on 29 May 1765 in protest against the imposition of stamp duties by the British government. In these resolutions Henry asserted that the power of taxation rested with the General Assembly, rather than with Parliament. The Virginia resolutions were reprinted in newspapers throughout the colonies and stiffened American resistance to the actions of George III's ministers.

THE REPORT OF THE PROCEEDINGS OF A MEETING OF REPRESENTATIVES IN WILLIAMSBURG ON **30 MAY 1774** was signed by twenty-five former members of the

House of Burgesses in response to news of the closing of the port of Boston after the Boston Tea Party. The former burgesses called their colleagues into extralegal session to seek redress of the colony's grievances. This convention, the first of Virginia's five revolutionary conventions, met from 1 August to 6 August 1774 and elected the colony's delegation to the First Continental Congress.

THE RESOLUTIONS OF THE VIRGINIA CONVENTION FOR INDEPENDENCE, passed on 15 May 1776, directed the Virginia delegation at the Continental Congress to move that Congress declare the colonies free and independent. On 7 June the ranking member of the Virginia delegation, Richard Henry Lee, moved "that these United Colonies are, and of right ought to be, free and independent States." On 2 July 1776 Congress passed Lee's motion.

THE VIRGINIA DECLARATION OF RIGHTS, also called the Virginia Bill of Rights, was written by George Mason, of Gunston Hall, and was adopted by Virginia's fifth revolutionary convention on 12 June 1776. Incorporated in the state constitution drafted that same month, it has been retained in all subsequent constitutions of the state, and it formed the basis of the first ten amendments to the federal Constitution, the French Declaration of the Rights of Man and of the Citizen adopted in 1789, and the United Nations' Universal Declaration of Human Rights of 1948.

Among the collections of The Library of Virginia is one of the only eleven existing copies of the United States Bill of Rights, adapted in part from the earlier Virginia Declaration of Rights.

THE VIRGINIA CONSTITUTION OF 1776, adopted by Virginia's fifth revolutionary convention on 29 June 1776, marked the completion of Virginia's transformation from royal colony to independent commonwealth. It vested most governmental powers in the General Assembly and provided that the governor be chosen by that body. It remained in force for fifty-four years. The state's constitution has been rewritten five times since.

THE DECLARATION OF INDEPENDENCE was drafted by a committee that included Thomas Jefferson, the document's principal author, and was adopted by the Continental Congress on 4 July 1776, two days after Congress had passed Richard Henry Lee's resolution for independence. Written with "a decent respect to the opinions of mankind," Jefferson's declaration explained the cause that impelled Americans to separate from Great Britain. Virginia's signers of the Declaration of Independence were: Carter Braxton, Benjamin Harrison, Thomas Jefferson, Francis Lightfoot Lee, Richard Henry Lee, Thomas Nelson Jr., and George Wythe.

THE VIRGINIA STATUTE FOR RELIGIOUS FREEDOM was Thomas Jefferson's eloquent statement of the principles of separation of church and state and of complete religious freedom. He drafted it as the Bill for Establishing Religious Freedom in 1777; it was introduced in the General Assembly on 12 June 1779, but it was not passed until 16 January 1786, having been guided through the assembly by James Madison. Without Madison's leadership, the bill probably would not have passed.

THE RESOLUTIONS FOR THE CESSION OF THE NORTHWEST TERRITORY, passed by the General Assembly on 2 January 1781, authorized the transfer to the United States of Virginia's territory north of the Ohio River. These resolutions included a stipulation that all states formed from the ceded territory should be admitted to the Union on the same basis as the original thirteen. The deed of cession, by which the transfer of about a quarter of a million square miles became final, was completed on 1 March 1784.

THE VIRGINIA PLAN (also known as the Randolph plan or the large-states' plan) was the set of fifteen proposals submitted to the Constitutional Convention at Philadelphia on 29 May 1787 by Edmund Randolph, then governor of Virginia. The plan had been drafted, however, by Randolph's fellow delegate James Madison. William Paterson submitted the New Jersey Plan (or small-states' plan), and in time the Connecticut Compromise resolved the problem of legislative representation by establishing state representation in the Senate and population-based representation in the House of Representatives. Most of the Virginia Plan was incorporated into the Constitution as finally adopted. At a convention called for the purpose, Virginia ratified the new Constitution on 25 June 1788 and was the tenth state to do so.

THE VIRGINIA AND KENTUCKY RESOLUTIONS were adopted late in 1798 by the Virginia and Kentucky legislatures as a formal protest against the restrictive Alien and Sedition Acts, which had been enacted earlier that year by the federal Congress. James Madison drafted the Virginia Resolutions, adopted on 24 December 1798, while the Kentucky Resolutions, adopted on 16 November 1798, were prepared by Thomas Jefferson and introduced by John Breckinridge.

THE CONSTITUTION OF **1830**, the second constitution of the commonwealth of Virginia, was adopted by a convention that met at Richmond from 5 October 1829 to 15 January 1830. It gave the western counties more equitable representation in the assembly and extended the franchise to white male leaseholders and householders. It remained in force for twenty-one years.

THE CONSTITUTION OF **1851**, the state's third constitution, was adopted by a convention that met at Richmond from 14 October 1850 to 1 August 1851. It established universal white, adult-male suffrage and provided that the governor, formerly chosen by the General Assembly, would henceforth be elected by popular vote. This constitution remained in force until after the Civil War.

THE VIRGINIA ORDINANCE OF SECESSION was adopted by the Convention of 1861 at Richmond on 17 April 1861, five days after Confederate forces fired on Fort Sumter and two days after President Abraham Lincoln called for troops to suppress the rebellion in the Southern states. Virginia then joined the newly established Confederate States of America.

THE CONSTITUTION OF **1869**, the fourth of Virginia's six constitutions, was adopted by the Convention of 1867–1868, which met at Richmond from 3 December 1867 to 17 April 1868. Also known as the Underwood Constitution because Judge John C. Underwood was president of the convention, this constitution was ratified by popular vote on 6 July 1869 and provided for universal manhood suffrage, for the establishment of Virginia's first statewide system of public schools, and for the division of each county into magisterial districts. Despite its Reconstruction origins, this constitution remained in force until 1902.

RUFFNER'S REPORT ON SCHOOLS, by William Henry Ruffner, Virginia's first superintendent of public instruction, included a plan for the establishment of free public schools in Virginia as required by the Constitution of 1869. Many of Ruffner's proposals, submitted to the General Assembly on 28 March 1870, were incorporated into the school law adopted on 11 July 1870.

THE CONSTITUTION OF **1902**, the fifth constitution of the commonwealth, was adopted by the Convention of 1901–1902, which met at Richmond from 12 June 1901 to 26 June 1902. The convention proclaimed the new constitution to be in force on 10 July 1902 without allowing the voters to ratify it. It established a poll tax as a prerequisite for voting, effectively disfranchising black voters, and created the State Corporation Commission. Carter Glass, of Lynchburg, played a leading role in the drafting of the constitution, which remained in force for sixty-nine years.

THE CONSTITUTION OF **1971**, the sixth and current constitution of the commonwealth, was drafted by Governor Mills E. Godwin's Commission on Constitutional Revision, approved by the General Assembly, and ratified by the voters on 3 November 1970. It went into effect on 1 July 1971. The present constitution includes provisions for environmental protection, annual legislative sessions, gubernatorial succession in case of disability or death, and state compliance with the federal Voting Rights Act of 1965, as well as a provision permitting increased state borrowing for capital improvements. Its bill of rights was amended to prohibit governmental discrimination on the basis of religious conviction, race, color, sex, or national origin.

Banner of Virginia's Ordinance of Secession, 1861, drawn by calligrapher William Flegenheimer, of Richmond

Inauguration parade of Governor John Garland Pollard, in Richmond's Capitol Square, January 1930

EXECUTIVE OFFICERS OF VIRGINIA

Governors of Virginia
1607–1994

The following list includes all governors, lieutenant governors, presidents of the Council, and other officials who are known to have served as chief executive of Virginia, whether by appointment, by election, or as temporary substitutes for the regularly chosen executives.

The list includes those who held the royal commission as governor but did not go to Virginia, as well as those who, under a variety of titles, actually discharged the governor's duties in Virginia.

Gaps in the records make it impossible to give an exact date for the beginning and end of every administration. Where there is any uncertainty, an approximate date is given.

Beginning with the administration of Governor Henry Lee in 1791, party affiliations are included at the end of the service date and reflect the governor's party affiliation at the time of election. In addition, life dates and place of residence at the time of election are also included. If the area of residence is now an independent city but was not at the time of election, the county is also included (for example: Winchester, Frederick County).

Governors under the Virginia Company of London, 1607–1624

The chief executive of Virginia during the first two years of the colony's existence was the president of the Council, who was chosen by the Council at Jamestown. With the appointment of Sir Thomas Gates, the Virginia Company of London began naming the governor. In the governor's absence, a deputy performed the functions of his office.

EDWARD MARIA WINGFIELD (ca. 1560–1613), president of the Council, 14 May–10 September 1607.

JOHN RATCLIFFE (d. winter 1609–1610), president of the Council, 10 September 1607–22 July 1608.

MATTHEW SCRIVENER (d. 1609), president of the Council, 22 July–10 September 1608.

JOHN SMITH (ca. 1580–1631), president of the Council, 10 September 1608–September 1609.

GEORGE PERCY (1580–ca. 1632), president of the Council, September 1609–23 May 1610.

Thomas West, baron De La Warr (1577–1618), oil painting, 1877,
by William Ludwell Sheppard, after an original portrait

SIR THOMAS GATES (ca. 1560–1622), governor, 23 May–10 June 1610.

THOMAS WEST, BARON DE LA WARR (1577–1618), governor, in Virginia 10 June 1610–28 March 1611. Held title until his death, 7 June 1618; represented for most of his term by deputies.

> **GEORGE PERCY** (1580–ca. 1632), deputy governor under De La Warr, 28 March–19 May 1611.

> **SIR THOMAS DALE** (ca.1565–1619), deputy governor under De La Warr, 19 May–August 1611.

> **SIR THOMAS GATES** (ca. 1560–1622), lieutenant governor under De La Warr, August 1611–March 1614.

> **SIR THOMAS DALE** (ca.1565–1619), deputy governor under De La Warr, March 1614–April 1616.

> **GEORGE YEARDLEY** (bap. 1588–1627), deputy governor under De La Warr, April 1616–15 May 1617.

> **SAMUEL ARGALL** (bap. 1580–1626), deputy governor under De La Warr, 15 May 1617–April 1619.

SIR GEORGE YEARDLEY (bap. 1588–1627), governor, 18 April 1619–18 November 1621.

SIR FRANCIS WYATT (ca. 1588–1644), governor, 18 November 1621–24 May 1624; last governor appointed by the Virginia Company, was continued in office by James I after revocation of the company's charter in 1624.

Governors under the Crown, 1624–1652

Unless otherwise noted, all governors during this period were appointed by the Crown.

SIR FRANCIS WYATT (ca. 1588–1644), governor, 24 May 1624–May 1626.

SIR GEORGE YEARDLEY (bap. 1588–1627), governor, June 1626–12 November 1627. Died in office.

FRANCIS WEST (1586–1634), governor, elected by the Council, 14 November 1627–February 1629.

JOHN POTT (d. before 1642), governor, elected by the Council, 5 March 1629–March 1630.

SIR JOHN HARVEY (d. ca. 1646), governor, March 1630–7 May 1635.

JOHN WEST (1590–1659), governor, elected by the Council, 7 May 1635–18 January 1637.

SIR JOHN HARVEY (d. ca. 1646), governor, 18 January 1637–November 1639.

SIR FRANCIS WYATT (ca. 1588–1644), governor, November 1639–February 1642.

SIR WILLIAM BERKELEY (1605–1677), governor, February 1642–12 March 1652; resident in Virginia except for the period June 1644–7 June 1645, when he was absent on a voyage to England. Relinquished his office when Virginia submitted to Parliament in 1652.

RICHARD KEMP (1600–1649), governor, acted during Berkeley's absence, June 1644–7 June 1645.

Governors under the Commonwealth of England, 1652–1660

During this period, in which Virginia was virtually self-governing, all governors were elected by the General Assembly.

RICHARD BENNETT (bap. 1609–1675), governor, 30 April 1652–31 March 1655.

EDWARD DIGGES (1620–1675), governor, 31 March 1655–December 1656.

SAMUEL MATHEWS (ca. 1630–1660), governor, December 1656–January 1660.

SIR WILLIAM BERKELEY (1605–1677), governor, March 1660–by October 1660, elected by the assembly.

Governors under the Crown, 1660–1775

After the restoration of the English monarchy, the governors were again appointed by the Crown. Many of these, particularly in the eighteenth century, never went to Virginia and were represented by deputies, usually designated as lieutenant governors. When there was no governor or lieutenant governor in residence, the functions of the office were performed by the president, or senior member, of the Council.

SIR WILLIAM BERKELEY (1605–1677), governor, by October 1660–27 April 1677; resident in Virginia except for the period 30 April 1661–November 1662, when he was absent on a voyage to England. Recalled in 1677.

> **FRANCIS MORYSON** (before 1628–ca. 1681), lieutenant governor, acted during Berkeley's absence, 30 April 1661–November 1662.

THOMAS CULPEPER, BARON CULPEPER OF THORESWAY (1635–1689), governor, 20 July 1677–August 1683; resident in Virginia 10 May–11 August 1680 and December 1682–22 May 1683; represented during rest of term by deputy.

> **HERBERT JEFFREYS** (d. 1678), appointed lieutenant governor after Berkeley's recall, served 27 April 1677–17 December 1678. Died in office.

> **SIR HENRY CHICHELEY** (1615–1683), deputy governor under Culpeper, 30 December 1678–10 May 1680 and 11 August 1680–December 1682.

> **NICHOLAS SPENCER** (ca. 1638–1689), president of the Council, 22 May 1683–21 February 1684.

FRANCIS HOWARD, BARON HOWARD OF EFFINGHAM (bap. 1643–1695), governor, 28 September 1683–1 March 1692; in Virginia 21 February 1684–February 1689, except for brief absences in New York during the summers of 1684 and 1687; represented during those intervals and for the remainder of his term by deputies.

> **NATHANIEL BACON SR.** (bap. 1620–1692), president of the Council, acted during Effingham's absences, June–September 1684 and July–September 1687; also served February 1689–3 June 1690.

> **FRANCIS NICHOLSON** (1655–1728), lieutenant governor, deputy to Effingham, 3 June 1690–20 September 1692.

SIR EDMUND ANDROS (1637–1714), governor, 20 September 1692–December 1698; in Virginia, except for a brief absence in Maryland, September–October 1698.

> **RALPH WORMELEY** (1650–1701), president of the Council, acted during Andros's absence, September–October 1698.

FRANCIS NICHOLSON (1655–1728), governor, 9 December 1698–15 August 1705; in Virginia except for brief absences in 1700, 1703, and 1704.

> **WILLIAM BYRD** (1652–1704), president of the Council, acted during Nicholson's absences, September–24 October 1700, April–June 1703, and August–September 1704.

EDWARD NOTT (1657–1706), governor, 15 August 1705–23 August 1706. Died in office.

EDMUND JENINGS (1659–1727), president of the Council, 27 August 1706–10 June 1708.

George Hamilton, earl of Orkney (1666–1737), engraving
by Jacobus Houbraken (1698–1780), Amsterdam, 1742

ROBERT HUNTER (1666–1734), governor, 22 April 1707–September 1709. Captured
by the French on his way to Virginia and never served in the colony.

    EDMUND JENINGS (1659–1727), lieutenant governor, deputy to Hunter, 10
June 1708–23 June 1710.

GEORGE HAMILTON, EARL OF ORKNEY (1666–1737), governor, 18 February
1710–29 January 1737. Never went to Virginia and was represented there by deputies.

    ALEXANDER SPOTSWOOD (1676–1740), lieutenant governor, deputy to
Orkney, 23 June 1710–27 September 1722.

    HUGH DRYSDALE (ca. 1670–1726), lieutenant governor, deputy to Orkney,
27 September 1722–22 July 1726. Died in office.

    ROBERT CARTER (1663–1732), president of the Council, 1 August 1726–11
September 1727.

SIR WILLIAM GOOCH (1681–1751), lieutenant governor, deputy to Orkney and to Albemarle, 11 September 1727–August 1749; in Virginia except for the period 15 October 1740–July 1741, when he was absent on the military expedition against Cartagena.

JAMES BLAIR (ca. 1655–1743), president of the Council, acted during Gooch's absence, 15 October 1740–July 1741.

WILLIAM ANNE KEPPEL, EARL OF ALBEMARLE (1702–1754), governor, 6 October 1737–22 December 1754. Never went to Virginia and was represented by deputies.

THOMAS LEE (1690–1750), president of the Council, 4 September 1749–14 November 1750. Died in office.

LEWIS BURWELL (1710–1756), president of the Council, 21 November 1750–21 November 1751.

ROBERT DINWIDDIE (1692–1770), lieutenant governor, deputy to Albemarle and to Loudoun, 21 November 1751–January 1758.

JOHN CAMPBELL, EARL OF LOUDOUN (1705–1782), governor, 8 March 1756–July 1759. Never went to Virginia and was represented by deputies.

JOHN BLAIR (ca. 1687–1771), president of the Council, 12 January–7 June 1758.

FRANCIS FAUQUIER (1703–1768), lieutenant governor, deputy to Loudoun and to Amherst, 7 June 1758–3 March 1768. Died in office.

SIR JEFFERY AMHERST (1717–1797), governor, 25 September 1759–July 1768. Never went to Virginia and was represented by deputies.

JOHN BLAIR (ca. 1687–1771), president of the Council, 4 March–26 October 1768.

NORBORNE BERKELEY, BARON DE BOTETOURT (1717–1770), governor, 26 October 1768–15 October 1770. Died in office.

WILLIAM NELSON (1711–1772), president of the Council, 15 October 1770–25 September 1771.

JOHN MURRAY, EARL OF DUNMORE (1732–1809), governor, 25 September 1771–June 1775. Dunmore left Williamsburg on 8 June 1775 and sought refuge aboard a British warship. After Dunmore's withdrawal, executive functions were performed by the eleven-man Committee of Safety, chaired by Edmund Pendleton, which was established on 19 August 1775 by Virginia's third revolutionary convention. The committee functioned from the date of its creation through 5 July 1776.

Governors under the Commonwealth, 1776–1865

Under the Constitution of 1776, the General Assembly elected Virginia's governors for one-year terms. No governor could serve more than three consecutive terms or be elected again until after an interval of four years. When the office became vacant by death or resignation, the president or senior member of the Council of State acted as governor until the assembly was able to choose a successor. The Constitution of 1830 left the election of the governor with the General Assembly but changed the term of office to three years with no eligibility for immediate reelection. Since the adoption of the Constitution of 1851, the voters have elected the governors for four-year terms with no eligibility for immediate reelection. The exception is the period of Reconstruction, 1865–1870, when the commanding general of the military district of Virginia named the governor.

PATRICK HENRY (1736–1799), from Hanover County, 6 July 1776–1 June 1779.

THOMAS JEFFERSON (1743–1826), from Albemarle County, 2 June 1779–3 June 1781.

WILLIAM FLEMING (1729–1795), from Botetourt County, member of the Council of State acting as governor, 4–12 June 1781.

THOMAS NELSON (1738–1789), from Yorktown, York County, 12 June–22 November 1781.

DAVID JAMESON (after 1720–1793), from Yorktown, York County, member of the Council of State acting as governor, 22–30 November 1781.

BENJAMIN HARRISON (1726–1791), from Charles City County, 1 December 1781–30 November 1784.

PATRICK HENRY (1736–1799), then resident in Henry County, 30 November 1784–30 November 1786.

EDMUND RANDOLPH (1753–1813), from Henrico County, 30 November 1786–12 November 1788.

BEVERLEY RANDOLPH (1754–1797), from Cumberland County, 12 November 1788–1 December 1791.

HENRY LEE (1756–1818), from Westmoreland County, 1 December 1791–1 December 1794, Federalist.

ROBERT BROOKE (1751–1800), from Spotsylvania County, 1 December 1794–30 November 1796, Democratic-Republican.

JAMES WOOD (1741–1813), from Frederick County, 30 November 1796–6 December 1799, Federalist.

HARDIN BURNLEY (1761–1809), from Orange County, member of the Council of State acting as governor, 7–9 December 1799.

JOHN PENDLETON (ca. 1749–1806), from Hanover County, member of the Council of State acting as governor, 11–19 December 1799.

JAMES MONROE (1758–1831), from Albemarle County, 19 December 1799–24 December 1802, Democratic-Republican.

JOHN PAGE (1744–1808), from Gloucester County, 24 December 1802–11 December 1805, Democratic-Republican.

WILLIAM H. CABELL (1772–1853), from Amherst County, 11 December 1805–12 December 1808, Democratic-Republican.

JOHN TYLER (1747–1813), from Charles City County, 12 December 1808–15 January 1811, Democratic-Republican. Resigned.

George William Smith (1762–1811), oil painting,
by an unknown artist

GEORGE WILLIAM SMITH (1762–1811), from Richmond, Henrico County, member of the Council of State acting as governor, 15–19 January 1811, Democratic-Republican.

JAMES MONROE (1758–1831), from Albemarle County, 19 January–3 April 1811, Democratic-Republican. Resigned.

GEORGE WILLIAM SMITH (1762–1811), from Richmond, Henrico County, member of the Council of State acting as governor, 3 April–6 December 1811; governor, 6–26 December 1811, Democratic-Republican. Died in the Richmond Theatre fire.

PEYTON RANDOLPH (ca. 1778–1828), from Richmond, Henrico County, member of the Council of State acting as governor, 27 December 1811–4 January 1812, Democratic-Republican.

JAMES BARBOUR (1775–1842), from Orange County, 4 January 1812–11 December 1814, Democratic-Republican.

WILSON CARY NICHOLAS (1761–1820), from Albemarle County, 11 December 1814–11 December 1816, Democratic-Republican.

JAMES PATTON PRESTON (1774–1843), from Montgomery County, 11 December 1816–11 December 1819, Democratic-Republican.

THOMAS MANN RANDOLPH (1768–1828), from Albemarle County, 11 December 1819–11 December 1822, Democratic-Republican.

JAMES PLEASANTS (1769–1836), from Goochland County, 11 December 1822–11 December 1825, Democratic-Republican.

JOHN TYLER (1790–1862), from Charles City County, 11 December 1825–4 March 1827, Democratic-Republican. Resigned.

WILLIAM BRANCH GILES (1762–1830), from Amelia County, 4 March 1827–4 March 1830, Democratic-Republican.

JOHN FLOYD (1783–1837), from Montgomery County, 4 March 1830–31 March 1834, Democrat.

LITTLETON WALLER TAZEWELL (1774–1860), from Norfolk, Norfolk County, 31 March 1834–30 March 1836, no party affiliation. Resigned.

WYNDHAM ROBERTSON (1803–1888), from Richmond, Henrico County, member of the Council of State acting as governor, 30 March 1836–31 March 1837, Whig.

DAVID CAMPBELL (1779–1859), from Washington County, 31 March 1837–31 March 1840, Whig.

THOMAS WALKER GILMER (1802–1844), from Albemarle County, 31 March 1840–20 March 1841, Whig. Resigned.

JOHN MERCER PATTON (1797–1858), from Richmond, Henrico County, member of the Council of State acting as governor, 20–31 March 1841, Whig.

JOHN RUTHERFOORD (1792–1866), from Richmond, Henrico County, member of the Council of State acting as governor, 31 March 1841–31 March 1842, Democrat.

JOHN MUNFORD GREGORY (1804–1888), from James City County, member of the Council of State acting as governor, 31 March 1842–5 January 1843, Whig.

JAMES McDOWELL (1795–1851), from Rockbridge County, 5 January 1843–1 January 1846, Democrat.

WILLIAM SMITH (1797–1887), from Fauquier County, 1 January 1846–1 January 1849, Democrat.

JOHN BUCHANAN FLOYD (1806–1863), from Washington County, 1 January 1849–1 January 1852, Democrat.

JOSEPH JOHNSON (1785–1877), from Harrison County (now West Virginia), 1 January 1852–1 January 1856, Democrat. The first governor elected by popular vote.

HENRY ALEXANDER WISE (1806–1876), from Accomack County, 1 January 1856–1 January 1860, Democrat.

JOHN LETCHER (1813–1884), from Rockbridge County, 1 January 1860–1 January 1864, Democrat.

WILLIAM SMITH (1797–1887), from Fauquier County, 1 January 1864–9 May 1865, Democrat. Smith did not formally surrender his office until 20 May.

Governor under the Restored Government, 1861–1865

During the Civil War, Virginia had two state governments, one at Richmond, under the Confederate States of America; and the other, first at Wheeling (until West Virginia became a state in 1863) and then at Alexandria, under the United States of America.

FRANCIS HARRISON PIERPONT (1814–1899), from Marion County (now West Virginia), governor of the Restored government at Wheeling, 20 June 1861–28 August 1863; governor of the Restored government at Alexandria, 28 August 1863–9 May 1865, Unionist.

Governors under the Commonwealth, 1865–1994

Between 1934 and 1958 the terms of the commonwealth's executive officers expired the day prior to the inauguration of their successors; thus for a twenty-four-year period the dates of term expiration and initiation do not agree. Until the General

Francis Harrison Pierpont (1814–1899), photograph

Assembly in 1956 remedied the discrepancy, with the voters' later approval of a constitutional amendment to take effect in 1958, Virginia was without an executive administration for approximately a half-day each inaugural year.

FRANCIS HARRISON PIERPONT (1814–1899), from Marion County (now West Virginia), provisional governor, 9 May 1865–4 April 1868, Republican.

HENRY HORATIO WELLS (1823–1900), a native of New York but resident in Alexandria County, provisional governor, 4 April 1868–21 September 1869, Republican.

GILBERT CARLTON WALKER (1833–1885), a native of New York but resident in the city of Norfolk, provisional governor, 21 September–31 December 1869; governor, 1 January 1870–1 January 1874, Republican.

JAMES LAWSON KEMPER (1823–1895), from Madison County, 1 January 1874–1 January 1878, Conservative.

FREDERICK WILLIAM MACKEY HOLLIDAY (1828–1899), from Frederick County, 1 January 1878–1 January 1882, Conservative.

WILLIAM EVELYN CAMERON (1842–1927), from the city of Petersburg, 1 January 1882–1 January 1886, Readjuster.

FITZHUGH LEE (1835–1905), from Stafford County, 1 January 1886–1 January 1890, Democrat.

PHILIP WATKINS McKINNEY (1832–1899), from Buckingham County, 1 January 1890–1 January 1894, Democrat.

CHARLES TRIPLETT O'FERRALL (1840–1905), from Rockingham County, 1 January 1894–1 January 1898, Democrat.

JAMES HOGE TYLER (1846–1925), from Pulaski County, 1 January 1898–1 January 1902, Democrat.

ANDREW JACKSON MONTAGUE (1862–1937), from the city of Danville, 1 January 1902–1 February 1906, Democrat.

CLAUDE AUGUSTUS SWANSON (1862–1939), from Pittsylvania County, 1 February 1906–1 February 1910, Democrat.

WILLIAM HODGES MANN (1843–1927), from Nottoway County, 1 February 1910–1 February 1914, Democrat.

HENRY CARTER STUART (1855–1933), from Russell County, 1 February 1914–1 February 1918, Democrat.

WESTMORELAND DAVIS (1859–1942), from Loudoun County, 1 February 1918–1 February 1922, Democrat.

ELBERT LEE TRINKLE (1876–1939), from Wythe County, 1 February 1922–1 February 1926, Democrat.

HARRY FLOOD BYRD (1887–1966), from the city of Winchester, 1 February 1926–15 January 1930, Democrat.

JOHN GARLAND POLLARD (1871–1937), from the city of Williamsburg, 15 January 1930–16 January 1934, Democrat.

Colgate Whitehead Darden Jr. (1897–1981), with wife, Constance du Pont, and daughter, Irene, leaving the governor's mansion at the end of his term, January 1946

GEORGE CAMPBELL PEERY (1873–1952), from Tazewell County, 17 January 1934–18 January 1938, Democrat.

JAMES HUBERT PRICE (1882–1943), from the city of Richmond, 19 January 1938–20 January 1942, Democrat.

COLGATE WHITEHEAD DARDEN JR. (1897–1981), from the city of Norfolk, 21 January 1942–15 January 1946, Democrat.

WILLIAM MUNFORD TUCK (1896–1983), from South Boston, Halifax County, 16 January 1946–17 January 1950, Democrat.

JOHN STEWART BATTLE (1890–1972), from the city of Charlottesville, 18 January 1950–19 January 1954, Democrat.

THOMAS BAHNSON STANLEY (1890–1970), from Henry County, 20 January 1954–11 January 1958, Democrat.

JAMES LINDSAY ALMOND JR. (1898–1986), from the city of Roanoke, 11 January 1958–13 January 1962, Democrat.

ALBERTIS SYDNEY HARRISON JR. (1907–), from Brunswick County, 13 January 1962–15 January 1966, Democrat.

MILLS EDWIN GODWIN JR. (1914–), from Nansemond County (now the city of Suffolk), 15 January 1966–17 January 1970, Democrat.

ABNER LINWOOD HOLTON JR. (1923–), from the city of Roanoke, 17 January 1970–12 January 1974, Republican.

MILLS EDWIN GODWIN JR. (1914–), from the city of Suffolk, 12 January 1974–14 January 1978, Republican.

JOHN NICHOLS DALTON (1931–1986), from the city of Radford, 14 January 1978–16 January 1982, Republican.

CHARLES SPITTAL ROBB (1939–), from Fairfax County, 16 January 1982–11 January 1986, Democrat.

GERALD LEE BALILES (1940–), from the city of Richmond, 11 January 1986–13 January 1990, Democrat.

LAWRENCE DOUGLAS WILDER (1931–), from the city of Richmond, 13 January 1990–15 January 1994, Democrat.

GEORGE FELIX ALLEN (1953–), from Albemarle County, 15 January 1994– , Republican.

Lieutenant Governors of Virginia
1852–1994

The Virginia Constitution of 1851 provided for the popular election of the governor and lieutenant governor and abolished the governor's Council of State. Prior to the creation of the office of lieutenant governor, a speaker chosen from the Virginia Senate's membership had presided over that body. Thereafter, the popularly elected lieutenant governor replaced the Senate's Speaker as its presiding officer with the title of president of the Senate. The lieutenant governor has few other official duties.

Lieutenant Governors under the Commonwealth, 1852–1865

SHELTON FARRAR LEAKE (1812–1884), from Albemarle County, 1 January 1852–1 January 1856, Democrat.

ELISHA W. McCOMAS (1820–1890), from Cabell County (now West Virginia), 1 January 1856–7 December 1857, Democrat. Resigned.

WILLIAM LOWTHER JACKSON (1825–1890), from Wood County (now West Virginia), 7 December 1857–1 January 1860, party affiliation unknown.

ROBERT LATANE MONTAGUE (1819–1880), from Middlesex County, 1 January 1860–1 January 1864, Democrat.

SAMUEL PRICE (1805–1877), from Greenbrier County (now West Virginia), 1 January 1864–9 May 1865, party affiliation unknown.

Lieutenant Governors under the Restored Government,
1861–1865

During the Civil War, Virginia had two state governments, one at Richmond, under the Confederate States of America; and the other, first at Wheeling (until West Virginia became a state in 1863) and then at Alexandria, under the United States of America.

DANIEL POLSLEY (1803–1877), from Mason County (now West Virginia), 20 June 1861–7 December 1863, Unionist.

LEOPOLD COPELAND PARKER COWPER (ca. 1814–1880), from Norfolk County, 7 December 1863–9 May 1865, Unionist.

Lieutenant Governors under the Commonwealth, 1865–1994

During the period of Reconstruction, 1865–1870, the commanding general of the military district of Virginia named the lieutenant governor. Upon Virginia's reentry into the federal Union (26 January 1870), the lieutenant governor was again popularly elected.

Between 1934 and 1958 the terms of the commonwealth's executive officers expired the day prior to the inauguration of their successors; thus for a twenty-four-year period the dates of term expiration and initiation do not agree. Until the General Assembly in 1956 remedied the discrepancy, with the voters' later approval of a constitutional amendment to take effect in 1958, Virginia was without an executive administration for approximately a half-day each inaugural year.

LEOPOLD COPELAND PARKER COWPER (ca. 1814–1880), from Norfolk County, 9 May 1865–19 August 1869, Republican.

JOHN FRANCIS LEWIS (1818–1895), from Rockingham County, 5 October 1869–1 January 1870, True Republican.

JOHN LAWRENCE MARYE JR. (1823–1902), from Spotsylvania County, 1 January 1870–1 January 1874, party affiliation unknown.

ROBERT ENOCH WITHERS (1821–1907), from Campbell County, 1 January 1874–1 March 1875, Conservative.

HENRY WIRTZ THOMAS (1812–1890), from Fairfax County, 1 March 1875–1 January 1878, Republican.

JAMES ALEXANDER WALKER (1832–1901), from Pulaski County, 1 January 1878–1 January 1882, Democrat.

JOHN FRANCIS LEWIS (1818–1895), from Rockingham County, 1 March 1882–1 January 1886, Readjuster Republican coalition.

JOHN EDWARD ("PARSON") MASSEY (1819–1901), from Albemarle County, 1 January 1886–1 January 1890, Democrat.

JAMES HOGE TYLER (1846–1925), from Pulaski County, 1 January 1890–1 January 1894, Democrat. Became governor 1 January 1898.

ROBERT CRAIG KENT (1828–1905), from Wythe County, 1 January 1894–1 January 1898, Democrat.

EDWARD ECHOLS (1849–1914), from the city of Staunton, 1 January 1898–1 January 1902, Democrat.

JOSEPH EDWARD WILLARD (1865–1924), from Fairfax County, 1 January 1902–1 February 1906, Democrat.

JAMES TAYLOR ELLYSON (1847–1919), from the city of Richmond, 1 February 1906–1 February 1918, Democrat.

BENJAMIN FRANKLIN BUCHANAN (1852–1932), from Smyth County, 1 February 1918–1 February 1922, Democrat.

JUNIUS EDGAR WEST (1866–1947), from the city of Suffolk, 1 February 1922–15 January 1930, Democrat.

JAMES HUBERT PRICE (1882–1943), from the city of Richmond, 15 January 1930–18 January 1938, Democrat. Became governor 19 January 1938.

SAXON WINSTON HOLT (1871–1940), from the city of Newport News, 19 January 1938–31 March 1940, Democrat. Died in office; unexpired term unfilled.

WILLIAM MUNFORD TUCK (1896–1983), from South Boston, Halifax County, 21 January 1942–15 January 1946, Democrat. Became governor 16 January 1946.

LEWIS PRESTON COLLINS II (1896–1952), from Smyth County, 16 January 1946–20 September 1952, Democrat. Died in office.

ALLIE EDWARD STOKES STEPHENS (1900–1973), from Isle of Wight County, elected 4 November 1952 to fill the unexpired term of Lewis Collins Preston II, took office on 2 December, and served until 13 January 1962, Democrat.

MILLS EDWIN GODWIN JR. (1914–), from Nansemond County, 13 January 1962–15 January 1966, Democrat. Became governor 15 January 1966.

FRED GRESHAM POLLARD (1918–), from the city of Richmond, 15 January 1966–17 January 1970, Democrat.

JULIAN SARGEANT REYNOLDS (1936–1971), from the city of Richmond, 17 January 1970–13 June 1971, Democrat. Died in office.

HENRY EVANS HOWELL JR., (1920–), from the city of Norfolk, elected 2 November 1971 to fill the unexpired term of Julian Sargeant Reynolds, took office on 4 December, and served until 12 January 1974, Independent.

JOHN NICHOLS DALTON (1931–1986), from the city of Radford, 12 January 1974–14 January 1978, Republican. Became governor 14 January 1978.

CHARLES SPITTAL ROBB (1939–), from Fairfax County, 14 January 1978–16 January 1982, Democrat. Became governor 16 January 1982.

RICHARD JOSEPH DAVIS (1921–), from the city of Portsmouth, 16 January 1982–11 January 1986, Democrat.

LAWRENCE DOUGLAS WILDER (1931–), from the city of Richmond, 11 January 1986–13 January 1990, Democrat. Became governor 13 January 1990.

DONALD STERNOFF BEYER JR. (1950–), from Fairfax County, 13 January 1990– , Democrat.

Attorneys General of Virginia
1643–1994

The list of colonial attorneys general is incomplete because of the loss of records. Dates of service are often inexact for the same reason. During the colonial period the king usually appointed the attorney general, but the governor and Council or the governor (or lieutenant governor) alone usually made interim appointments when the office became vacant. There was no set term of office, and upon occasion there was not even an incumbent. Records are sparse for the period 1652–1660, during the Interregnum, when Virginia was virtually self-governing. For these years under the Commonwealth of England, there appears to have been no incumbent attorney general.

Between 1776 and 1851, the General Assembly elected the attorney general, but the governors filled vacancies. There was still no term limit. Since 1852, in accordance with the state constitution of 1851, the voters elect the attorneys general for four-year terms. Attorneys general are also eligible for reelection. Should the office become vacant, the General Assembly, if in session, is empowered to elect an attorney general to serve until the next general election; otherwise, the governor appoints a replacement to serve until the next session of the General Assembly or the next general election, whichever occurs first. The only exception was in the period 1865–1870, during Reconstruction, when the commanding general of the military district of Virginia named the attorney general.

Attorneys General under the Crown, 1643–1652 and 1660–1775

RICHARD LEE (1613–1664), from York County, appointed by Governor William Berkeley and Council on 12 October 1643, length of service unknown.

PETER JENINGS (1631–1671), from Gloucester County, already serving by 25 June 1670, reappointed by Charles II on 15 September 1670, probably served until 12 October 1670.

GEORGE JORDAN (1617–1678), from James City County, appointed by Governor William Berkeley and Council on 12 October 1670, served until after 3 October 1672.

ROBERT BEVERLEY (d. 1687), from Middlesex County, appointed by Governor William Berkeley and Council on 10 March 1676 to serve for "this present Court."

WILLIAM SHERWOOD (d. 1697), from James City County, already serving by early March 1677 and still serving on 25 November 1678.

EDMUND JENINGS (1659–1727), from James City County, appointed in 1680, served until shortly before 10 June 1691.

GEORGE BRENT (d. 1699), from Stafford County, acting as attorney general, probably during an absence of Edmund Jenings, from before 16 November 1686 until sometime before 1 May 1688.

EDWARD CHILTON (ca. 1656–ca. 1707), from Jamestown, James City County, sworn into office 20 October 1691, served until he left Virginia sometime before 14 June 1694.

WILLIAM RANDOLPH (ca. 1651–1711), from Henrico County, sworn into office 14 June 1694, served until 29 October 1698. Resigned.

BARTHOLOMEW FOWLER (d. ca. 1703), from Henrico County, appointed by Governor Francis Nicholson on 29 October 1698, served until 4 September 1700. Resigned.

BENJAMIN HARRISON (1673–1710), from Charles City County, appointed by Governor Francis Nicholson and Council on 17 October 1700, served until about 1702.

STEVENS THOMSON (1674–1714), from Williamsburg, James City and York Counties, appointment approved by Privy Council 30 July 1703, sworn into office 2 March 1704, served until February 1714. Died in office.

JOHN CLAYTON (1665–1737), from James City County, appointed by Lieutenant Governor Alexander Spotswood in 1714, given leave to go to England for one year on

22 April 1726, returned to Virginia late in 1727 or early 1728, reappointed by royal warrant upon the proclamation of the accession of George II, 29 February 1728, served until 18 November 1737. Died in office.

SIR JOHN RANDOLPH (1693–1737), from Williamsburg, James City and York Counties, appointed by Lieutenant Governor William Gooch and Council on 22 April 1726 during absence of John Clayton, served until return of Clayton late in 1727 or early 1728.

EDWARD BARRADALL (1704–1743), from Williamsburg, James City and York Counties, appointed by Lieutenant Governor William Gooch between 17 and 25 November 1737, royal warrant issued 7 March 1738, sworn in 26 October 1738, served until 19 June 1743. Died in office.

THOMAS NELSON (1716–1782), from Yorktown, York County, apparently appointed acting attorney general by Lieutenant Governor William Gooch between 19 and 27 June 1743, served until sometime in midsummer 1744.

PEYTON RANDOLPH (1721–1775), from Williamsburg, James City and York Counties, royal warrant issued 7 May 1744, sworn in sometime in midsummer 1744, served until departed Virginia without royal permission sometime shortly before 29 January 1754; Board of Trade declared office forfeit on 20 June 1754; royal warrant issued 13 May 1755, reinstated between 20 January and 10 February 1755, served until shortly after 22 November 1766. Resigned.

GEORGE WYTHE (1726–1806), from Williamsburg, James City and York Counties, appointed acting attorney general by Lieutenant Governor Robert Dinwiddie on or shortly before 29 January 1754, served until sometime between 20 January and 10 February 1755; appointed acting attorney general by Lieutenant Governor Francis Fauquier sometime shortly after 22 November 1766, served until sometime between 4 and 11 June 1767.

JOHN RANDOLPH (1729–1784), from Williamsburg, James City and York Counties, sworn in under royal commission between 4 and 11 June 1767, fled Virginia in early September 1775.

Attorneys General under the Commonwealth, 1776–1865

EDMUND JENINGS RANDOLPH (1753–1813), from Williamsburg, James City and York Counties, elected by convention 29 June 1776, served from early July 1776 until 30 November 1786.

JAMES INNES (1754–1798), from Williamsburg, James City and York Counties, elected by General Assembly, served 30 November 1786 until 13 November 1796. Resigned.

> **JOHN MARSHALL** (1755–1835), from Richmond, Henrico County, acting in absence of James Innes from mid-October 1794 until late March 1795.

ROBERT BROOKE (1751–1800), from Spotsylvania County, elected by General Assembly, served mid-November 1796–27 February 1800, Democratic-Republican. Died in office.

PHILIP NORBORNE NICHOLAS (1776–1849), from Richmond, Henrico County, appointed by Governor James Monroe 15 March 1800, elected by General Assembly 4 December 1800, served until 7 January 1819, Democratic-Republican. Resigned.

JOHN ROBERTSON (1787–1873), from Richmond, Henrico County, elected by General Assembly 21 January 1819, served until mid-October 1834, Republican. Resigned.

SIDNEY SMITH BAXTER (1802–1879), from Richmond, Henrico County, elected by General Assembly 11 December 1834, served until 1 January 1852, Democrat.

WILLIS PERRY BOCOCK (1806–1887), from Appomattox County, elected by the voters, 1 January 1852–20 March 1857, Democrat. Resigned.

JAMES LYONS (1801–1882), from the city of Richmond, apparently appointed acting attorney general by Governor Henry A. Wise 20 March 1857, served until 13 June 1857.

JOHN RANDOLPH TUCKER (1823–1897), from Winchester, Frederick County, elected by the voters, served 13 June 1857–9 May 1865, Democrat. Relinquished office.

Attorneys General under the Restored Government, 1861–1865

During the Civil War, Virginia had two state governments, one at Richmond, under the Confederate States of America; and the other, first at Wheeling (until West Virginia became a state in 1863) and then at Alexandria, under the United States of America.

JAMES S. WHEAT (ca. 1813–before 1880), from Ohio County (now West Virginia), elected by the Wheeling Convention 21 June 1861 and again by the people in May 1862 and served until 7 December 1863.

THOMAS RUSSELL BOWDEN (1841–1893), from Williamsburg, James City and York Counties, elected attorney general by the people; served 7 December 1863–9 May 1865, Unionist.

Attorneys General under the Commonwealth, 1865–1994

Between 1934 and 1958 the terms of the commonwealth's executive officers expired the day prior to the inauguration of their successors; thus for a twenty-four-year period the dates of term expiration and initiation do not agree. Until the General Assembly in 1956 remedied the discrepancy, with the voters' later approval of a constitutional amendment to take effect in 1958, Virginia was without an executive administration for approximately a half-day each inaugural year.

THOMAS RUSSELL BOWDEN (1841–1893), from Williamsburg, James City and York Counties, 9 May 1865–1 August 1869, Republican. Resigned.

CHARLES WHITTLESEY (ca. 1820–1874), from the city of Alexandria, appointed by Brigadier General Edward Richard Sprigg Canby, served 10 September 1869–19 January 1870, Republican. Removed from office by General Canby.

JAMES CRAIG TAYLOR (1826–1887), from Montgomery County, appointed by Brigadier General Edward Richard Sprigg Canby 19 January 1870 and, having been elected by the voters, served until 1 January 1874, Conservative.

RALEIGH TRAVERS DANIEL (1805–1877), from the city of Richmond, 1 January 1874–16 August 1877, Conservative. Died in office.

JAMES GAVEN FIELD (1826–1902), from Orange County, appointed by Governor James Lawson Kemper 29 August 1877 to fill the unexpired term of Raleigh Travers Daniel and, having been elected by the voters on 6 November 1877 to a term beginning 1 January 1878, served until 1 January 1882, Conservative.

FRANK SIMPSON BLAIR (1839–1899), from Wythe County, 1 January 1882–1 January 1886, Readjuster.

RUFUS ADOLPHUS AYERS (1849–1926), from Wise County, 1 January 1886–1 January 1890, Democrat.

ROBERT TAYLOR SCOTT (1834–1897), from Fauquier County, 1 January 1890–5 August 1897, Democrat. Died in office.

RICHARD CARTER SCOTT (d. 1928), from the city of Richmond, appointed by Governor Charles T. O'Ferrall 11 August 1897 to fill the unexpired term of Robert Taylor Scott and served until 1 January 1898, Democrat.

ANDREW JACKSON MONTAGUE (1862–1937), from the city of Richmond, 1 January 1898–1 January 1902, Democrat. Became governor 1 January 1902.

WILLIAM ALEXANDER ANDERSON (1842–1930), from Rockbridge County, 1 January 1902–1 February 1910, Democrat.

SAMUEL WALKER WILLIAMS (1848–1920), from Wythe County, 1 February 1910–2 February 1914, Democrat.

JOHN GARLAND POLLARD (1871–1937), from the city of Williamsburg, 2 February 1914–5 January 1918, Democrat. Resigned. Became governor 15 January 1930.

JOSEPH DICKENSON HANKS JR. (1875–1924), from the city of Richmond, appointed by Governor Henry C. Stuart 5 January 1918 to fill the unexpired term of John Garland Pollard and served until 1 February 1918, Democrat.

JOHN RICHARDSON SAUNDERS (1869–1934), from Middlesex County, 1 February 1918–17 March 1934, Democrat. Died in office.

ABRAM PENN STAPLES (1885–1951), from the city of Roanoke, appointed by Governor George C. Peery 22 March 1934 and elected by the General Assembly 10 January 1936 to fill the unexpired term of John Richardson Saunders, subsequently elected by the voters 3 November 1937 to a term beginning 19 January 1938, and served until 7 October 1947, Democrat. Resigned.

HARVEY BLACK APPERSON (1890–1948), from Roanoke County, appointed by Governor William M. Tuck 7 October 1947 to fill the unexpired term of Abram Penn Staples and served until 2 February 1948, Democrat. Died in office.

JAMES LINDSAY ALMOND JR. (1898–1986), from the city of Roanoke, appointed by the General Assembly 11 February 1948 to fill the unexpired term of Harvey Black Apperson, subsequently elected by the voters 8 November 1949 to a term beginning 18 January 1950, and served until 16 September 1957, Democrat. Resigned. Became governor 11 January 1958.

KENNETH CARTRIGHT PATTY (1891–1967), from the city of Richmond, appointed by Governor Thomas B. Stanley 16 September 1957 to fill the unexpired term of James Lindsay Almond Jr. and served until 13 January 1958, Democrat.

ALBERTIS SYDNEY HARRISON JR. (1907–), from Brunswick County, 13 January 1958–20 April 1961, Democrat. Resigned. Became governor 13 January 1962.

FREDERICK THOMAS GRAY (1918–1992), from Chesterfield County, appointed by Governor J. Lindsay Almond Jr. 1 May 1961 to fill the unexpired term of Albertis Sydney Harrison Jr. and served until 13 January 1962, Democrat.

ROBERT YOUNG BUTTON (1899–1977), from Culpeper County, 13 January 1962–17 January 1970, Democrat.

ANDREW PICKENS MILLER (1932–), from Washington County, 17 January 1970–17 January 1977, Democrat. Resigned.

ANTHONY FRANCIS TROY (1941–), from Chesterfield County, appointed by the General Assembly 25 January 1977 to fill the unexpired term of Andrew Pickens Miller and served until 14 January 1978, Democrat.

JOHN MARSHALL COLEMAN (1942–), from the city of Staunton, 14 January 1978–16 January 1982, Republican.

GERALD LEE BALILES (1940–), from the city of Richmond, 16 January 1982–1 July 1985, Democrat. Resigned. Became governor 11 January 1986.

WILLIAM GRAY BROADDUS (1942–), from Henrico County, appointed by Governor Charles S. Robb 3 July 1985 to fill the unexpired term of Gerald Lee Baliles and served until 11 January 1986, Democrat.

MARY SUE TERRY (1947–), from Patrick County, 11 January 1986–27 January 1993, Democrat. Resigned.

STEPHEN DOUGLAS ROSENTHAL (1949–), from the city of Lynchburg, elected by the General Assembly 29 January 1993 to fill the unexpired term of Mary Sue Terry and served until 15 January 1994, Democrat.

JAMES STUART GILMORE III (1949–), from Henrico County, 15 January 1994– , Republican.

The first woman to serve as an executive officer of Virginia, Mary Sue Terry takes the oath as attorney general, 13 January 1990.

George Washington at Princeton, oil on canvas, 1779, by Charles Willson Peale
(Courtesy of the Pennsylvania Academy of the Fine Arts, Philadelphia. Gift of Maria McKean Allen and Phebe Warren Downes through the bequest of their mother, Elizabeth Warton McKean)

VIRGINIANS IN THE NATION'S SERVICE

Presidents of the United States

GEORGE WASHINGTON, the first president, was born on 22 February 1732 at his father's plantation on Popes Creek, in Westmoreland County. He married Martha Dandridge Custis, a widow with two small children, on 6 January 1759. He commanded Virginia troops during the French and Indian War and represented first Frederick and afterward Fairfax County in the House of Burgesses. He also represented Fairfax County in the first two revolutionary conventions in 1774 and 1775. In 1775 Washington became commander of the Continental army, which he led to final victory at Yorktown six years later. He also presided over the constitutional convention that met at Philadelphia in 1787. The Father of His Country, as Washington was often called, served two presidential terms. He was inaugurated on 30 April 1789 and retired on 3 March 1797, after declining a third term. Washington died 14 December 1799 at Mount Vernon and is buried there.

THOMAS JEFFERSON, the third president, was born on 13 April 1743 at Shadwell, in Albemarle County. He married Martha Wayles Skelton in 1772, and they had five daughters and one son. Before his election to the presidency in 1801, Jefferson had served in the colonial and state legislatures, as governor of Virginia (1779–1781), as minister to France (1784–1789), as secretary of state (1790–1793), and as vice president of the United States (1797–1801). Jefferson served two terms as president from 1801 to 1809. He was also the author of the Declaration of Independence and of the Virginia Statute for Religious Freedom, and the founder of the University of Virginia. Jefferson died on 4 July 1826 at Monticello, where he is buried.

JAMES MADISON, the fourth president, was born on 16 March 1751 near Port Conway, in King George County. He married Dolley Payne Todd in 1794. They had no children. Madison first served in the state legislature in 1776. As a member of the constitutional convention at Philadelphia in 1787, Madison played a leading role in the drafting and adoption of the United States Constitution and became known as the Father of the Constitution. He served as secretary of state under Jefferson and succeeded the latter as president. Madison's two terms lasted from 1809 to 1817, during which time the United States fought the War of 1812 with Great Britain. Madison died at Montpelier, in Orange County, on 28 June 1836, and is buried there.

JAMES MONROE, the fifth president, was born on 28 April 1758 in Westmoreland County and lived at various times in Fredericksburg, in Albemarle County, and at Oak Hill, in Loudoun County. He married Elizabeth Kortright, of New York, in 1786, and they had two daughters. He was twice governor of Virginia, held various diplomatic posts, and served under Madison as secretary of state and as secretary of war before his election as president. During his service as secretary of war, he continued to act as secretary of state. Monroe served two terms as president from 1817 to 1825. He died in New York City on 4 July 1831 and was buried there. On 5 July 1858 his body was reinterred in Richmond's Hollywood Cemetery.

WILLIAM HENRY HARRISON, the ninth president, was born on 9 February 1773 at Berkeley, in Charles City County. He married Anna Symes, of New Jersey, and they had six sons and four daughters. Harrison spent most of his adult life in the Northwest Territory and in Ohio. He won fame in the Indian wars and was the victor at the Battle of Tippecanoe in 1811. He also commanded American troops in the War of 1812. Inaugurated on 4 March 1841, Harrison served only one month before dying in the White House on 4 April. He is buried in North Bend, Ohio.

JOHN TYLER, the tenth president, was born on 29 March 1790 at Greenway, in Charles City County. He was married twice, first to Letitia Christian, of New Kent County, and then to Julia Gardiner, of New York, and he had a total of eight sons and six daughters. Tyler lived at Sherwood Forest, in Charles City County. He served as a representative and a senator from Virginia to the United States Congress and as governor of the commonwealth. Elected vice president in 1840, Tyler succeeded Harrison as president after the latter's death and served from 4 April 1841 until 3 March 1845. The former president supported Virginia's secession from the Union in 1861 and was elected to the Confederate House of Representatives. On 18 January 1862 he died in Richmond, where he had gone to attend the opening session of that body. He is buried in Hollywood Cemetery.

ZACHARY TAYLOR, the twelfth president, was born on 24 November 1784 in Orange County and grew up in Kentucky. He married Margaret Smith, of Maryland, in 1810, and they had five daughters and one son. Taylor fought in various Indian wars and won his greatest fame in the Mexican War with his victories at Palo Alto, Monterrey, and Buena Vista. Inaugurated on 5 March 1849, he served only sixteen months and died in office on 9 July 1850. He is buried in Louisville, Kentucky.

THOMAS WOODROW WILSON, the twenty-eighth president, was born in Staunton on 28 December 1856 and grew up in Georgia and in South Carolina. Wilson and his first wife, Ellen Louise Axson, of Rome, Georgia, who died in 1914, had three daughters. Wilson married Edith Bolling Galt, of Wytheville, in 1915. He served as president of Princeton University (1902–1910), governor of New Jersey (1911–1913), and president of the United States for two terms (1913–1921). During his administration the United States entered World War I on the side of the Allies. As part of the peace settlement, Wilson proposed the foundation of the League of Nations, and he fought unsuccessfully for American participation in that organization. He died in Washington, D.C., on 3 February 1924 and is buried in the National Cathedral.

Vice Presidents of the United States

THOMAS JEFFERSON (1743–1826), 4 March 1797–3 March 1801, during administration of John Adams.

JOHN TYLER (1790–1862), 4 March 1841–4 April 1841, during administration of William Henry Harrison.

also included (for example: Winchester, Frederick County). Prior to 1795, party allegiances were often imprecise, thus for the earliest sessions of Congress no affiliation is listed. Moreover, during the early nineteenth century, members of Congress frequently changed political parties; those evolving affiliations are provided whenever possible.

To reconcile numerous discrepancies in members' full names, dates, or affiliations, comparative references were made to the United States Congress Joint Committee on Printing, *Biographical Directory of the United States Congress, 1774–1989, Bicentennial Edition* (Washington, D.C., 1989); Stanley B. Parsons, William W. Beach, and Dan Hermann, *United States Congressional Districts, 1788–1841* (Westport, Conn., 1978); Postmaster of the United States House of Representatives, *Congressional Directory for the First Session of the Twenty-Eighth Congress of the United States of America* (Washington, D.C., 1843–1844) and subsequent edition of 1860; U.S. Congress Joint Committee on Printing, *Congressional Directory for the Second Session of the Forty-First Congress of the United States* (Washington, D.C., 1870) and subsequent editions of 1871 and 1877; U.S. Congress Joint Committee on Printing, *Official Congressional Directory for the Use of the United States Congress* (Washington, D.C., 1882) and subsequent editions of 1887, 1890–1946, 1959–1993; U.S. Congress Joint Committee on Printing, *Pocket Congressional Directory, January 1955* (Washington, D.C., 1955) and subsequent editions issued in odd-numbered years 1957–1991. See also Kenneth C. Martis, ed., *Historical Atlas of Political Parties in the United States Congress, 1789–1989* (New York, 1989); Daniel P. Jordan, "Virginia Congressmen, 1801–1825" (Ph.D. diss., University of Virginia, 1970); W. Buck Yearns, *The Confederate Congress* (Athens, Ga., 1960); and Ezra J. Warner and W. Buck Yearns, *Biographical Register of the Confederate Congress* (Baton Rouge, 1975). Additional sources within The Library of Virginia included research files of the *Dictionary of Virginia Biography* Project and period census, tax, deed, and estate records.

Members of the Continental Congress
1774–1789

THOMAS ADAMS (1730–1788), from New Kent County, 1778–1779.

JOHN BANISTER (1734–1788), from Dinwiddie County, 1778.

RICHARD BLAND (1710–1776), from Prince George County, 1774–1775.

THEODORICK BLAND (1742–1790), from Prince George County, 1780–1783.

CARTER BRAXTON (1736–1797), from King William County, 1776.

JOHN BROWN (1757–1837), from the district of Kentucky (now Kentucky), 1787–1788.

EDWARD CARRINGTON (1748–1810), from Cumberland County, 1786–1788.

JOHN DAWSON (1762–1814), from Spotsylvania County, 1788–1789.

WILLIAM FITZHUGH (1741–1809), from Stafford County, 1779.

WILLIAM FLEMING (1736–1824), from Cumberland County, 1779.

WILLIAM GRAYSON (1740–1790), from Prince William County, 1784–1787.

CYRUS GRIFFIN (1748–1810), from Lancaster County, 1778–1781, 1787–1789.

SAMUEL HARDY (1758–1785), from Isle of Wight County, 1783–1785.

BENJAMIN HARRISON (1726–1791), from Charles City County, 1774–1778.

JOHN HARVIE (1742–1807), from West Augusta (now Pennsylvania), 1777–1778.

JAMES HENRY (1731–1804), from Accomack County, 1780.

PATRICK HENRY (1736–1799), from Hanover County, 1774–1775.

THOMAS JEFFERSON (1743–1826), from Albemarle County, 1775–1776, 1783–1784.

JOSEPH JONES (1727–1805), from King George County, 1777, 1780–1783.

ARTHUR LEE (1740–1792), from Prince William County, 1782–1784.

FRANCIS LIGHTFOOT LEE (1734–1797), from Richmond County, 1775–1779.

HENRY LEE (1756–1818), from Westmoreland County, 1786–1788.

RICHARD HENRY LEE (1732–1794), from Westmoreland County, 1774–1779, 1784–1787.

JAMES MADISON (1751–1836), from Orange County, 1780–1783, 1787–1788.

JAMES MERCER (1736–1793), from Hampshire County (now West Virginia), 1779.

JOHN FRANCIS MERCER (1759–1821), from Stafford County, 1783–1784.

JAMES MONROE (1758–1831), from Fredericksburg, Spotsylvania County, 1783–1786.

THOMAS NELSON (1738–1789), from Yorktown, York County, 1775–1777, 1779.

MANN PAGE (1749–1781), from Spotsylvania County, 1777.

EDMUND PENDLETON (1721–1803), from Caroline County, 1774–1775.

EDMUND JENINGS RANDOLPH (1753–1813), from Williamsburg, James City and York Counties, 1779, 1781–1782.

PEYTON RANDOLPH (ca. 1721–1775), from Williamsburg, James City and York Counties, 1774–1775.

MERIWETHER SMITH (1730–1790), from Essex County, 1778–1781.

JOHN WALKER (1744–1809), from Albemarle County, 1780.

GEORGE WASHINGTON (1732–1799), from Fairfax County, 1774–1775.

GEORGE WYTHE (1726–1806), from Williamsburg, James City and York Counties, 1775–1776.

Members of the United States Congress
1789–1994
House of Representatives

WATKINS MOORMAN ABBITT (1908–), from Appomattox County, 1948–1973, Democrat.

MARK ALEXANDER (1792–1883), from Mecklenburg County, 1819–1833, Jacksonian.

GEORGE FELIX ALLEN (1953–), from Albemarle County, 1991–1993, Republican.

JOHN JAMES ALLEN (1797–1871), from Harrison County (now West Virginia), 1833–1835, Anti-Jacksonian.

ROBERT ALLEN (1794–1859), from Shenandoah County, 1827–1833, Jacksonian.

JAMES LINDSAY ALMOND JR. (1898–1986), from the city of Roanoke, 1946–1948, Democrat.

WILLIAM SEGAR ARCHER (1789–1855), from Amelia County, 1820–1823, Democratic-Republican; 1823–1825, Crawford Republican; 1825–1835, Jacksonian.

WILLIAM ARMSTRONG (1782–1865), from Hampshire County (now West Virginia), 1825–1829, pro-administration (John Quincy Adams); 1829–1833, Anti-Jacksonian.

ARCHIBALD ATKINSON (1792–1872), from Isle of Wight County, 1843–1849, Democrat.

ARCHIBALD AUSTIN (1772–1837), from Buckingham County, 1817–1819, Democratic-Republican.

THOMAS HAMLET AVERETT (1800–1855), from Halifax County, 1849–1853, Democrat.

RICHARD SMALL AYER (1829–1896), from Richmond County, 1870–1871, Republican.

JOHN BAKER (ca. 1769–1823), from Jefferson County (now West Virginia), 1811–1813, Federalist.

WILLIAM LEE BALL (1781–1824), from Lancaster County, 1817–1824, Democratic-Republican.

LINN BANKS (1784–1842), from Culpeper County, 1838–1841, Democrat.

JOHN STRODE BARBOUR (1790–1855), from Culpeper County, 1823–1825, Crawford Republican; 1825–1833, Jacksonian.

JOHN STRODE BARBOUR JR. (1820–1892), from the city of Alexandria, 1881–1887, Democrat.

PHILIP PENDLETON BARBOUR (1783–1841), from Orange County, 1814–1823, Democratic-Republican; 1823–1825, Crawford Republican; 1827–1830, Jacksonian.

RICHARD WALKER BARTON (1800–1859), from Winchester, Frederick County, 1841–1843, Democrat.

BURWELL BASSETT (1764–1841), from Williamsburg, James City and York Counties, 1805–1813, 1815–1819, 1821–1823, Democratic-Republican; 1823–1825, Crawford Republican; 1825–1829, Jacksonian.

HERBERT HARVELL BATEMAN (1928–), from the city of Newport News, 1983– , Republican.

THOMAS HENRY BAYLY (1810–1856), from Accomack County, 1844–1856, Democrat.

THOMAS MONTEAGLE BAYLY (1775–1834), from Accomack County, 1813–1815, Federalist.

JAMES MADISON HITE BEALE (1786–1866), from Shenandoah County, 1833–1837, Jacksonian; 1849–1853, Democrat.

RICHARD LEE TURBERVILLE BEALE (1819–1893), from Westmoreland County, 1847–1849, 1879–1881, Democrat.

HENRY BEDINGER (1812–1858), from Jefferson County (now West Virginia), 1845–1849, Democrat.

James Monroe (1758–1831), oil on canvas, by Rembrandt Peale (1778–1860)
(James Monroe Museum and Memorial Library)

ANDREW BEIRNE (1771–1845), from Monroe County (now West Virginia), 1837–1841, Democrat.

JACOB BEESON BLAIR (1821–1901), from Wood County (now West Virginia), 1861–1863, Unionist.

SCHUYLER OTIS BLAND (1872–1950), from the city of Newport News, 1918–1950, Democrat.

THEODORICK BLAND (1742–1790), from Prince George County, 1789–1790.

THOMAS JEROME BLILEY JR. (1932–), from the city of Richmond, 1981– , Republican.

TAZEWELL ELLETT (1856–1914), from the city of Richmond, 1895–1897, Democrat.

JAMES FLETCHER EPES (1842–1910), from Nottoway County, 1891–1895, Democrat.

SYDNEY PARHAM EPES (1865–1900), from Nottoway County, 1897–1898, 1899–1900, Democrat.

JOHN WAYLES EPPES (1773–1823), from Chesterfield County, 1803–1811, Democratic-Republican; from Buckingham County, 1813–1815, Democratic-Republican.

BENJAMIN ESTIL (1780–1853), from Washington County, 1825–1827, pro-administration (John Quincy Adams).

THOMAS EVANS (d. 1815), from Accomack County, 1797–1801, Federalist.

CHARLES JAMES FAULKNER (1806–1884), from Berkeley County (now West Virginia), 1851–1855, Whig; 1855–1859, Democrat.

JOHN WOOD FISHBURNE (1888–1937), from the city of Charlottesville, 1931–1933, Democrat.

JOSEPH LYMAN FISHER (1914–), from Arlington County, 1975–1981, Democrat.

JOHN WILLIAM FLANNAGAN JR. (1885–1955), from the city of Bristol, 1931–1949, Democrat.

HENRY DELAWARE FLOOD (1865–1921), from Appomattox County, 1901–1921, Democrat.

JOEL WEST FLOOD (1894–1964), from Appomattox County, 1932–1933, Democrat.

THOMAS STANHOPE FLOURNOY (1811–1883), from Halifax County, 1847–1849, Whig.

JOHN FLOYD (1783–1837), from Montgomery County, 1817–1823, Democratic-Republican; 1823–1825, Crawford Republican; 1825–1829, Jacksonian.

THOMAS BACON FUGATE (1899–1980), from Lee County, 1949–1953, Democrat.

ABRAM FULKERSON (1834–1902), from Bristol, Washington County, 1881–1883, Readjuster.

ANDREW STEELE FULTON (1800–1884), from Wythe County, 1847–1849, Whig.

JOHN HALL FULTON (d. 1836), from Washington County, 1833–1835, Jacksonian.

WILLIAM EMBRE GAINES (1844–1912), from Nottoway County, 1887–1889, Republican.

JACOB AARON GARBER (1879–1953), from Rockingham County, 1929–1931, Republican.

DAVID SHEPHERD GARLAND (1769–1841), from Amherst County, 1810–1811, Democratic-Republican.

JAMES GARLAND (1791–1885), from Nelson County, 1835–1837, Jacksonian; 1837–1839, Democrat; 1839–1841, Conservative.

JAMES MERCER GARNETT (1770–1843), from Essex County, 1805–1809, Democratic-Republican.

MUSCOE RUSSELL HUNTER GARNETT (1821–1864), from Essex County, 1856–1861, Democrat.

John Tyler Jr. (1790–1862), oil painting, 1841, by [J.?] Hart

ROBERT SELDEN GARNETT (1789–1840), from Essex County, 1817–1823, Democratic-Republican; 1823–1825, Crawford Republican; 1825–1827, Jacksonian.

GEORGE TANKARD GARRISON (1835–1889), from Accomack County, 1881–1883, 1884–1885, Democrat.

JULIAN VAUGHAN GARY (1892–1973), from the city of Richmond, 1945–1965, Democrat.

JAMES HERBERT GHOLSON (1798–1848), from Brunswick County, 1833–1835, Anti-Jacksonian.

THOMAS GHOLSON JR. (d. 1816), from Brunswick County, 1808–1816, Democratic-Republican.

JAMES KING GIBSON (1812–1879), from Washington County, 1870–1871, Conservative.

WILLIAM BRANCH GILES (1762–1830), from Amelia County, 1790–1795; 1795–1798, 1801–1803, Democratic-Republican.

THOMAS WALKER GILMER (1802–1844), from Charlottesville, Albemarle County, 1841–1843, Whig; 1843–1844, Democrat.

CARTER GLASS (1858–1946), from the city of Lynchburg, 1902–1918, Democrat.

WILLIAM LEFTWICH GOGGIN (1807–1870), from Bedford County, 1839–1843, 1844–1845, 1847–1849, Whig.

JOHN GOODE JR. (1829–1909), from the city of Norfolk, 1875–1881, Democrat.

SAMUEL GOODE (1756–1822), from Mecklenburg County, 1799–1801, Democratic-Republican.

WILLIAM OSBORNE GOODE (1798–1859), from Mecklenburg County, 1841–1843, 1853–1859, Democrat.

ROBERT WILLIAM GOODLATTE (1952–), from the city of Roanoke, 1993– , Republican.

PETERSON GOODWYN (1745–1818), from Petersburg, Dinwiddie County, 1803–1818, Democratic-Republican.

WILLIAM FITZHUGH GORDON (1787–1858), from Albemarle County, 1830–1835, Jacksonian.

EDWIN GRAY (ca. 1769–by 1822), from Southampton County, 1799–1813, Federalist.

JOHN COWPER GRAY (1783–1823), from Southampton County, 1820–1821, Democratic-Republican.

SAMUEL GRIFFIN (1746–1810), from James City County, 1789–1795.

THOMAS GRIFFIN (1773–1837), from Yorktown, York County, 1803–1805, Federalist.

NORMAN ROND HAMILTON (1877–1964), from the city of Portsmouth, 1937–1939, Democrat.

GEORGE HANCOCK (1754–1820), from Botetourt County, 1793–1795; 1795–1797, Federalist.

PORTER HARDY JR. (1903–), from Norfolk County (now the city of Chesapeake), 1947–1969, Democrat.

HERBERT EUGENE HARRIS II (1926–), from Fairfax County, 1975–1981, Democrat.

JOHN THOMAS HARRIS (1823–1899), from Harrisonburg, Rockingham County, 1859–1861, 1871–1881, Democrat.

WILLIAM ALEXANDER HARRIS (1805–1864), from Page County, 1841–1843, Democrat.

WINDER RUSSELL HARRIS (1888–1973), from the city of Norfolk, 1941–1944, Democrat.

BURR POWELL HARRISON (1904–1973), from the city of Winchester, 1946–1963, Democrat.

CARTER BASSETT HARRISON (1763–1808), from Prince George County, 1793–1795; 1795–1799, Democratic-Republican.

THOMAS WALTER HARRISON (1856–1935), from the city of Winchester, 1916–1922, 1923–1929, Democrat.

AYLETT HAWES (1768–1833), from Culpeper County, 1811–1817, Democratic-Republican.

JAMES HAY (1856–1931), from Madison County, 1897–1916, Democrat.

THOMAS SHERWOOD HAYMOND (1794–1869), from Marion County (now West Virginia), 1849–1851, Whig.

SAMUEL LEWIS HAYS (1794–1871), from Lewis County (now West Virginia), 1841–1843, Democrat.

JOHN HEATH (1758–1810), from Northumberland County, 1793–1795; 1795–1797, Democratic-Republican.

JOHN HILL (1800–1880), from Buckingham County, 1839–1841, Whig.

ALEXANDER RICHMOND HOLLADAY (1811–1877), from Spotsylvania County, 1849–1853, Democrat.

EDWARD EVERETT HOLLAND (1861–1941), from the city of Suffolk, 1911–1921, Democrat.

JOEL HOLLEMAN (1799–1844), from Isle of Wight County, 1839–1840, Democrat.

DAVID HOLMES (1770–1832), from Harrisonburg, Rockingham County, 1797–1809, Democratic-Republican.

JAMES MURRAY HOOKER (1873–1940), from Patrick County, 1921–1925, Democrat.

BENJAMIN STEPHEN HOOPER (1835–1898), from Prince Edward County, 1883–1885, Readjuster.

GEORGE WASHINGTON HOPKINS (1804–1861), from Washington County, 1835–1847, 1857–1859, Democrat.

SAMUEL ISAAC HOPKINS (1843–1914), from the city of Lynchburg, 1887–1889, Labor.

EDMUND WILCOX HUBARD (1806–1872), from Buckingham County, 1841–1847, Democrat.

JOHN PRATT HUNGERFORD (1761–1833), from Westmoreland County, 1811, 1813–1817, Democratic-Republican.

ROBERT MERCER TALIAFERRO HUNTER (1809–1887), from Essex County, 1837–1841, Whig; 1841–1843, Independent; 1845–1847, Democrat.

EPPA HUNTON (1822–1908), from Fauquier County, 1873–1881, Democrat.

EDWARD BRAKE JACKSON (1793–1826), from Harrison County (now West Virginia), 1820–1823, Democratic-Republican.

GEORGE JACKSON (1757–1831), from Harrison County (now West Virginia), 1795–1797, 1799–1803, Democratic-Republican.

JOHN GEORGE JACKSON (1774–1825), from Harrison County (now West Virginia), 1803–1810, 1813–1817, Democratic-Republican.

RORER ABRAHAM JAMES (1859–1921), from the city of Danville, 1920–1921, Democrat.

ALBERT GALLATIN JENKINS (1830–1864), from Kanawha County (now West Virginia), 1857–1861, Democrat.

WILLIAM PAT JENNINGS (1919–1994), from Smyth County, 1955–1967, Democrat.

JAMES JOHNSON (d. 1825), from Suffolk, Nansemond County, 1813–1820, Democratic-Republican.

JOSEPH JOHNSON (1785–1877), from Harrison County (now West Virginia), 1823–1827, Jackson Republican; 1833, party affiliation unknown; 1835–1837, Jacksonian; 1837–1841, 1845–1847, Democrat.

CHARLES CLEMENT JOHNSTON (1795–1832), from Washington County, 1831–1832, Jacksonian.

JOSEPH EGGLESTON JOHNSTON (1807–1891), from the city of Richmond, 1879–1881, Democrat.

JAMES JONES (1772–1848), from Nottoway County, 1819–1823, Democratic-Republican.

JOHN WINSTON JONES (1791–1848), from the city of Petersburg, 1835–1837, Jacksonian; 1837–1845, Democrat.

WALTER JONES (1745–1815), from Northumberland County, 1797–1799, 1803–1811, Democratic-Republican.

WILLIAM ATKINSON JONES (1849–1918), from Richmond County, 1891–1918, Democrat.

JOSEPH JORGENSEN (1844–1888), from the city of Petersburg, 1877–1883, Republican.

JOHN KERR (1782–1842), from Halifax County, 1813–1815, 1815–1817, Democratic-Republican.

ZEDEKIAH KIDWELL (1814–1872), from Marion County (now West Virginia), 1853–1857, Democrat.

JOHN LAMB (1840–1924), from the city of Richmond, 1897–1913, Democrat.

JOHN MERCER LANGSTON (1829–1897), from the city of Petersburg, 1890–1891, Republican.

MENALCUS LANKFORD (1883–1937), from the city of Norfolk, 1929–1933, Republican.

FRANCIS RIVES LASSITER (1866–1909), from the city of Petersburg, 1900–1903, 1907–1909, Democrat.

JOHN WILLIAM LAWSON (1837–1905), from Isle of Wight County, 1891–1893, Democrat.

SHELTON FARRAR LEAKE (1812–1884), from Charlottesville, Albemarle County, 1845–1847, Democrat; 1859–1861, Independent Democrat.

HENRY LEE (1756–1818), from Westmoreland County, 1799–1801, Federalist.

RICHARD BLAND LEE (1761–1827), from Prince William County, 1789–1795.

WILLIAM HENRY FITZHUGH LEE (1837–1891), from Fairfax County, 1887–1891, Democrat.

ISAAC LEFFLER (1788–1853), from Ohio County (now West Virginia), 1827–1829, pro-administration (John Quincy Adams).

JABEZ LEFTWICH (1766–1855), from Bedford County, 1821–1823, Democratic-Republican; 1823–1825, Crawford Republican.

POSEY GREEN LESTER (1850–1929), from Floyd County, 1889–1893, Democrat.

JOHN LETCHER (1813–1884), from Lexington, Rockbridge County, 1851–1859, Democrat.

CHARLES SWEARINGER LEWIS (1821–1878), from Harrison County (now West Virginia), 1854–1855, Democrat.

JOSEPH LEWIS JR. (1772–1834), from Fauquier County, 1803–1817, Federalist.

THOMAS LEWIS (ca. 1749–1847), from Kanawha County (now West Virginia), 1803–1804, Federalist.

WILLIAM I. LEWIS (1766–1828), from Lynchburg, Campbell County, 1817–1819, Democratic-Republican.

HARRY LIBBEY (1843–1913), from Hampton, Elizabeth City County, 1883–1885, Readjuster; 1885–1887, Republican.

JOHN LOVE (d. 1822), from Alexandria, Fairfax County, 1807–1811, Democratic-Republican.

GEORGE LOYALL (1789–1868), from Norfolk, Norfolk County, 1830–1831, 1833–1837, Jacksonian.

EDWARD LUCAS (1790–1858), from Jefferson County (now West Virginia), 1833–1837, Jacksonian.

WILLIAM LUCAS (1800–1877), from Jefferson County (now West Virginia), 1839–1841, 1843–1845, Democrat.

WILLIAM MASON McCARTY (ca. 1789–1863), from Alexandria, Fairfax County, 1840–1841, Whig.

WILLIAM McCOMAS (1795–1865), from Cabell County (now West Virginia), 1833–1835, Jacksonian; 1835–1837, Anti-Jacksonian.

WILLIAM McCOY (d. 1864), from Pendleton County (now West Virginia), 1811–1823, Democratic-Republican; 1823–1825, Crawford Republican; 1825–1833, Jacksonian.

JAMES McDOWELL (1795–1851), from Rockbridge County, 1846–1851, Democrat.

JAMES MACHIR (d. 1827), from Hardy County (now West Virginia), 1797–1799, Federalist.

WILLIAM ROBERTSON McKENNEY (1851–1916), from the city of Petersburg, 1895–1896, Democrat.

LEWIS McKENZIE (1810–1895), from the city of Alexandria, 1863, Unionist; 1870–1871, Union Conservative.

WILLIAM McKINLEY (ca. 1762–ca. 1826), from Ohio County (now West Virginia), 1810–1811, Democratic-Republican.

FAYETTE McMULLEN (1805–1880), from Scott County, 1849–1857, Democrat.

Zachary Taylor (1784–1850), a ca. 1850 daguerreotype by Albert Sands Southworth and Josiah Johnson Hawes *(The Metropolitan Museum of Art, Gift of I. N. Phelps Stokes, Edward S. Hawes, Alice Mary Hawes, Marion Augusta Hawes, 1937. [37.14.32])*

JAMES MADISON (1751–1836), from Orange County, 1789–1795; 1795–1797, Democratic-Republican.

FRANCIS MALLORY (1807–1860), from Hampton, Elizabeth City County, 1837–1839, 1840–1843, Whig.

JOHN OTHO MARSH JR. (1926–), from Shenandoah County, 1963–1971, Democrat.

JAMES WILLIAM MARSHALL (1843–1911), from Craig County, 1893–1895, Democrat.

JOHN MARSHALL (1755–1835), from Richmond, Henrico County, 1799–1800, Federalist.

ELBERT SEVIER MARTIN (ca. 1829–1876), from Lee County, 1859–1861, Independent Democrat.

JAMES MURRAY MASON (1798–1871), from Winchester, Frederick County, 1837–1839, Democrat.

JOHN YOUNG MASON (1799–1859), from Greensville County, 1831–1837, Jacksonian.

LEWIS MAXWELL (1790–1862), from Lewis County (now West Virginia), 1827–1829, pro-administration (John Quincy Adams); 1829–1833, Anti-Jacksonian.

HARRY LEE MAYNARD (1861–1922), from the city of Portsmouth, 1901–1911, Democrat.

ROBERT MURPHY MAYO (1836–1896), from Westmoreland County, 1883–1884, Readjuster.

RICHARD KIDDER MEADE (1803–1862), from the city of Petersburg, 1847–1853, Democrat.

CHARLES FENTON MERCER (1778–1858), from Loudoun County, 1817–1823, Federalist; 1823–1825, Crawford Republican; 1825–1829, pro-administration (John Quincy Adams); 1829–1837, Anti-Jacksonian; 1837–1839, Whig.

ELISHA EDWARD MEREDITH (1848–1900), from Prince William County, 1891–1897, Democrat.

JOHN SINGLETON MILLSON (1808–1874), from the city of Norfolk, 1849–1861, Democrat.

WILLIAM MILNES JR. (1827–1889), from Page County, 1870–1871, Conservative Republican.

ANDREW JACKSON MONTAGUE (1862–1937), from the city of Richmond, 1913–1937, Democrat.

ANDREW MOORE (1752–1821), from Rockbridge County, 1789–1795; 1795–1797, 1804, Democratic-Republican.

ROBERT WALTON MOORE (1859–1941), from Fairfax County, 1919–1931, Democrat.

SAMUEL McDOWELL MOORE (1796–1875), from Rockbridge County, 1833–1835, Anti-Jacksonian.

THOMAS LOVE MOORE (d. 1862), from Fauquier County, 1820–1823, Democratic-Republican.

JAMES PATRICK MORAN (1945–), from the city of Alexandria, 1991– , Democrat.

DANIEL MORGAN (1736–1802), from Frederick County, 1797–1799, Federalist.

WILLIAM STEPHEN MORGAN (1801–1876), from Monongalia County (now West Virginia), 1835–1837, Jacksonian; 1837–1839, Democrat.

JOHN MORROW (fl. 1787–1819), from Jefferson County (now West Virginia), 1805–1809, Democratic-Republican.

JEREMIAH MORTON (1799–1878), from Culpeper County, 1849–1851, Whig.

HUGH NELSON (1768–1836), from Albemarle County, 1811–1823, Democratic-Republican.

THOMAS MADUIT NELSON (1782–1853), from Mecklenburg County, 1816–1819, Democratic-Republican.

JOSEPH NEVILLE (1730–1819), from Hampshire County (now West Virginia), 1793–1795.

ANTHONY NEW (1747–1833), from Caroline County, 1793–1795; 1795–1805, Democratic-Republican.

ALEXANDER NEWMAN (1804–1849), from Ohio County (now West Virginia), 1849, Democrat.

THOMAS NEWTON JR. (1768–1847), from Norfolk, Norfolk County, 1801–1823, Democratic-Republican; 1823–1825, Adams-Clay Republican; 1825–1829, pro-administration (John Quincy Adams); 1829–1830, 1831–1833, Anti-Jacksonian.

WILLOUGHBY NEWTON (1802–1874), from Westmoreland County, 1843–1845, Whig.

JOHN NICHOLAS (1764–1819), from Stafford County, 1793–1795; 1795–1801, Democratic-Republican.

WILSON CARY NICHOLAS (1761–1820), from Albemarle County, 1807–1809, Democratic-Republican.

CHARLES TRIPLETT O'FERRALL (1840–1905), from Harrisonburg, Rockingham County, 1884–1893, Democrat.

JAMES RANDOLPH OLIN (1920–), from the city of Roanoke, 1983–1993, Democrat.

PETER JOHNSTON OTEY (1840–1902), from the city of Lynchburg, 1895–1902, Democrat.

JOHN PAGE (1744–1808), from Gloucester County, 1789–1795; 1795–1797, Democratic-Republican.

ROBERT PAGE (1765–1840), from Frederick County, 1799–1801, Federalist.

JOSIAH PARKER (1751–1810), from Isle of Wight County, 1789–1795; 1795–1801, Federalist.

RICHARD PARKER (1810–1893), from Clarke County, 1849–1851, Democrat.

SEVERN EYRE PARKER (1787–1836), from Northampton County, 1819–1821, Democratic-Republican.

STANFORD ELMER PARRIS (1929–), from Fairfax County, 1973–1975, 1981–1991, Republican.

JOHN MERCER PATTON (1797–1858), from Fredericksburg, Spotsylvania County, 1830–1837, Jacksonian; 1837–1838, Democrat.

JOHN PAUL (1839–1901), from Harrisonburg, Rockingham County, 1881–1883, Readjuster.

JOHN PAUL JR. (1883–1964), from the city of Harrisonburg, 1922–1923, Republican.

LEWIS FRANKLIN PAYNE JR. (1945–), from Nelson County, 1988– , Democrat.

GEORGE CAMPBELL PEERY (1873–1952), from Tazewell County, 1923–1929, Democrat.

JOHN PEGRAM (1773–1831), from Dinwiddie County, 1818–1819, Democratic-Republican.

JOHN STROTHER PENDLETON (1802–1868), from Culpeper County, 1845–1849, Whig.

ISAAC SAMUELS PENNYBACKER (1805–1847), from Harrisonburg, Rockingham County, 1837–1839, Democrat.

OWEN BRADFORD PICKETT (1930–), from the city of Virginia Beach, 1987– , Democrat.

JAMES PINDALL (ca. 1783–1825), from Harrison County (now West Virginia), 1817–1820, Federalist.

JAMES HENRY PLATT JR. (1837–1894), from the city of Petersburg, 1870–1875, Radical Republican.

JAMES PLEASANTS (1769–1836), from Goochland County, 1811–1819, Democratic-Republican.

RICHARD HARDING POFF (1923–), from the city of Radford, 1953–1972, Republican.

CHARLES HOWELL PORTER (1833–1897), from the city of Richmond, 1870–1873, Republican.

ALFRED HARRISON POWELL (1781–1831), from Winchester, Frederick County, 1825–1827, pro-administration (John Quincy Adams).

CUTHBERT POWELL (1775–1849), from Fauquier County, 1841–1843, Whig.

LEVIN POWELL (1737–1810), from Loudoun County, 1799–1801, Federalist.

PAULUS POWELL (1809–1874), from Amherst County, 1849–1859, Democrat.

FRANCIS PRESTON (1765–1836), from Montgomery County, 1793–1795; 1795–1797, Democratic-Republican.

WILLIAM BALLARD PRESTON (1805–1862), from Montgomery County, 1847–1849, Whig.

AUBURN LORENZO PRIDEMORE (1837–1900), from Lee County, 1877–1879, Democrat.

ROGER ATKINSON PRYOR (1828–1919), from the city of Petersburg, 1859–1861, Democrat.

JULIAN MINOR QUARLES (1848–1929), from the city of Staunton, 1899–1901, Democrat.

JOHN RANDOLPH (1773–1833), from Charlotte County, 1799–1813, 1815–1817, 1819–1823, Democratic-Republican; 1823–1825, Crawford Republican; 1827–1829, Jacksonian; 1833, party affiliation unknown.

THOMAS MANN RANDOLPH (1768–1828), from Albemarle County, 1803–1807, Democratic-Republican.

WILLIAM FRANCIS RHEA (1858–1931), from the city of Bristol, 1899–1903, Democrat.

JAMES BUCHANAN RICHMOND (1842–1910), from Scott County, 1879–1881, Democrat.

Thomas Woodrow Wilson (1856–1924), oil painting, by Staunton artist
Frank Graham Cootes (1879–1960) *(Courtesy of the Woodrow Wilson
Birthplace Foundation, Inc., Staunton, Va.)*

ROBERT RIDGWAY (1828–1870), from Amherst County, 1870, Conservative.

FRANCIS EVEROD RIVES (1792–1861), from Sussex County, 1837–1841, Democrat.

WILLIAM CABELL RIVES (1793–1868), from Albemarle County, 1823–1825,
Crawford Republican; 1825–1829, Jacksonian.

JOHN FRANKLIN RIXEY (1854–1907), from Culpeper County, 1897–1907, Democrat.

JOHN ROANE (1766–1838), from King William County, 1809–1815, Democratic-
Republican; 1827–1831, 1835–1837, Jacksonian.

JOHN JONES ROANE (1794–1869), from King William County, 1831–1833,
Jacksonian.

WILLIAM HENRY ROANE (1787–1845), from King and Queen County, 1815–1817,
Democratic-Republican.

ABSALOM WILLIS ROBERTSON (1887–1971), from the city of Lexington, 1933–1946, Democrat.

JOHN ROBERTSON (1787–1873), from Richmond, Henrico County, 1834–1837, Anti-Jacksonian; 1837–1839, Whig.

EDWARD JOHN ROBESON JR. (1890–1966), from the city of Newport News, 1950–1959, Democrat.

JAMES KENNETH ROBINSON (1916–), from the city of Winchester, 1971–1985, Republican.

ROBERT RUTHERFORD (1728–1803), from Frederick County, 1793–1795; 1795–1797, Democratic-Republican.

GREEN BERRY SAMUELS (1806–1859), from Shenandoah County, 1839–1841, Democrat.

DAVID EDWARD SATTERFIELD JR. (1894–1946), from the city of Richmond, 1937–1945, Democrat.

DAVID EDWARD SATTERFIELD III (1920–1988), from the city of Richmond, 1965–1981, Democrat.

EDWARD WATTS SAUNDERS (1860–1921), from Franklin County, 1906–1920, Democrat.

ROBERT CORTEZ SCOTT (1947–), from the city of Newport News, 1993– , Democrat.

WILLIAM LLOYD SCOTT (1915–), from the city of Fairfax, 1967–1973, Republican.

JAMES ALEXANDER SEDDON (1815–1880), from the city of Richmond, 1845–1847, 1849–1851, Democrat.

JOSEPH EGGLESTON SEGAR (1804–1880), from Hampton, Elizabeth City County, 1862–1863, Unionist.

JAMES BEVERLEY SENER (1837–1903), from Fredericksburg, Spotsylvania County, 1873–1875, Republican.

JOSEPH CROCKETT SHAFFER (1880–1958), from Wythe County, 1929–1931, Republican.

DANIEL SHEFFEY (1770–1830), from Wythe County, 1809–1817, Federalist.

NORMAN SISISKY (1927–), from the city of Petersburg, 1983– , Democrat.

DANIEL FRENCH SLAUGHTER JR. (1925–), from Culpeper County, 1985–1991, Republican.

CAMPBELL SLEMP (1839–1907), from Wise County, 1903–1907, Republican.

CAMPBELL BASCOM SLEMP (1870–1943), from Wise County, 1907–1923, Republican.

ARTHUR SMITH (1785–1853), from Isle of Wight County, 1821–1823, Democratic-Republican; 1823–1825, Crawford Republican.

BALLARD SMITH (1782–1870), from Greenbrier County (now West Virginia), 1815–1821, Democratic-Republican.

HOWARD WORTH SMITH (1883–1976), from the city of Alexandria, 1931–1967, Democrat.

JOHN SMITH (1750–1836), from Frederick County, 1801–1815, Democratic-Republican.

JOHN AMBLER SMITH (1847–1892), from New Kent County, 1873–1875, Republican.

WILLIAM SMITH (1774–1859), from Greenbrier County (now West Virginia), 1821–1823, Democratic-Republican; 1823–1825, Crawford Republican; 1825–1827, Jacksonian.

WILLIAM SMITH (1797–1887), from Culpeper County, 1841–1843, 1853–1861, Democrat.

ALEXANDER SMYTH (1765–1830), from Wythe County, 1817–1823, Democratic-Republican; 1823–1825, Crawford Republican; 1827–1830, Jacksonian.

JOHN FRYALL SNODGRASS (1804–1854), from Wood County (now West Virginia), 1853–1854, Democrat.

ROBERT GOODE SOUTHALL (1852–1924), from Amelia County, 1903–1907, Democrat.

THOMAS BAHNSON STANLEY (1890–1970), from Henry County, 1946–1953, Democrat.

LEWIS STEENROD (1810–1862), from Ohio County (now West Virginia), 1839–1845, Democrat.

JAMES STEPHENSON (1764–1833), from Berkeley County (now West Virginia), 1803–1805, 1809–1811, 1822–1823, Federalist; 1823–1825, Crawford Federalist.

ANDREW STEVENSON (1784–1857), from Richmond, Henrico County, 1821–1823, Democratic-Republican; 1823–1825, Crawford Republican; 1825–1834, Jacksonian.

WILLIAM HENRY HARRISON STOWELL (1840–1922), from Halifax County, 1871–1877, Republican.

JOHN STRATTON (1769–1804), from Northampton County, 1801–1803, Federalist.

GEORGE FRENCH STROTHER (1783–1840), from Culpeper County, 1817–1820, Democratic-Republican.

JAMES FRENCH STROTHER (1811–1860), from Rappahannock County, 1851–1853, Whig.

ALEXANDER HUGH HOLMES STUART (1807–1891), from Staunton, Augusta County, 1841–1843, Whig.

ARCHIBALD STUART (1795–1855), from Patrick County, 1837–1839, Democrat.

GEORGE WILLIAM SUMMERS (1804–1868), from Kanawha County (now West Virginia), 1841–1845, Whig.

CLAUDE AUGUSTUS SWANSON (1862–1939), from Pittsylvania County, 1893–1906, Democrat.

JACOB SWOOPE (ca. 1768–1832), from Augusta County, 1809–1811, Federalist.

JOHN TALIAFERRO (1768–1852), from King George County, 1801–1803, 1811–1813, Democratic-Republican; 1824–1825, Crawford Republican; 1825–1829, pro-administration (John Quincy Adams); 1829–1831, 1835–1837, Anti-Jacksonian; 1837–1843, Whig.

MAGNUS TATE (1760–1823), from Berkeley County (now West Virginia), 1815–1817, Federalist.

ROBERT TAYLOR (1763–1845), from Orange County, 1825–1827, pro-administration (John Quincy Adams).

WILLIAM TAYLOR (1788–1846), from Lexington, Rockbridge County, 1843–1846, Democrat.

WILLIAM PENN TAYLOR (ca. 1791–1865), from Caroline County, 1833–1835, Anti-Jacksonian.

LITTLETON WALLER TAZEWELL (1774–1860), from Williamsburg, James City and York Counties, 1800–1801, Democratic-Republican.

WILLIAM TERRY (1824–1888), from Wythe County, 1871–1873, 1875–1877, Conservative.

CHRISTOPHER YANCY THOMAS (1818–1879), from Martinsville, Henry County, 1874–1875, Republican.

GEORGE WESTERN THOMPSON (1806–1888), from Ohio County (now West Virginia), 1851–1852, Democrat.

PHILIP ROOTES THOMPSON (1766–1837), from Culpeper County, 1801–1807, Democratic-Republican.

ROBERT AUGUSTINE THOMPSON (1805–1876), from Kanawha County (now West Virginia), 1847–1849, Democrat.

ROBERT TAYLOR THORP (1850–1938), from Mecklenburg County, 1896–1897, 1898–1899, Republican.

WILLIAM MARSHALL TREDWAY (1807–1891), from Danville, Pittsylvania County, 1845–1847, Democrat.

JAMES TREZVANT (d. 1841), from Southampton County, 1825–1831, Jacksonian.

PAUL SEWARD TRIBLE JR. (1946–), from Essex County, 1977–1983, Republican.

ABRAM TRIGG (1750–after 1813), from Montgomery County, 1797–1809, Democratic-Republican.

CONNALLY FINDLAY TRIGG (1847–1907), from Washington County, 1885–1887, Democrat.

JOHN JOHNS TRIGG (1748–1804), from Bedford County, 1797–1804, Democratic-Republican.

WILLIAM MUNFORD TUCK (1896–1983), from South Boston, Halifax County, 1953–1969, Democrat.

GEORGE TUCKER (1775–1861), from Lynchburg, Campbell County, 1819–1823, Democratic-Republican; 1823–1825, Crawford Republican.

HENRY ST. GEORGE TUCKER (1780–1848), from Winchester, Frederick County, 1815–1819, Democratic-Republican.

HENRY ST. GEORGE TUCKER (1853–1932), from the city of Staunton, 1889–1897, Democrat; from the city of Lexington, 1922–1932, Democrat.

JOHN RANDOLPH TUCKER (1823–1897), from the city of Lexington, 1875–1887, Democrat.

ROBERT TURNBULL (1850–1920), from Brunswick County, 1910–1913, Democrat.

SMITH SPANGLER TURNER (1842–1898), from Warren County, 1894–1897, Democrat.

DAVID GARDINER TYLER (1846–1927), from Charles City County, 1893–1897, Democrat.

JOHN TYLER (1790–1862), from Charles City County, 1817–1821, Democratic-Republican.

CHARLES HORACE UPTON (1812–1877), from Fairfax County, 1861–1862, Unionist.

THOMAS VAN SWEARINGEN (1784–1822), from Jefferson County (now West Virginia), 1819–1822, Federalist.

ABRAHAM BEDFORD VENABLE (1758–1811), from Prince Edward County, 1791–1795; 1795–1799, Democratic-Republican.

EDWARD CARRINGTON VENABLE (1853–1908), from the city of Petersburg, 1889–1890, Democrat.

EDMUND WADDILL JR. (1855–1931), from Henrico County, 1890–1891, Republican.

FRANCIS WALKER (1764–1806), from Albemarle County, 1793–1795.

GILBERT CARLTON WALKER (1833–1885), from the city of Norfolk, 1875–1879, Democrat.

JAMES ALEXANDER WALKER (1832–1901), from Wythe County, 1895–1899, Republican.

WILLIAM CREED WAMPLER (1926–), from the city of Bristol, 1953–1955, 1967–1983, Republican.

WALTER ALLEN WATSON (1867–1919), from Nottoway County, 1913–1919, Democrat.

KELLIAN VAN RENSALEAR WHALEY (1821–1876), from Wayne County (now West Virginia), 1861–1863, Unconditional Unionist.

ALEXANDER WHITE (ca. 1738–1804), from Frederick County, 1789–1793.

FRANCIS WHITE (d. 1826), from Hampshire County (now West Virginia), 1813–1815, Federalist.

JOSEPH WHITEHEAD (1867–1938), from Pittsylvania County, 1925–1931, Democrat.

THOMAS WHITEHEAD (1825–1901), from Amherst County, 1873–1875, Democrat.

GEORGE WILLIAM WHITEHURST (1925–), from the city of Norfolk, 1969–1987, Republican.

JARED WILLIAMS (1766–1831), from Frederick County, 1819–1823, Democratic-Republican; 1823–1825, Crawford Republican.

ALEXANDER WILSON (d. after 1812), from Botetourt County, 1804–1809, Democratic-Republican.

EDGAR CAMPBELL WILSON (1800–1860), from Monongalia County (now West Virginia), 1833–1835, Anti-Jacksonian.

THOMAS WILSON (1765–1826), from Monongalia County (now West Virginia), 1811–1813, Federalist.

GEORGE DOUGLAS WISE (1831–1898), from the city of Richmond, 1881–1890, 1891–1895, Democrat.

HENRY ALEXANDER WISE (1806–1876), from Accomack County, 1833–1837, Jacksonian; 1837–1843, Whig; 1843–1844, Democrat.

JOHN SERGEANT WISE (1846–1913), from the city of Richmond, 1883–1885, Readjuster.

RICHARD ALSOP WISE (1843–1900), from the city of Williamsburg, 1898–1899, 1900, Republican.

FRANK RUDOLPH WOLF (1939–), from Fairfax County, 1981– , Republican.

CLIFTON ALEXANDER WOODRUM (1887–1950), from the city of Roanoke, 1923–1945, Democrat.

JAMES PLEASANT WOODS (1868–1948), from the city of Roanoke, 1919–1923, Democrat.

JACOB YOST (1853–1933), from the city of Staunton, 1887–1889, 1897–1899, Republican.

WILLIAM ALBIN YOUNG (1860–1928), from the city of Norfolk, 1897–1898, 1899–1900, Democrat.

Senate

WILLIAM SEGAR ARCHER (1789–1855), from Amelia County, 1841–1847, Whig.

JAMES BARBOUR (1775–1842), from Orange County, 1815–1823, Democratic-Republican; 1823–1825, Crawford Republican.

JOHN STRODE BARBOUR JR. (1820–1892), from the city of Alexandria, 1889–1892, Democrat.

LEMUEL JACKSON BOWDEN (1815–1864), from Williamsburg, James City and York Counties, 1863–1864, Republican.

RICHARD BRENT (1757–1814), from Prince William County, 1809–1814, Democratic-Republican.

THOMAS GRANVILLE BURCH (1869–1951), from Martinsville, Henry County, 1946, Democrat.

HARRY FLOOD BYRD (1887–1966), from the city of Winchester, 1933–1965, Democrat.

HARRY FLOOD BYRD JR. (1914–), from the city of Winchester, 1965–1971, Democrat; 1971–1983, Independent.

JOHN SNYDER CARLILE (1817–1878), from Harrison County (now West Virginia), 1861–1865, Unionist.

JOHN WARWICK DANIEL (1842–1910), from the city of Lynchburg, 1887–1910, Democrat.

JOHN WAYLES EPPES (1773–1823), from Buckingham County, 1817–1819, Democratic-Republican.

WILLIAM BRANCH GILES (1762–1830), from Amelia County, 1804–1815, Democratic-Republican.

CARTER GLASS (1858–1946), from the city of Lynchburg, 1920–1946, Democrat.

WILLIAM GRAYSON (1740–1790), from Prince William County, 1789–1790.

ROBERT MERCER TALIAFERRO HUNTER (1809–1887), from Essex County, 1847–1861, Democrat.

EPPA HUNTON (1822–1908), from Fauquier County, 1892–1895, Democrat.

JOHN WARFIELD JOHNSTON (1818–1889), from Washington County, 1870–1883, Democrat.

RICHARD HENRY LEE (1732–1794), from Westmoreland County, 1789–1792.

BENJAMIN WATKINS LEIGH (1781–1849), from Richmond, Henrico County, 1834–1836, Anti-Jacksonian.

JOHN FRANCIS LEWIS (1818–1895), from Rockingham County, 1870–1875, Republican.

WILLIAM MAHONE (1826–1895), from the city of Petersburg, 1881–1887, Readjuster.

THOMAS STAPLES MARTIN (1847–1919), from Albemarle County, 1895–1919, Democrat.

ARMISTEAD THOMSON MASON (1787–1819), from Louisa County, 1816–1817, Democratic-Republican.

JAMES MURRAY MASON (1798–1871), from Winchester, Frederick County, 1847–1861, Democrat.

STEVENS THOMSON MASON (1760–1803), from Loudoun County, 1794–1795; 1795–1803, Democratic-Republican.

JAMES MONROE (1758–1831), from Albemarle County, 1790–1794.

ANDREW MOORE (1752–1821), from Rockbridge County, 1804–1809, Democratic-Republican.

WILSON CARY NICHOLAS (1761–1820), from Albemarle County, 1799–1804, Democratic-Republican.

RICHARD ELLIOTT PARKER (1783–1840), from Frederick (now Clarke) County, 1836–1837, Jacksonian.

ISAAC SAMUELS PENNYBACKER (1805–1847), from Harrisonburg, Rockingham County, 1845–1847, Democrat.

JAMES PLEASANTS (1769–1836), from Goochland County, 1819–1822, Democratic-Republican.

JOHN RANDOLPH (1773–1833), from Charlotte County, 1825–1827, Jacksonian.

HARRISON HOLT RIDDLEBERGER (1844–1890), from Shenandoah County, 1883–1889, Readjuster.

WILLIAM CABELL RIVES (1793–1868), from Albemarle County, 1832–1834, 1836, Jacksonian; 1837–1839, Democrat; 1841–1845, Whig.

WILLIAM HENRY ROANE (1787–1845), from Hanover County, 1837–1841, Democrat.

CHARLES SPITTAL ROBB (1939–), from Fairfax County, 1989– , Democrat.

ABSALOM WILLIS ROBERTSON (1887–1971), from the city of Lexington, 1946–1967, Democrat.

WILLIAM LLOYD SCOTT (1915–), from the city of Fairfax, 1973–1979, Republican.

WILLIAM BELSER SPONG JR. (1920–), from the city of Portsmouth, 1966–1973, Democrat.

CLAUDE AUGUSTUS SWANSON (1862–1939), from Pittsylvania County, 1910–1933, Democrat.

JOHN TAYLOR (1753–1824), from Caroline County, 1792–1794; 1803, 1822–1823, Democratic-Republican; 1823–1824, Crawford Republican.

HENRY TAZEWELL (1753–1799), from Williamsburg, James City and York Counties, 1794–1795; 1795–1799, Democratic-Republican.

LITTLETON WALLER TAZEWELL (1774–1860), from Norfolk, Norfolk County, 1824–1825, Jackson Republican; 1825–1832, Jacksonian.

PAUL SEWARD TRIBLE JR. (1946–), from the city of Newport News, 1983–1989, Republican.

JOHN TYLER (1790–1862), from Charles City County, 1827–1833, Jacksonian; 1833–1836, Anti-Jacksonian.

ABRAHAM BEDFORD VENABLE (1758–1811), from Prince Edward County, 1803–1804, Democratic-Republican.

JOHN WALKER (1744–1809), from Albemarle County, 1790.

JOHN WILLIAM WARNER (1927–), from Fauquier County, 1979– , Republican.

WAITMAN THOMAS WILLEY (1811–1900), from Monongalia County (now West Virginia), 1861–1863, Unionist.

ROBERT ENOCH WITHERS (1821–1907), from the city of Lynchburg, 1875–1881, Democrat.

Members of the Provisional Confederate Congress February 1861–February 1862

When the Provisional Confederate Congress met in 1861, its members consisted of two or three representatives chosen by each participating state's legislature. Thus the congress was unicameral. When the members of the First and Second Confederate Congresses were chosen, however, both senators and representatives were elected from each Confederate state.

THOMAS SALEM BOCOCK (1815–1891), from Appomattox County, July 1861–February 1862.

ALEXANDER ROBINSON BOTELER (1815–1892), from Jefferson County (now West Virginia), November 1861–February 1862.

JOHN WHITE BROCKENBROUGH (1806–1877), from Rockbridge County, May 1861–February 1862.

ROBERT MERCER TALIAFERRO HUNTER (1809–1887), from Essex County, May 1861–February 1862.

ROBERT JOHNSTON (1818–1885), from Harrison County (now West Virginia), July 1861–February 1862.

WILLIAM HAMILTON MacFARLAND (1799–1872), from the city of Richmond, July 1861–February 1862.

JAMES MURRAY MASON (1798–1871), from Winchester, Frederick County, July 1861–August 1861.

WALTER PRESTON (1819–1867), from Washington County, July 1861–February 1862.

WILLIAM BALLARD PRESTON (1805–1862), from Montgomery County, July 1861–February 1862.

ROGER ATKINSON PRYOR (1828–1919), from the city of Petersburg, July 1861–February 1862.

WILLIAM CABELL RIVES (1793–1868), from Albemarle County, May 1861–February 1862.

CHARLES WELLS RUSSELL (1818–1867), from Ohio County (now West Virginia), July 1861–February 1862.

ROBERT EDEN SCOTT (1803–1862), from Fauquier County, July 1861–February 1862.

JAMES ALEXANDER SEDDON (1815–1880), from the city of Richmond, July 1861–February 1862.

WALLER REDD STAPLES (1826–1897), from Montgomery County, May 1861–February 1862.

JOHN TYLER (1790–1862), from Charles City County, August 1861–January 1862.

Members of the First and Second
Confederate Congresses
February 1862–March 1865
House of Representatives

JOHN BROWN BALDWIN (1820–1873), from Staunton, Augusta County, February 1862–March 1865.

THOMAS SALEM BOCOCK (1815–1891), from Appomattox County, February 1862–March 1865.

ALEXANDER ROBINSON BOTELER (1815–1892), from Jefferson County (now West Virginia), February 1862–February 1864.

JOHN RANDOLPH CHAMBLISS (1809–1875), from Greensville County, February 1862–February 1864.

CHARLES FENTON COLLIER (1817–1899), from the city of Petersburg, August 1862–February 1864.

DANIEL COLEMAN DEJARNETTE (1822–1881), from Caroline County, February 1862–March 1865.

DAVID FUNSTEN (1819–1866), from the city of Alexandria, December 1863–March 1865.

MUSCOE RUSSELL HUNTER GARNETT (1821–1864), from Essex County, February 1862–February 1864.

THOMAS SAUNDERS GHOLSON (1809–1868), from the city of Petersburg, May 1864–March 1865.

JOHN GOODE JR. (1829–1909), from Bedford County, February 1862–March 1865.

JAMES PHILEMON HOLCOMBE (1820–1873), from Albemarle County, February 1862–February 1864.

FREDERICK WILLIAM MACKEY HOLLIDAY (1828–1899), from Winchester, Frederick County, May 1864–March 1865.

ALBERT GALLATIN JENKINS (1830–1864), from Kanawha County (now West Virginia), February 1862–August 1862.

ROBERT JOHNSTON (1818–1885), from Harrison County (now West Virginia), February 1862–March 1865.

JAMES LYONS (1801–1882), from the city of Richmond, February 1862–February 1864.

FAYETTE McMULLEN (1805–1880), from Scott County, May 1864–March 1865.

SAMUEL AUGUSTINE MILLER (1819–1890), from Kanawha County (now West Virginia), February 1863–March 1865.

ROBERT LATANÉ MONTAGUE, from Middlesex County, May 1864–January 1865.

WALTER PRESTON (1819–1867), from Washington County, February 1862–February 1864.

ROGER ATKINSON PRYOR (1828–1919), from the city of Petersburg, February 1862–April 1862.

WILLIAM CABELL RIVES (1793–1868), from Albemarle County, May 1864–March 1865.

CHARLES WELLS RUSSELL (1818–1867), from Ohio County (now West Virginia), February 1862–March 1865.

WILLIAM SMITH (1797–1887), from Fauquier County, February 1862–April 1863.

WALLER REDD STAPLES (1826–1897), from Montgomery County, February 1862–March 1865.

JOHN TYLER (1790–1862), from Charles City County, was elected but died before being seated.

ROBERT HENRY WHITFIELD (1814–1868), from Isle of Wight County, May 1864–March 1865.

WILLIAMS CARTER WICKHAM (1820–1888), from Hanover County, May 1864–March 1865.

Senate

ALLEN TAYLOR CAPERTON (1810–1876), from Monroe County (now West Virginia), January 1863–March 1865.

ROBERT MERCER TALIAFERRO HUNTER (1809–1887), from Essex County, February 1862–March 1865.

WILLIAM BALLARD PRESTON (1805–1862), from Montgomery County, February 1862–October 1862.

The design by Albert Lybrock for a cast-iron monument to mark James Monroe's tomb in Richmond's Hollywood Cemetery appeared on an 1858 bid from the Baltimore firm of Hayward, Bartlett & Co. to "furnish and set up complete the Monroe Monument in accordance with the drawing."

The Roman Revival Lunenburg County courthouse, reflecting Thomas Jefferson's strictly interpreted classicism, was completed in 1827. Exterior stairs were added later in the century when the courtroom was divided into two levels.

COUNTIES OF VIRGINIA

Since early colonial days, the county has been the basic unit of local government in Virginia. In 1634 the General Assembly at Jamestown established eight shires, similar to those in England. These were Accomack, Charles City, Charles River, Elizabeth City, Henrico, James City, Warrosquyoake, and Warwick River. Since that time, an additional 158 counties have been created by legislative action. Of these, 59 were established under the colonial government, and the remaining 99 have been created since the establishment of the commonwealth in 1776. The youngest county, Dickenson, was established in 1880. Ninety-five of the total of 166 counties are still in existence within Virginia. Sixty-one are now in other states.

The paragraphs below contain brief sketches of the counties now in existence in Virginia, those that have become extinct, and those that have undergone name changes. The date given for the formation of each county is that of the passage of the act of assembly creating the county, rather than the date of the actual beginning of county government. Often the latter event occurred in the year following legislative establishment. The population figures are those given in the 1990 census.

Counties of Virginia

ACCOMACK COUNTY was named for the Accomac Indians, who lived on the Eastern Shore at the time of the first English settlement in Virginia. One of the original eight shires established in 1634, Accomac County (spelled without a *k*) became Northampton County in 1643. The present county was formed from Northampton about 1663. In 1940 the General Assembly adopted the county's present spelling. Its area is 476 square miles, and the county seat is Accomac. Population 31,703.

ALBEMARLE COUNTY was named for William Anne Keppel, second earl of Albemarle and governor of the Virginia colony from 1737 to 1754. It was formed from Goochland County in 1744, and part of Louisa County and certain islands in the Fluvanna River, now called the James, were added later. Its area is 740 square miles, and the county seat is Charlottesville. Population 68,040.

ALEXANDRIA COUNTY was named for the town of Alexandria. It was formed from a portion of Fairfax County that had been ceded by Virginia in 1789 to the federal government for use as the site of a new national capital. In 1801 the area officially became part of the District of Columbia, although Congress named it Alexandria County. Congress returned the county to Virginia in 1846, and the following year the General Assembly extended the commonwealth's jurisdiction over the region. In 1920 the county's name was changed to Arlington County. *See* Arlington County

ALLEGHANY COUNTY bears a variant spelling derived from the name of the Allegheny Mountains, a range of which passes along the county's western boundary. It was formed from Bath, Botetourt, and Monroe (now in West Virginia) Counties in 1822, and additional parts of Monroe and Bath were added later. Its area is 444.44 square miles, and the county seat is Covington. Population 13,176.

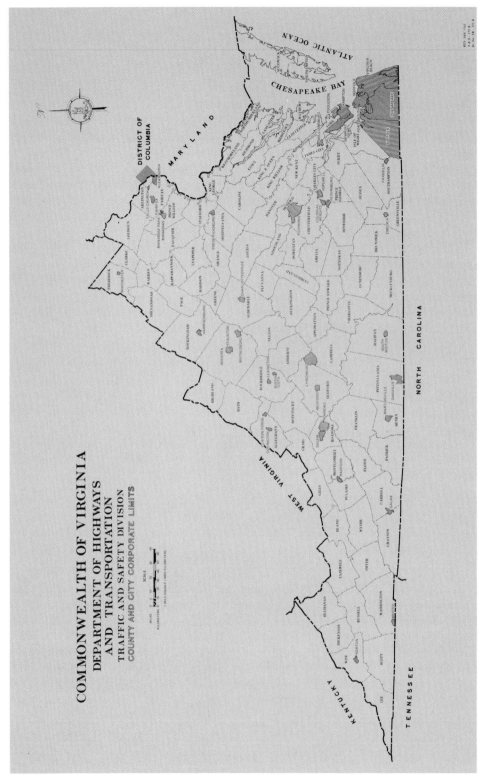

COMMONWEALTH OF VIRGINIA
DEPARTMENT OF HIGHWAYS
AND TRANSPORTATION
TRAFFIC AND SAFETY DIVISION
COUNTY AND CITY CORPORATE LIMITS

(Courtesy of the Virginia Department of Transportation)

AMELIA COUNTY was named for Amelia Sophia Eleanora, daughter of George II of England. It was formed from Prince George and Brunswick Counties in 1734. Its area is 366 square miles, and the county seat is Amelia. Population 8,787.

AMHERST COUNTY was named for Major General Jeffery Amherst, British commander in North America during the latter part of the French and Indian War and governor of Virginia from 1759 to 1768. It was formed from Albemarle County in 1761. Its area is 470 square miles, and the county seat is Amherst. Population 28,578.

APPOMATTOX COUNTY was named for the Appomattox River, which rises in the county. The name was borne earlier by an Indian tribe living near the mouth of the river. The county was formed from parts of Buckingham, Prince Edward, Charlotte, and Campbell Counties in 1845, and another part of Campbell was added in 1848. Its area is 345 square miles, and the county seat is Appomattox. Population 12,298.

ARLINGTON COUNTY originally was named Alexandria County. It was formed from a part of Fairfax County that was ceded to the United States government in 1789 but was returned to Virginia in 1846. The county's name was changed in 1920 to Arlington, the name of the Custis family mansion (the home of Robert E. Lee), which is located in the county. Its area is 25 square miles, and the county seat is Arlington. Population 170,936.

AUGUSTA COUNTY was named in honor of Augusta of Saxe-Gotha, wife of Frederick Louis, Prince of Wales, and mother of George III. It was formed from Orange County in 1738, but, because the region was sparsely inhabited, county government was not actually established there until 1745. Its area is 968 square miles, and the county seat is Staunton. Population 54,677.

BATH COUNTY was given its name either for the many mineral springs found in the county or for the town of Bath in England. It was formed from Augusta, Botetourt, and Greenbrier (now in West Virginia) Counties in 1790. Its area is 540 square miles, and the county seat is Warm Springs. Population 4,799.

BEDFORD COUNTY probably was named for John Russell, fourth duke of Bedford, who, as secretary of state for the southern department from 1748 to 1751, had general supervision of colonial affairs. It was formed from Lunenburg County in 1753, and parts of Albemarle and Lunenburg Counties were added later. Its area is 764 square miles, and the county seat is Bedford. Population 45,656.

BLAND COUNTY is said to have been named for Richard Bland, a leader of colonial Virginia's resistance to Great Britain in the 1760s and 1770s. It was formed from Giles, Wythe, and Tazewell Counties in 1861, and another part of Giles was added later. Its area is 369 square miles, and the county seat is Bland. Population 6,514.

BOTETOURT COUNTY was named for Norborne Berkeley, baron de Botetourt, the royal governor who served from 1768 to 1770. It was formed from Augusta County in 1769, and a part of Rockbridge County was added later. Its area is 549 square miles, and the county seat is Fincastle. Population 24,992.

BRUNSWICK COUNTY was named for the duchy of Brunswick-Lüneburg, one of the German possessions of George I. It was formed in 1720 from Prince George County, but, because of the sparse population, county government was not organized until 1732. In the latter year Brunswick County was enlarged by the addition of parts of Surry and Isle of Wight Counties. Its area is 579 square miles, and the county seat is Lawrenceville. Population 15,987.

BUCHANAN COUNTY was named for United States president James Buchanan and was formed from Tazewell and Russell Counties in 1858. Its area is 508 square miles, and the county seat is Grundy. Population 31,333.

BUCKINGHAM COUNTY probably was named either for the English county or for the duke of Buckingham. According to some sources, however, the name came from Archibald Cary's tract of land called Buckingham, on what was then Willis's Creek. It was formed from Albemarle County in 1761. Its area is 582 square miles, and the county seat is Buckingham. Population 12,873.

CAMPBELL COUNTY was named for William Campbell, one of the heroes of the Battle of Kings Mountain in 1780. The county was formed from Bedford County in 1781. Its area is 511 square miles, and the county seat is Rustburg. Population 47,572.

CAROLINE COUNTY was named for Caroline of Anspach, consort of George II. It was formed from Essex, King and Queen, and King William Counties in 1728, and additional parts of King and Queen were added later. Its area is 549 square miles, and the county seat is Bowling Green. Population 19,217.

CARROLL COUNTY was named for Charles Carroll of Carrollton, a signer of the Declaration of Independence from Maryland. It was formed from Grayson County in 1842, and part of Patrick County was added later. Its area is 497.58 square miles, and the county seat is Hillsville. Population 26,594.

CHARLES CITY COUNTY was named for Charles I of England and was one of the eight shires established in 1634. Its area is 204 square miles, and the county seat is Charles City. Population 6,282.

CHARLES RIVER COUNTY was named for Charles I of England and was one of the eight shires established in 1634. It was renamed York County in 1643, probably in honor of James, duke of York, the second son of Charles I. *See* York County

CHARLOTTE COUNTY was named for Charlotte of Mecklenburg-Strelitz, consort of George III. It was formed from Lunenburg County in 1764. Its area is 471 square miles, and the county seat is Charlotte Court House. Population 11,688.

CHESTERFIELD COUNTY was named for Philip Dormer Stanhope, fourth earl of Chesterfield, British statesman and diplomat, and was formed from Henrico County in 1749. Its area is 446.41 square miles, and the county seat is Chesterfield Court House. Population 209,274.

CLARKE COUNTY was named for George Rogers Clark, who helped win the Northwest Territory for Virginia during the Revolution (and who spelled his name without the *e*). The county was formed from Frederick County in 1836, and part of Warren County was added later. Its area is 174 square miles, and the county seat is Berryville. Population 12,101.

CRAIG COUNTY was named for Robert Craig, a nineteenth-century Virginia congressman. The county was formed from Botetourt, Roanoke, Giles, and Monroe (now in West Virginia) Counties in 1851, and several subsequent additions were made from Alleghany, Giles, Monroe, and Montgomery Counties. Its area is 336 square miles, and the county seat is New Castle. Population 4,372.

Nineteenth-century photograph of the Clarke County courthouse in Berryville

CULPEPER COUNTY probably was named for Catherine Culpeper, or for her mother, Margaret Lady Culpeper, or for Thomas Culpeper, second baron Culpeper of Thoresway, governor of Virginia from 1677 to 1683, or for their family, which long held proprietary rights in the Northern Neck. It was formed from Orange County in 1749. Its area is 389 square miles, and the county seat is Culpeper. Population 27,791.

CUMBERLAND COUNTY was named for William Augustus, duke of Cumberland, third son of George II. It was formed from Goochland County in 1749. Its area is 298.5 square miles, and the county seat is Cumberland. Population 7,825.

DICKENSON COUNTY was named for William J. Dickenson, delegate to the General Assembly from Russell County in 1880 when Dickenson was formed from Russell, Wise, and Buchanan Counties. Its area is 335 square miles, and the county seat is Clintwood. Population 17,620.

DINWIDDIE COUNTY was named for Robert Dinwiddie, lieutenant governor of Virginia from 1751 to 1758, and was formed from Prince George County in 1752. Its area is 501.28 square miles, and the county seat is Dinwiddie. Population 20,960.

DUNMORE COUNTY was named for John Murray, fourth earl of Dunmore and governor of Virginia from 1771 to 1775. It was formed from Frederick County in May 1772. Lord Dunmore's actions at the outbreak of the American Revolution made him so unpopular with Virginians, however, that the General Assembly changed the county's name to Shanando (now Shenandoah) County, effective 1 February 1778. *See* Shenandoah County

ELIZABETH CITY COUNTY (extinct) was named for Elizabeth, daughter of James I, and was one of the eight shires established in 1634. It became extinct in 1952, when it was incorporated into the city of Hampton, which was the county seat. *See* Hampton

ESSEX COUNTY probably was named for the English county. It was formed from old Rappahannock County in 1692. Its area is 261 square miles, and the county seat is Tappahannock. Population 8,689.

FAIRFAX COUNTY was named for Thomas Fairfax, sixth baron Fairfax of Cameron, proprietor of the Northern Neck. It was formed from Prince William County in 1742. Its area is 410 square miles, and the county seat is Fairfax. Population 818,584.

FAUQUIER COUNTY was named for Francis Fauquier, lieutenant governor of Virginia from 1758 to 1768. It was formed in 1759 from Prince William County. Its area is 651 square miles, and the county seat is Warrenton. Population 48,741.

FINCASTLE COUNTY (extinct) was named either for George, Lord Fincastle, Lord Dunmore's son; for John Murray, fourth earl of Dunmore, Viscount Fincastle; or for the town of Fincastle, Virginia, which was established in 1772 and named after Lord Botetourt's home in England. The county was created from Botetourt County in 1772. It became extinct in 1776 when it was divided to form Montgomery, Washington, and Kentucky (now the state of Kentucky) Counties. *See* Kentucky County; Montgomery County; Washington County

FLOYD COUNTY was named for John Floyd, governor of Virginia from 1830 to 1834. It was formed from Montgomery County in 1831, and part of Franklin County was added later. Its area is 383 square miles, and the county seat is Floyd. Population 12,005.

FLUVANNA COUNTY takes its name from an eighteenth-century term for the upper James River. The name, meaning river of Anne, was originally bestowed in honor of Queen Anne of England. The county was formed from Albemarle County in 1777. Its area is 282 square miles, and the county seat is Palmyra. Population 12,429.

FRANKLIN COUNTY was named for Benjamin Franklin and was formed from Bedford and Henry Counties in 1785. Its area is 711.5 square miles, and the county seat is Rocky Mount. Population 39,549.

FREDERICK COUNTY was named in honor of Frederick Louis, Prince of Wales and eldest son of George II. It was formed from Orange County in 1738, but, because the region was sparsely settled, county government was not organized until 1743. Part of Augusta County was added later. Its area is 426 square miles, and the county seat is Winchester. Population 45,723.

GILES COUNTY was named for William Branch Giles, United States senator from Virginia in 1806 when the county was created. It was formed from Montgomery,

Monroe (now in West Virginia), and Tazewell Counties, and parts of Wythe, Monroe, Mercer (now in West Virginia), Craig, and Tazewell Counties were added later. Its area is 363 square miles, and the county seat is Pearisburg. Population 16,366.

GLOUCESTER COUNTY probably was named for the English county, although it may also have been intended to honor Henry, duke of Gloucester, the third son of Charles I. It was formed from York County in 1651. Its area is 225 square miles, and the county seat is Gloucester. Population 30,131.

GOOCHLAND COUNTY was named for Sir William Gooch, lieutenant governor of Virginia from 1727 to 1749. It was formed from Henrico County in 1728. Its area is 289 square miles, and the county seat is Goochland. Population 14,163.

GRAYSON COUNTY was named for William Grayson, a delegate to the Continental Congress from 1784 to 1787 and one of the first two United States senators from Virginia. It was formed from Wythe County in 1792, and a portion of Patrick County was added later. Its area is 454 square miles, and the county seat is Independence. Population 16,278.

GREENE COUNTY was named for Nathanael Greene, American commander of the Army of the South in the Revolutionary War. It was formed from Orange County in 1838. Its area is 153 square miles, and the county seat is Stanardsville. Population 10,297.

GREENSVILLE COUNTY was named either for Revolutionary War general Nathanael Greene or for Sir Richard Grenville, leader of the Roanoke Island settlement of 1585. The county was formed from Brunswick County in 1780. Parts of Brunswick and Sussex Counties were added later. Its area is 300 square miles, and the county seat is Emporia. Population 8,853.

HALIFAX COUNTY was named for George Montagu Dunk, second earl of Halifax, who was president of the Board of Trade from 1748 to 1761. It was formed from Lunenburg County in 1752. Its area is 805.7 square miles, and the county seat is Halifax. Population 29,033.

HANOVER COUNTY was named for George I, who at the time of his accession to the English throne was elector of Hanover in Germany. The county was formed from New Kent County in 1720. Its area is 471 square miles, and the county seat is Hanover. Population 63,306.

HENRICO COUNTY was named for Henry, Prince of Wales, the oldest son of James I. It was one of the eight original shires established in 1634. Its area is 244.06 square miles, and the county seat is located in the western part of the county, near Richmond. Population 217,881.

HENRY COUNTY was named for Patrick Henry, revolutionary leader and first governor of the commonwealth of Virginia. It was formed from Pittsylvania County in 1776. Its area is 385 square miles, and the county seat is Martinsville. Population 56,942.

HIGHLAND COUNTY was so named because of its mountainous terrain, and it is sometimes called the Little Switzerland of America. It was formed from Pendleton (now in West Virginia) and Bath Counties in 1847. Its area is 416 square miles, and the county seat is Monterey. Population 2,635.

ISLE OF WIGHT COUNTY probably was named for the Isle of Wight off the south coast of England. It was first known as Warrosquyoake and was one of the eight shires established in 1634. The present name was given in 1637. Part of Nansemond County was added in 1769. Its area is 319 square miles, and the county seat is Isle of Wight. Population 25,053.

JAMES CITY COUNTY was named for James I. It was one of the eight shires established in 1634. Parts of New Kent and York Counties were added later. Its area is 144.1 square miles, and the county seat is in the city of Williamsburg. Population 34,859.

KING AND QUEEN COUNTY was named for William III and Mary II, who were called to the English throne in 1688. It was formed from New Kent County in 1691. Its area is 327 square miles, and the county seat is King and Queen Court House. Population 6,289.

KING GEORGE COUNTY was named in honor of George I of England and was formed from Richmond County in 1720. Part of Westmoreland County was added later. Its area is 181 square miles, and the county seat is King George. Population 13,527.

KING WILLIAM COUNTY was named for William III and was formed from King and Queen County in 1701. Its area is 285.7 square miles, and the county seat is King William. Population 10,913.

LANCASTER COUNTY probably was named for the English county. It was formed from Northumberland and York Counties in 1651. Its area is 136.5 square miles, and the county seat is Lancaster. Population 10,896.

LEE COUNTY was named for Henry ("Light-Horse Harry") Lee, governor of Virginia from 1791 to 1794. It was formed from Russell County in 1792, and part of Scott County was added later. Its area is 438 square miles, and the county seat is Jonesville. Population 24,496.

LOUDOUN COUNTY was named for John Campbell, fourth earl of Loudoun, who was commander of British forces in North America during the early part of the French and Indian War and governor of Virginia from 1756 to 1759. It was formed from Fairfax County in 1757. Its area is 512 square miles, and the county seat is Leesburg. Population 86,129.

LOUISA COUNTY was named for Louisa, a daughter of George II. It was formed from Hanover County in 1742. Its area is 514 square miles, and the county seat is Louisa. Population 20,325.

LOWER NORFOLK COUNTY. *See* Norfolk County

LUNENBURG COUNTY was named for George II, duke of Brunswick-Lüneburg, a German possession of England's Hanoverian kings. It was formed from Brunswick County in 1745. Its area is 443 square miles, and the county seat is Lunenburg. Population 11,419.

MADISON COUNTY was named for James Madison, a prominent Virginian and member of Congress in 1792 when the county was formed from Culpeper County. Its area is 327 square miles, and the county seat is Madison. Population 11,949.

MATHEWS COUNTY was named for Thomas Mathews, of Norfolk, the Speaker of the Virginia House of Delegates in 1790 when the county was formed from Gloucester County. Its area is 85.7 square miles, and the county seat is Mathews. Population 8,348.

MECKLENBURG COUNTY was named, like Charlotte County, for Charlotte of Mecklenburg-Strelitz, consort of George III. It was formed from Lunenburg County in 1764. Its area is 675 square miles, and the county seat is Boydton. Population 29,241.

MIDDLESEX COUNTY probably was named for the English county. It was formed from Lancaster County about 1669. Its area is 142 square miles, and the county seat is Saluda. Population 8,653.

MONTGOMERY COUNTY was named for Richard Montgomery, who was killed in the American assault on Quebec late in 1775. It was formed from Fincastle County in 1776, and parts of Botetourt and Pulaski Counties were added later. Its area is 391.1 square miles, and the county seat is Christiansburg. Population 73,913.

NANSEMOND COUNTY (extinct) was named for the Nansemond Indians, who lived in the area in the early seventeenth century. The word *nansemond* means fishing point or angle. When first established in 1637, the county was known as Upper Norfolk, but the name Nansemond was adopted in 1646. The county seat was Suffolk. The county became the independent city of Nansemond in July 1972, and on 1 January 1974 Nansemond merged with the city of Suffolk. The entire area is now known as Suffolk. *See* Suffolk

NELSON COUNTY was named for Thomas Nelson Jr., governor of Virginia from June to November 1781. It was formed in 1807 from Amherst County. Its area is 471 square miles, and the county seat is Lovingston. Population 12,778.

NEW KENT COUNTY was named either for the English county of Kent or for Kent Island, in the upper waters of the Chesapeake Bay. William Claiborne, a native of Kent who had been driven from Kent Island by Lord Baltimore, was a prominent resident of the New Kent area about 1654 when the county was formed from York County. Its area is 221 square miles, and the county seat is New Kent. Population 10,445.

NEW NORFOLK COUNTY (extinct) was named by Charles I and was created from Elizabeth City County in 1636. It became extinct when it was divided into Upper and Lower Norfolk Counties in 1637. *See* Nansemond County; Norfolk County

NORFOLK COUNTY (extinct) probably was named by Adam Thoroughgood, a local resident, for his native county in England. It was formed from Lower Norfolk County in 1691. Norfolk County became extinct in 1963, when it was consolidated with the city of South Norfolk to form the city of Chesapeake. The county seat was Portsmouth. *See* Chesapeake

NORTHAMPTON COUNTY probably was named for the English county, of which Obedience Robins, a prominent early resident of the Eastern Shore, was a native. The county, which originally included all of the peninsula south of Maryland and which was one of the eight shires established in 1634, was first called Accomac. The name was changed by legislative action in 1643. Its area is 357 square miles, and the county seat is Eastville. Population 13,061. *See also* Accomack County

NORTHUMBERLAND COUNTY probably was named for the English county. It was formed about 1645 from the district of Chickacoan, the early-seventeenth-century name for the region between the Potomac and the Rappahannock Rivers. Its area is 223 square miles, and the county seat is Heathsville. Population 10,524.

NOTTOWAY COUNTY was named for the Nadowa Indian tribe. The word *nadowa*, anglicized to *nottoway*, means snake, or enemy. The county was formed from Amelia County in 1788. Its area is 308 square miles, and the county seat is Nottoway. Population 14,993.

ORANGE COUNTY, according to most accounts, was named for William of Orange, the Dutch prince who became William III of England in 1688. It is more probable, however, that the name honored William IV, prince of Orange-Nassau, who married Anne, eldest daughter of George II, in 1734—the year Orange County was formed from Spotsylvania County. Its area is 355 square miles, and the county seat is Orange. Population 21,421.

PAGE COUNTY was named, according to most sources, for John Page, revolutionary patriot, congressman, and governor of Virginia from 1802 to 1805. It was formed from Rockingham and Shenandoah Counties in 1831. Its area is 316 square miles, and the county seat is Luray. Population 21,690.

PATRICK COUNTY, like Henry County, was named for Patrick Henry. It was formed from Henry County in 1790. Its area is 469 square miles, and the county seat is Stuart. Population 17,473.

PITTSYLVANIA COUNTY was named in honor of William Pitt, first earl of Chatham, a great English statesman. It was formed from Halifax County in 1766. Its area is 982.89 square miles, and the county seat is Chatham. Population 55,655.

POWHATAN COUNTY was named for the Indian chieftain who ruled the Native American inhabitants of tidewater Virginia in the early seventeenth century. It was formed from Cumberland County in 1777, and part of Chesterfield County was added later. Its area is 272 square miles, and the county seat is Powhatan. Population 15,328.

PRINCE EDWARD COUNTY was named in honor of Edward Augustus, a son of Prince Frederick Louis, a grandson of George II, and a younger brother of George III. The county was formed from Amelia County in 1753. Its area is 357 square miles, and the county seat is Farmville. Population 17,320.

PRINCE GEORGE COUNTY was named for Prince George of Denmark, husband of Queen Anne of England. It was formed from Charles City County in 1702. Its area is 276 square miles, and the county seat is Prince George. Population 27,394.

PRINCESS ANNE COUNTY (extinct) was named for Anne, daughter of James II, who became queen of England in 1702. The county was formed from Lower Norfolk County in 1691 and became extinct in 1963, after its consolidation with the city of Virginia Beach. The county seat was Princess Anne. *See* Virginia Beach

PRINCE WILLIAM COUNTY was named for William Augustus, duke of Cumberland and third son of George II. It was formed from Stafford and King George Counties in 1730. Its area is 347 square miles, and the county seat is Manassas. Population 215,686.

PULASKI COUNTY was named for Casimir Pulaski, the Polish patriot who served in the American army during the Revolutionary War and who was killed during the siege of Savannah in 1779. It was formed from Montgomery and Wythe Counties in 1839. Its area is 318 square miles, and the county seat is Pulaski. Population 34,496.

RAPPAHANNOCK COUNTY was named for the Rappahannock River, which in turn received its name from an Indian tribe that lived along its banks. There have been two Virginia counties named Rappahannock. The first was created from Lancaster in 1656 and became extinct in 1692 when it was divided into Essex and Richmond Counties. The present county was formed from Culpeper County in 1833. Its area is 267 square miles, and the county seat is Washington. Population 6,622.

RICHMOND COUNTY was named either for Richmond borough in Surrey, England, or for the late-seventeenth-century duke of Richmond. It was formed from old Rappahannock County in 1692. Its area is 193 square miles, and the county seat is Warsaw. Population 7,273.

ROANOKE COUNTY was named for the Roanoke River. The name is an Indian word meaning shell money. The county was formed from Botetourt County in 1838, and part of Montgomery County was added later. Its area is 248.28 square miles, and the county seat is Salem. Population 79,332.

ROCKBRIDGE COUNTY was named for Natural Bridge, an exceptional rock formation located in the county. The county was formed from Augusta and Botetourt Counties in 1778, and another part of Botetourt was added later. Its area is 600 square miles, and the county seat is Lexington. Population 18,350.

ROCKINGHAM COUNTY was named for Charles Watson-Wentworth, second marquis of Rockingham, who supported the colonists in their disputes with Great Britain. It was formed from Augusta County in 1778. Its area is 871 square miles, and the county seat is Harrisonburg. Population 57,482.

RUSSELL COUNTY was named for William Russell, a Clinch Valley pioneer and the member of the House of Delegates who introduced the legislation forming the county from Washington County in 1786. Its area is 483 square miles, and the county seat is Lebanon. Population 28,667.

SCOTT COUNTY was named for Winfield Scott, a native of Virginia, in recognition of his victories during the War of 1812. It was formed from Lee, Russell, and Washington Counties in 1814. Its area is 539 square miles, and the county seat is Gate City. Population 23,204.

SHENANDOAH COUNTY was named for the Shenandoah River, which passes through the county. *Shenandoah* is an Indian word meaning beautiful daughter of the stars. The county was named Dunmore when it was formed from Frederick County in 1772. The present name was adopted in 1778. Its area is 507 square miles, and the county seat is Woodstock. Population 31,636.

SMYTH COUNTY was named in 1832 for Alexander Smyth, a former congressman from Virginia who had died in 1830 while efforts were underway to create the new county. The county was formed from Washington and Wythe Counties. Its area is 435 square miles, and the county seat is Marion. Population 32,370.

SOUTHAMPTON COUNTY was named, in the opinion of many authorities, for Henry Wriothesley, third earl of Southampton and treasurer of the London Company from 1620 to 1624. It is more likely, however, that the county was named for the borough of Southampton in England. Southampton County was formed in 1749 from Isle of Wight County, and part of Nansemond County was added later. Its area is 599.26 square miles, and the county seat is Courtland. Population 17,550.

SPOTSYLVANIA COUNTY was named for Alexander Spotswood, lieutenant governor of Virginia from 1710 to 1722. It was formed from Essex, King William, and King and Queen Counties in 1720. Its area is 407 square miles, and the county seat is Spotsylvania. Population 57,403.

STAFFORD COUNTY was named for the English county. It was formed from Westmoreland County in 1664. Its area is 277 square miles, and the county seat is Stafford. Population 61,236.

SURRY COUNTY was named for the county of Surrey in England, and was formed from James City County about 1652. Its area is 306 square miles, and the county seat is Surry. Population 6,145.

SUSSEX COUNTY was named for the English county, and was formed from Surry County in 1753. Its area is 496 square miles, and the county seat is Sussex. Population 10,248.

TAZEWELL COUNTY was named for Henry Tazewell, United States senator from Virginia from 1794 until his death in 1799. It was formed from Wythe and Russell Counties in 1799, and parts of Logan (now in West Virginia), Russell, Wythe, and Washington Counties were added later. Its area is 522 square miles, and the county seat is Tazewell. Population 45,960.

UPPER NORFOLK COUNTY (extinct) was established in 1637. In 1646 it was renamed Nansemond County for the Nansemond Indians, who lived in the area. The county seat was Suffolk. The county became the independent city of Nansemond in July 1972, and on 1 January 1974 Nansemond merged with the city of Suffolk. The entire area is now known as Suffolk. *See* Suffolk

WARREN COUNTY was named for Joseph Warren, the revolutionary patriot who sent Paul Revere and William Dawes on their famous rides and who was killed at the Battle of Bunker Hill. The county was formed from Shenandoah and Frederick Counties in 1836. Its area is 219 square miles, and the county seat is Front Royal. Population 26,142.

WARROSQUYOAKE COUNTY was named for the Indian tribe. It was formed in 1634 as one of the original eight shires. In 1637 it was renamed Isle of Wight County. *See* Isle of Wight County

WARWICK COUNTY (extinct) was named either for Robert Rich, earl of Warwick, a prominent member of the London Company, or for the county of Warwick in England. The county was originally called Warwick River and was one of the eight shires formed in 1634. The shorter name was adopted in 1643. Warwick County became extinct in 1952, when it became the city of Warwick. The new city was consolidated with the city of Newport News in 1958 and took the latter's name. Denbigh was the county seat. *See* Newport News

WARWICK RIVER COUNTY. *See* Warwick County

WASHINGTON COUNTY is the first locality in the United States known to have been named for George Washington. It was formed from Fincastle County in 1776, and a part of Montgomery County was added later. Its area is 560 square miles, and the county seat is Abingdon. Population 45,887.

WESTMORELAND COUNTY was named for the English county. It was formed from Northumberland County in 1653, and part of King George County was added later. Its area is 252 square miles, and the county seat is Montross. Population 15,480.

WISE COUNTY was named for Henry Alexander Wise, governor of Virginia from 1856 to 1860. It was formed in 1856 from Lee, Scott, and Russell Counties. Its area is 415.6 square miles, and the county seat is Wise. Population 39,573.

WYTHE COUNTY was named for George Wythe, a signer of the Declaration of Independence and chancellor of Virginia in 1789 when Wythe County was formed from Montgomery County. Part of Grayson County was added later. Its area is 459 square miles, and the county seat is Wytheville. Population 25,466.

YORK COUNTY originally was named Charles River County, for Charles I, and was one of the eight shires formed in 1634. The present name was given in 1643, probably in honor of James, duke of York, the second son of Charles I. Its area is 108.5 square miles, and the county seat is Yorktown. Population 42,422.

Counties Formerly in Virginia

Prior to 1784 the commonwealth of Virginia consisted of a vast territory extending west from the Atlantic Ocean to the Mississippi River and north from the North Carolina line to the Great Lakes. Starting in 1784, however, the size of the commonwealth decreased: in 1784 the United States Congress accepted Virginia's cession of its northwestern lands; parts of three Virginia counties were added to the commonwealth of Pennsylvania between 1776 and 1785; and between 1784 and 1792 residents of the area known as the district of Kentucky held ten conventions on the question of statehood. On 18 December 1789 the General Assembly of Virginia passed an act to allow Kentucky to apply for statehood, and on 1 June 1792 Kentucky's nine counties became a state. With the start of the Civil War in 1861, fifty of Virginia's western counties voted to remain in the Union, and on 23 June 1863 West Virginia became a state.

Illinois County Formerly in Virginia

ILLINOIS COUNTY was named for the Illini, a confederacy of woodland tribes. The French changed the name, which means "the men," to Illinois. Illinois County was created in December 1778 after George Rogers Clark had captured several British posts on the Mississippi River within Virginia's boundaries. The county included all of that territory between the Ohio and Mississippi Rivers that now constitutes the states of Ohio, Indiana, Illinois, Michigan, and Wisconsin, as well as a small part of Minnesota. The General Assembly continued the county's existence until 5 January 1782. On 1 March 1784 the Illinois territory was ceded to Congress and ceased to be part of the commonwealth of Virginia.

Pennsylvania County Formerly in Virginia

YOHOGANIA COUNTY (extinct) was given its name from the Indian word meaning a stream flowing in a roundabout course. It was created in 1776 when the district of West Augusta was divided into three new counties: Monongalia, Ohio, and Yohogania. Within nine years, almost all of Yohogania, and much of Ohio and Monongalia Counties, became part of the commonwealth of Pennsylvania. The remaining portions of Ohio and Monongalia Counties in 1863 became part of the new state of West Virginia. Yohogania remained a Virginia county until the October 1785 session of the General Assembly, at which time the assembly recognized that since the western boundary of Pennsylvania had been extended and had taken in most of Yohogania, the area left was too small to remain a separate county. Thus the rest of Yohogania was added to Ohio County.

Kentucky Counties Formerly in Virginia

BOURBON COUNTY was named for the royal family of France in recognition of French aid to the colonies during the Revolution. It was formed in 1785 from Kentucky County. Its area is 292 square miles. The county seat was established in 1789 and named Hopewell; in 1790 its name was changed briefly to Bourbonton and then to its present name, Paris.

FAYETTE COUNTY was named for the Marquis de Lafayette. It was created in 1780 and was one of the three original counties that made up the district of Kentucky. Fayette County consisted of the northern and eastern portions of the present state. Its area is 285 square miles, and the county seat is Lexington.

JEFFERSON COUNTY was named for Thomas Jefferson, governor of Virginia from 1779 to 1781. Established in 1780, it was one of the three original counties that made up the district of Kentucky. Jefferson County consisted of the middle section of the present state. Its area is 386 square miles, and the county seat is Louisville.

KENTUCKY COUNTY (extinct) was given its name from the Wyandot word for plain or broad plains. It was created in 1776 from Fincastle County. Kentucky County became extinct in November 1780 when it was divided into Fayette, Jefferson, and Lincoln Counties.

LINCOLN COUNTY was named for Major General Benjamin Lincoln, whose army was captured by the British at Charleston in 1779. Formed in 1780, Lincoln County was the third of the original counties established in the district of Kentucky. It consisted of the western portion of the present state. Its area is 337 square miles. Harrodsburg was the first county seat until it became the center of government for Mercer County, which was created in 1785. Stanford then became the county seat of Lincoln.

MADISON COUNTY was named for Virginia statesman James Madison and was created in 1785 out of part of Lincoln County. Its area is 443 square miles. Milford was the original county seat, but the county's government was moved to Richmond, Kentucky, in 1798.

MASON COUNTY was named for George Mason, author of the Virginia Declaration of Rights. It was formed from Bourbon County in 1788. Its area is 241 square miles. Washington was the county seat until 1848 when Maysville became the new center of county government.

PARISHES OF THE ESTABLISHED CHURCH
1607–1785

When the first English settlers came to Virginia in 1607 they followed the familiar patterns of the Church of England and established parishes that served as local units of ecclesiastical and community organization. Parish boundaries in England had been established by custom, not by acts of Parliament. In colonial Virginia, however, the General Assembly established parishes and fixed their boundaries, often at the same time that it created or altered counties. A decade after independence, on 16 January 1786, the General Assembly passed Thomas Jefferson's Bill for Establishing Religious Freedom, ending state-enforced support for the formerly established church and its parishes.

The following two lists of the parishes in Virginia from 1607 to 1785 are: first, an alphabetical list of counties together with the parishes associated with them; and second, an alphabetical list of parishes and the counties associated with them. Dates are given for the pre-1785 formations and extinctions of parishes and for the years during which a parish was associated with one or more counties. Dates of parishes that continued to exist after 1785 are left open. Unknown dates are represented by question marks.

For additional information about parishes, see Charles Francis Cocke's *Parish Lines, Diocese of Virginia* (Richmond, 1967); *Parish Lines, Diocese of Southern Virginia* (Richmond, 1960); and *Parish Lines, Diocese of Southwestern Virginia* (Richmond, 1960).

PARISHES
COUNTY—PARISH
1607–1785

Accomack County
Accomack, Saint George's

Albemarle County
Fredericksville, Saint Anne's, Tillotson

Amelia County
Nottoway, Raleigh

Amherst County
Amherst, Lexington

Augusta County
Augusta

Bedford County
Cumberland, Russell

Botetourt County
Botetourt

Brunswick County
Meherrin, Saint Andrew's

Buckingham County
Tillotson

Campbell County
Russell

Caroline County
Drysdale, Saint Anne's, Saint Asaph's, Saint Margaret's, Saint Mary's

Charles City County
Bristol, Charles City, Chickahominy, Flowerdew Hundred, Jordan's Journey, Martin's Brandon, Smith's Hundred, Southampton, Wallingford, West and Shirley, Westover, Weyanoke, Wilmington

Charles River County. *See* York County

Charlotte County
Cornwall
Chesterfield County
Dale, King William, Manchester
Culpeper County
Bromfield, Saint Mark's
Cumberland County
King William, Littleton, Saint James
Southam
Dinwiddie County
Bath, Bristol
Dunmore County
Beckford
Elizabeth City County
Elizabeth City, Kecoughtan, Lower
Parish of Elizabeth City County,
Nutmeg Quarter, Stanley Hundred,
Upper Parish of Elizabeth City
County, Waters Creek
Essex County
Saint Anne's, Saint George's, Saint
Mary's, Sittenburne, South Farnham
Fairfax County
Cameron, Fairfax, Truro
Fauquier County
Hamilton, Leeds
Fluvanna County
Fluvanna
Franklin County
Patrick, Russell
Frederick County
Beckford, Frederick, Norborne
Gloucester County
Abingdon, Kingston, Petsworth,
Ware
Goochland County
King William, Saint James Northam,
Saint James's, Saint James Southam
Greensville County
Meherrin, Saint Andrew's
Halifax County
Antrim
Hanover County
Saint Martin's, Saint Paul's
Henrico County
Bristol, Dale, Henrico or Varina,
King William, Saint James's

Henry County
Camden, Patrick
Isle of Wight County
Lower, Newport, Nottoway, Upper,
Warrosquyoake
James City County
Argall's Gift, Blisland, Bruton,
Chickahominy, Chippokes, Harrop,
Hog Island, James City, Lawnes
Creek, Martin's Hundred, Middle
Plantation, Middletowne, Saint
Peter's, Southwark, Wallingford,
Wilmington, Yorkhampton
King and Queen County
Drysdale, Saint John's, Saint
Stephen's, Stratton Major
King George County
Brunswick, Hanover, Overwharton,
Saint Paul's, Sittenburne
King William County
Saint David's, Saint John's, Saint
Margaret's
Lancaster County
Christ Church, Great Christ Church
or Christ Church, Lancaster, Lower,
Piankatank, Poropotank, Saint
Mary's Whitechapel, Trinity, Upper
Loudoun County
Cameron, Shelburne
Louisa County
Fredericksville, Saint Martin's,
Trinity
Lower Norfolk County
Elizabeth River, Lynnhaven
Lunenburg County
Cornwall, Cumberland, Saint
James's
Mecklenburg County
Saint James's
Middlesex County
Christ Church
Montgomery County
Montgomery
Nansemond County
Chuckatuck, East, Lower, Lower
Suffolk, South, Suffolk, Upper,
Upper Suffolk, West

New Kent County
Blisland, Saint John's, Saint Paul's, Saint Peter's, Saint Stephen's, Stratton Major

New Norfolk County
Elizabeth River

Norfolk County
Elizabeth River, Portsmouth, Saint Brides

Northampton County
Hungars, Lower, Northampton, Occohannock, Upper

Northumberland County
Boutracy, Chickacoan, Fairfield, Lee, Nomini, Saint Stephen's, Wicomico

Old Rappahannock County
Farnham, North Farnham, Piscataway, Saint Mary's, Sittenburne, South Farnham

Orange County
Saint Mark's, Saint Thomas

Pittsylvania County
Camden

Powhatan County
King William, Saint James Southam

Prince Edward County
Nottoway, Saint Patrick's

Prince George County
Bath, Bristol, Martin's Brandon, Westover, Weyanoke

Princess Anne County
Lynnhaven

Prince William County
Dettingen, Hamilton, Leeds, Truro

Richmond County
Hanover, Lunenburg, North Farnham, Richmond, Saint Mary's, Sittenburne

Rockbridge County
Rockbridge

Rockingham County
Rockingham

Shenandoah County
Beckford

Southampton County
Nottoway, Saint Luke's

Spotsylvania County
Berkeley, Saint George's, Saint Mark's

Stafford County
Brunswick, Chotank, Hamilton, Lower, Overwharton, Potomac, Saint Paul's, Stafford, Upper

Surry County
Albemarle, Lawnes Creek, Southwark

Sussex County
Albemarle

Upper Norfolk County
East, Elizabeth River, Lower, South, Upper, West

Warrosquyoake County
Warrosquyoake

Warwick County
Blount Point, Denbigh, Elizabeth City, Mulberry Island, Nutmeg Quarter, Stanley Hundred, Warwick, Waters Creek

Warwick River County. *See* Warwick County

Washington County
Washington

Westmoreland County
Appomattox, Chickacoan, Cople, Machodick, Nomini, Potomac, Washington, Westbury

York County
Blisland, Bruton, Charles, Charles River, Chiskiack, Hampton, Marston, Middle Plantation, Middletowne, New Poquoson, York, Yorkhampton

PARISHES
PARISH—COUNTY
1607–1785

Abingdon Parish, about 1653–
Gloucester County, about 1653–
Accomack Parish, 1634–1643
Accomack County, 1634–1643
Accomack Parish, 1663–
Accomack County, 1663–
Albemarle Parish, 1738–
Surry County, 1738–1753; Sussex
County, 1753–
Amherst Parish, 1761–
Amherst County, 1761–
Antrim Parish, 1752–
Halifax County, 1752–
Appomattox Parish, after 1653–1664
Westmoreland County, after
1653–1664
**Argall's Gift Parish, 1618–before 1640
(called Chickahominy by 1640)**
James City County, 1618–before
1640
Augusta Parish, 1738–
Augusta County, 1738–
Bath Parish, 1742–
Prince George County, 1742–1752;
Dinwiddie County, 1752–
Beckford Parish, 1769–
Frederick County, 1769–1772;
Dunmore County, 1772–1778;
Shenandoah County, 1778–
Berkeley Parish, 1769–
Spotsylvania County, 1769–
Blisland Parish, about 1653–
James City County, about 1653– ;
York County, about 1653–1654; New
Kent County, 1654–
Blount Point Parish, before 1634– ?
Warwick County, before 1634– ?
Botetourt Parish, 1769–
Botetourt County, 1769–
Boutracy Parish, before 1679–before 1716
Northumberland County, before
1679–before 1716

Bristol Parish, 1643–
Charles City County, 1643–1702;
Henrico County, 1643–1735; Prince
George County, 1702– ; Dinwiddie
County, 1752–
Bromfield Parish, 1752–
Culpeper County, 1752–
Brunswick Parish, 1732–
King George County, 1732– ;
Stafford County, 1776–
Bruton Parish, by 1674–
James City County, by 1674– ; York
County, by 1674–
Camden Parish, 1766–
Pittsylvania County, 1766– ; Henry
County, 1776–1778
Cameron Parish, 1748–
Fairfax County, 1748–1763;
Loudoun County, 1757–
Charles City Parish, 1613– ?
Charles City County, 1613– ?
Charles Parish, about 1692–
York County, about 1692–
**Charles River Parish, about 1634–1642
(name changed to York Parish by
1642)**
York County, about 1634–1642
Chickacoan Parish, about 1645–1664
Northumberland County,
1645–1664; Westmoreland County,
1653–1664
**Chickahominy Parish, before
1640–1643 (later Wallingford
Parish)**
Charles City County, before
1640–1643; James City County,
before 1640–1643
Chippokes Parish, 1643–1647
James City County, 1643–1647
**Chiskiack Parish, 1640–1643 (name
changed to Hampton Parish)**
York County, 1640–1643

Chotank Parish, about 1680–before 1702
Stafford County, about 1680–before 1702

Christ Church Parish, 1666–
Lancaster County, 1666–about 1669; Middlesex County, about 1669–

Christ Church Parish (also referred to as Great Christ Church Parish), about 1670–
Lancaster County, about 1670–

Chuckatuck Parish, after 1643–1737
Nansemond County, after 1643–1737

Cople Parish, about 1664–
Westmoreland County, about 1664–

Cornwall Parish, 1757–
Lunenburg County, 1757–1764; Charlotte County, 1764–

Cumberland Parish, 1745–
Lunenburg County, 1745– ; Bedford County, 1753–1756

Dale Parish, 1734–
Henrico County, 1734–1749; Chesterfield County, 1749–

Denbigh Parish, about 1635–about 1730
Warwick County, about 1635–about 1730

Dettingen Parish, 1744–
Prince William County, 1744–

Drysdale Parish, 1723–
King and Queen County, 1723– ; Caroline County, 1728–

East Parish, 1643–1744
Upper Norfolk County, 1643–1646; Nansemond County, 1646–1744

Elizabeth City Parish, 1619– . *See also* Kecoughtan Parish
Elizabeth City County, 1619– ; Warwick County, 1619–

Elizabeth River Parish, before 1643–
New Norfolk County, 1636–1637; Upper Norfolk County, before 1643–1643; Lower Norfolk County, before 1643–1691; Norfolk County, 1691–

Fairfax Parish, 1764–
Fairfax County, 1764–

Fairfield Parish, 1664–before 1699
Northumberland County, 1664–before 1699

Farnham Parish, about 1656–before 1683
Old Rappahannock County, about 1656–before 1683

Flowerdew Hundred Parish. *See* Jordan's Journey Parish

Fluvanna Parish, 1777–
Fluvanna County, 1777–

Frederick Parish, 1738–
Frederick County, 1738–

Fredericksville Parish, 1742–
Louisa County, 1742– ; Albemarle County, 1744–

Great Christ Church Parish. *See* Christ Church Parish (Lancaster)

Hamilton Parish, 1730–
Stafford County, 1730–about 1731; Prince William County, 1730–1769; Fauquier County, 1759–

Hampton Parish, 1643–1707
York County, 1643–1707

Hanover Parish, 1713–
Richmond County, 1713–1720; King George County, 1720–

Harrop Parish, 1645–1658
James City County, 1645–1658

Henrico Parish, about 1611– (Varina used interchangeably, about 1680–1714)
Henrico County, about 1611–

Hog Island Parish, about 1624– ?
James City County, about 1624– ?

Hungars Parish, 1691–
Northampton County, 1691–

James City Parish, 1607–
James City County, 1607–

Jordan's Journey (or Flowerdew Hundred) Parish, about 1620s–1688
Charles City County, about 1620s–1688

Kecoughtan Parish, about 1610–1619 (name changed to Elizabeth City Parish)
Elizabeth City County, about 1610–1619

Kingston Parish, about 1652–
Gloucester County, about 1652–

King William Parish, 1700–
Henrico County, 1700–1749;
Goochland County, 1728–1749;
Cumberland County, 1749–1777;
Chesterfield County, 1749– ;
Powhatan County, 1777–

Lancaster Parish, 1651–1654, 1657–1666
Lancaster County, 1651–1654,
1657–1666

Lawnes Creek Parish, 1640–1738
James City County, 1640–1652;
Surry County, 1652–1738

Lee Parish, 1664–before 1680
(Wicomico Parish called Lee Parish
for a short time)
Northumberland County,
1664–before 1680

Leeds Parish, 1769–
Fauquier County, 1769– ; Prince
William County, 1769–

Lexington Parish, 1778–
Amherst County, 1778–

Littleton Parish, 1772–
Cumberland County, 1772–

Lower Parish, 1643–1691
Northampton County, 1643–1691

Lower Parish, 1643–1734. *See also*
Newport Parish
Isle of Wight County, 1643–1734

Lower Parish, after 1643–1737
Upper Norfolk County, after
1643–1646; Nansemond County,
1646–1737

Lower Parish, 1654–1656
Lancaster County, 1654–1656

**Lower Parish, about 1664–about
1680**
Stafford County, about 1664–about
1680

Lower Parish, 1744–
Nansemond County, 1744–

**Lower Parish of Elizabeth City County,
before 1632–1636**
Elizabeth City County, before
1632–1636

Lower Suffolk Parish, after 1744–
Nansemond County, after 1744–

Lunenburg Parish, 1732–
Richmond County, 1732–

Lynnhaven Parish, 1643–
Lower Norfolk County, 1643–1691;
Princess Anne County, 1691–

Machodick Parish, after 1653–1664
Westmoreland County, after
1653–1664

Manchester Parish, 1772–
Chesterfield County, 1772–

Marston Parish, 1654–1674
York County, 1654–1674

Martin's Brandon Parish, 1655–
Charles City County, 1655–1702;
Prince George County, 1702–

Martin's Hundred Parish, 1622–1712
James City County, 1622–1712

Meherrin Parish, 1753–
Brunswick County, 1753– ;
Greensville County, 1780–

Middle Plantation Parish, 1633–1658
James City County, 1633–1658; York
County, 1634–1658

Middletowne Parish, 1658–1674
James City County, 1658–1674; York
County, 1658–1674

Montgomery Parish, 1776–
Montgomery County, 1776–

**Mulberry Island Parish, about
1635–about 1730**
Warwick County, about 1635–about
1730

New Poquoson Parish, about 1635–1692
York County, about 1635–1692

**Newport Parish, name in use before
1734–**
Isle of Wight County, before 1734–

Nomini Parish, before 1653–by 1660
Northumberland County, before
1653–1653; Westmoreland County,
1653–by 1660

Norborne Parish, 1769–1772
Frederick County, 1769–1772

Northampton Parish, about 1643–1663
Northampton County, about
1643–1663

North Farnham Parish, about 1683–
Old Rappahannock County, about
1683–1692; Richmond County, 1692–

Nottoway Parish, 1734–
Isle of Wight County, 1734–1749;
Southampton County, 1749–

Nottoway Parish, 1748–
Amelia County, 1748– ; Prince
Edward County, 1753–1755

**Nutmeg Quarter Parish, about
1630s–1657**
Elizabeth City County, 1630s;
Warwick County, 1630s–1657

Occohannock Parish, 1652–1663
Northampton County, 1652–1663

Overwharton Parish, about 1702–
Stafford County, about 1702– ; King
George County, 1776–

Patrick Parish, 1778–
Henry County, 1778– ; Franklin
County, 1785–

Petsworth Parish, about 1652–
Gloucester County, about 1652–

Piankatank Parish, 1657–1666
Lancaster County, 1657–1666

**Piscataway Parish, about 1681– ?
(mentioned in a deed of 1681)**
Old Rappahannock County, about
1681– ?

Poropotank Parish, before 1661–1666
Lancaster County, before 1661–1666

Portsmouth Parish, 1761–
Norfolk County, 1761–

Potomac Parish, about 1653–before 1680
Westmoreland County, about
1653–1664; Stafford County,
1664–before 1680

Raleigh Parish, 1734–
Amelia County, 1734–

Richmond Parish, 1692–at least 1693
Richmond County, 1692–at least 1693

Rockbridge Parish, 1777–
Rockbridge County, 1777–

Rockingham Parish, 1777–
Rockingham County, 1777–

Russell Parish, 1754–
Bedford County, 1754– ; Campbell
County, 1781– ; Franklin County,
1785–

Saint Andrew's Parish, 1720–
Brunswick County, 1720– ;
Greensville County, 1781–

Saint Anne's Parish, 1704–
Essex County, 1704– ; Caroline
County, 1728–

Saint Anne's Parish, 1744–
Albemarle County, 1744–

Saint Asaph's Parish, 1779–
Caroline County, 1779–

Saint Brides Parish, 1761–
Norfolk County, 1761–

Saint David's Parish, 1744–
King William County, 1744–

Saint George's Parish, 1714–
Essex County, 1714–1720;
Spotsylvania County, 1720–

Saint George's Parish, 1762–
Accomack County, 1762–

Saint James Northam Parish, 1744–
Goochland County, 1744–

Saint James Southam Parish, 1744–
Goochland County, 1744–1749;
Cumberland County, 1749–1777;
Powhatan County, 1777–

Saint James's Parish, 1720–1744
Henrico County, 1720–1728;
Goochland County, 1728–1744

Saint James's Parish, 1761–
Lunenburg County, 1761–1764;
Mecklenburg County, 1764–

Saint John's Parish, 1680–
New Kent County, 1680–1691; King
and Queen County, 1691–1701; King
William County, 1701–

Saint Luke's Parish, 1762–
Southampton County, 1762–

Saint Margaret's Parish, 1720–
King William County, 1720–1744;
Caroline County, 1728–

Saint Mark's Parish, 1730–
Spotsylvania County, 1730–1734;
Orange County, 1734–1752;
Culpeper County, 1748–

Saint Martin's Parish, 1726–
Hanover County, 1726– ; Louisa
County, 1742–

Saint Mary's Parish, about 1677–
Old Rappahannock County, about
1677–1692; Richmond County,
1692–1713; Essex County,
1692–1728; Caroline County, 1728–

**Saint Mary's Whitechapel Parish,
before 1669–1752**
Lancaster County, before 1669–1752

Saint Patrick's Parish, 1755–
Prince Edward County, 1755–

Saint Paul's Parish, before 1702–
Stafford County, before 1702–1776;
King George County, 1776–

Saint Paul's Parish, 1704–
New Kent County, 1704–1720;
Hanover County, 1720–

Saint Peter's Parish, 1679–
James City County, 1679–1767; New
Kent County, 1679–

Saint Stephen's Parish, before 1674–
New Kent County, before
1674–1691; King and Queen County,
1691–

Saint Stephen's Parish, about 1698–
Northumberland County, about
1698–

Saint Thomas Parish, 1740–
Orange County, 1740–

Shelburne Parish, 1769–
Loudoun County, 1769–

Sittenburne Parish, before 1664–1732
Old Rappahannock County, before
1664–1692; Essex County,
1692–1704; Richmond County,
1692–1732; King George County,
1720–1732

**Smith's Hundred Parish, about
1617–about 1619**
Charles City County, about
1617–about 1619

South Parish, 1643–1744
Upper Norfolk County, 1643–1646;
Nansemond County, 1646–1744

Southampton Parish, 1619–1622
Charles City County, 1619–1622

South Farnham Parish, about 1683–
Old Rappahannock County, about
1683–1692; Essex County, 1692–

Southwark Parish, 1647–
James City County, 1647–1652;
Surry County, 1652–

**Stafford Parish, about 1680–before
1702**
Stafford County, about 1680–before
1702

**Stanley Hundred Parish, about
1628–about 1635**
Elizabeth City County, about
1628–about 1635; Warwick County,
about 1628–about 1635

Stratton Major Parish, 1655–
New Kent County, 1655–1691; King
and Queen County, 1691–

Suffolk Parish, 1737–
Nansemond County, 1737–

Tillotson Parish, 1757–
Albemarle County, 1757–1761;
Buckingham County, 1761–

**Trinity Parish, about 1670–about 1724
(parish name used but parish not
officially established)**
Lancaster County, about 1670–about
1724

Trinity Parish, 1761–
Louisa County, 1761–

Truro Parish, 1732–
Prince William County, 1732–1742;
Fairfax County, 1742–

Upper Parish, 1643–1691
Northampton County, 1643–1691

Upper Parish, 1643–1734
Isle of Wight County, 1643–1734

Upper Parish, after 1643–after 1744
Upper Norfolk County, after
1643–1646; Nansemond County,
1646–after 1744

Upper Parish, 1654–1656
Lancaster County, 1654–1656

Upper Parish, about 1664–before 1680
Stafford County, about 1664–before
1680

**Upper Parish of Elizabeth City County,
before 1632–about 1636**
Elizabeth City County, before
1632–about 1636

Upper Suffolk Parish, after 1744–
Nansemond County, after 1744–

Varina Parish. *See* Henrico Parish

Wallingford Parish, 1643–1720 (first called Chickahominy Parish)
Charles City County, 1643–1720; James City County, 1643–1720

Ware Parish, about 1652–
Gloucester County, about 1652–

Warrosquyoake Parish, before 1629–1734
Warrosquyoake County, before 1629–1637; Isle of Wight County, 1637–1734

Warwick Parish, about 1725–
Warwick County, about 1725–

Washington Parish, 1664–
Westmoreland County, 1664–

Washington Parish, 1776–
Washington County, 1776–

Waters Creek Parish, 1629–about 1643
Elizabeth City County, 1629–1634; Warwick County, 1629–about 1643

West Parish, 1643–before 1737
Upper Norfolk County, 1643–1646; Nansemond County, 1646–before 1737

West and Shirley Parish, about 1613–1622
Charles City County, about 1613–1622

Westbury Parish, 1664–before 1680
Westmoreland County, 1664–before 1680

Westover Parish, by 1625–1720
Charles City County, by 1625–1702; Prince George County, 1702–1720

Weyanoke Parish, about 1618–1720
Charles City County, about 1618–1702; Prince George County, 1702–1720

Wicomico Parish, about 1648– . *See also* Lee Parish
Northumberland County, about 1648–

Wilmington Parish, about 1658–1723
Charles City County, about 1658–1723; James City County, about 1658–1723

York Parish, about 1638–1707
York County, about 1638–1707

Yorkhampton Parish, 1707–
York County, 1707– ; James City County, 1712–

Early-twentieth-century view of City Hall Avenue in Norfolk, photographed by Harry C. Mann

CITIES OF VIRGINIA

Virginia's forty-one independent cities are politically and administratively independent of the county or counties in which they are geographically situated. This separation of cities and counties in Virginia local government has no statewide parallel elsewhere in the United States. Virginia towns, on the other hand, exercise only some functions of self-government and are in most respects subordinate to the counties in which they are located. Until 1892 towns became cities only by act of the General Assembly; after 1892 a town could also incorporate as a city by petition to the circuit court. In recent years, five Virginia cities—Chesapeake, Hampton, Newport News, Suffolk, and Virginia Beach—have expanded their boundaries to subsume the now-extinct counties in which they were geographically situated. (A useful history of the commonwealth's unusual practice of city-county separation is Chester W. Bain, "*A Body Incorporate*": *The Evolution of City-County Separation in Virginia* [Charlottesville, 1967].) The capital city of Richmond has been the seat of government since 1780.

ALEXANDRIA, in Fairfax and Arlington Counties, was named for John Alexander, an early owner of the tract on which the town was located. Alexandria was established in 1749. Its site had been known as Hunting Creek Warehouse and as Belhaven. Alexandria was incorporated as a town in 1779 and as a city in 1852. Its area is 15.75 square miles. Population 111,183.

BEDFORD, in Bedford County, originally was known as Liberty. It became the county seat in 1782, when the court was moved there from New London. Liberty was incorporated as a town in 1839. Its name was changed to Bedford City in 1890 and to Bedford in 1912. Bedford was incorporated as a city by court order in 1969. Its area is 6.77 square miles. Population 6,073.

BRISTOL, on the Tennessee-Virginia border in Washington County, originally was called Goodson, for Samuel Goodson, its founder. Goodson was established in 1850 and incorporated as a town in 1856. In 1852 the town of Bristol, Tennessee, was laid out contiguous to Goodson. In 1890, Goodson was incorporated as a city, and its name was changed to Bristol, for its Tennessee neighbor. Today the two cities have separate governments but share a public library and a local planning commission. Its area is 11.53 square miles. Population 18,426.

BUENA VISTA, in Rockbridge County, was built on the site of the abandoned Buena Vista iron furnace. This furnace, which was in operation as late as 1855, probably was named for the Mexican village near which General Zachary Taylor won an important battle in the Mexican War in 1847. Buena Vista was established in 1889 and incorporated as a town in 1890. It was incorporated as a city in 1892. Its area is 6.53 square miles. Population 6,406.

CHARLOTTESVILLE, in Albemarle County, was named for Charlotte Sophia of Mecklenburg-Strelitz (1744–1818), the wife of George III, and was established in 1762. Charlottesville was incorporated as a town in 1801 and as a city in 1888. Its area is 10 square miles. Population 40,341.

CHESAPEAKE, which is named for the Chesapeake Bay, comprises the former Norfolk County and the former city of South Norfolk. It was formed by court order in 1963 by a merger of these two entities, both of which thereby became extinct. Its area is 353 square miles. Population 151,976.

CLIFTON FORGE, in Alleghany County, was named for James Clifton's iron furnace, which was located in the Iron Gate Gorge by 1828. Known as Williamson's Station in 1857 when the railroad arrived, it was established as a town in 1861 and took the name Clifton Forge when it was incorporated in 1884. Clifton Forge became a city by court order in 1906. Its area is 4.297 square miles. Population 4,679.

COLONIAL HEIGHTS, in Chesterfield County, is located on the heights overlooking the Appomattox River and takes its name from the fact that the Marquis de Lafayette placed his artillerymen, known as the Colonials, on the heights to shell British positions in Petersburg in 1781. Colonial Heights was established in 1910 and incorporated as a town in 1926; it became a city by court order in 1948. Its area is 8.15 square miles. Population 16,064.

COVINGTON, in Alleghany County, was named for Peter Covington, an early settler. It was established in 1818 and first incorporated as a town in 1833. Covington became a city by court order in 1953. Its area is 4.5 square miles. Population 6,991.

DANVILLE, in Pittsylvania County, was named for the Dan River on which the city is located. Danville was established in 1793; it was incorporated as a town in 1830 and as a city in 1890. North Danville was added in 1896. Its area is 43.8 square miles. Population 53,056.

EMPORIA, in Greensville County, was formed in 1887 from the merger of Hicksford and Belfield. Because of friction between the two villages, Benjamin D. Tillar, a county native and member of the Virginia House of Delegates, named the town after Emporia, Kansas, the hometown of one of his associates in the Atlantic and Danville Railroad. Emporia comes from the Latin word meaning place of plenty where business is transacted. The General Assembly revoked the town charter in 1888, a year after it had incorporated Emporia, and did not reincorporate the town until 1892. Emporia became a city by court order in 1967. Its area is 6.5 square miles. Population 5,306.

FAIRFAX, in Fairfax County, was first called Providence. It was established at the site of the county courthouse in 1805. After the town named Fairfax in Culpeper County was renamed Culpeper in 1859, Fairfax County took the name Fairfax for its county seat. Fairfax was incorporated as a town in 1874, and became a city by court order in 1961. Its area is 6.26 square miles. Population 19,622.

FALLS CHURCH, in Fairfax County, was named for an Anglican church erected in the area about 1769. The church was so called because of its proximity to the Little Falls of the Potomac. Falls Church was established in 1850, was incorporated as a town in 1875, and became a city by court order in 1948. Its area is 2.2 square miles. Population 9,578.

FRANKLIN, in Southampton County, came into existence during the 1830s as a stop along the Portsmouth and Roanoke Railroad line then under construction. The origin of the name is unclear. It could have been named for Benjamin Franklin, patriot and statesman; for a man named Franklin who kept a store in the area; or for the exclamation of a railroad section foreman who drove a spike into a crosstie and said, "This shall be Franklin!" It was a post village in 1855 and was incorporated as a town in 1876. Franklin became a city by court order in 1961. Its area is 7.74 square miles. Population 7,864.

FREDERICKSBURG, in Spotsylvania County, was named for Frederick Louis, Prince of Wales, eldest son of George II. Fredericksburg was established in 1728, was incorporated as a town in 1782, and became a city in 1879. Its area is 10 square miles. Population 19,027.

GALAX, in Grayson and Carroll Counties, was first called Bonaparte. It received its present name from the mountain evergreen that grows profusely in the surrounding area. It was incorporated as a town in 1906 and became a city by court order in 1954. Its area is 8.25 square miles. Population 6,670.

HAMPTON was located in Elizabeth City County, which is now extinct. It takes its name from Hampton Creek, earlier called Southampton River in honor of the earl of Southampton, an important figure in the Virginia Company of London. An Indian village stood on the site in 1607, when John Smith visited the area. The English established a village there in 1610 and a trading post in 1630. Hampton was established by an act of assembly in 1680 and was designated as a port in 1708. It was first incorporated as a town in 1849, then incorporated again in 1852, but the act of incorporation was repealed in 1860. The General Assembly again incorporated the town of Hampton in 1887, and it became a city by court order in 1908. It was greatly enlarged in 1952 by a merger with Elizabeth City County and the town of Phoebus; the county and town thereby became extinct. Its area is 52 square miles. Population 133,793.

HARRISONBURG, in Rockingham County, was named for Thomas Harrison, who gave fifty acres for the town site. It was established in 1780, was incorporated as a town in 1849, and became a city by court order in 1916. It was enlarged by an annexation from Rockingham County in 1982. Its area is 17.394 square miles. Population 30,707.

HOPEWELL, in Prince George County, was established as Charles City Point by Sir Thomas Dale in 1613. Francis Eppes, who arrived in Virginia on the ship *Hopewell*, patented land near Charles City Point in 1635. He named part of his property Hopewell Farm. The town was known as City Point until 1913 when E. I. Du Pont de Nemours and Company purchased Hopewell Farm and established a factory and a settlement for munitions workers there. Hopewell was never incorporated as a town but was incorporated as a city by an act of the General Assembly in 1916. It was enlarged by the annexation of City Point in 1923 and by further annexations from Prince George County in 1952 and 1969. Its area is 11.3 square miles. Population 23,101.

LEXINGTON, in Rockbridge County, probably was named for the village in Massachusetts where the first battle of the American Revolution was fought. The town was established in 1778 as the county seat for newly created Rockbridge County. It is believed that Thomas Jefferson suggested the name for the town. Lexington was incorporated as a town in 1874 and became a city by court order in 1965. Its area is 2.5 square miles. Population 6,959.

LYNCHBURG, in Campbell County, was named for John Lynch, the owner of the original town site. It was established in 1786, was incorporated as a town in 1805, and became a city in 1852. Parts of Campbell and Bedford Counties were annexed to the city in 1976. Its area is 50 square miles. Population 66,049.

MANASSAS, in Prince William County, began in 1852 as Manassas Junction at the intersection of the Manassas Gap Railroad and the Orange and Alexandria Railroad. It was incorporated as the town of Manassas in 1873 and became a city by court order in 1975. Its area is 10 square miles. Population 27,957.

MANASSAS PARK, in Prince William County, was established in 1955 as an outgrowth of Manassas. It was incorporated as a town by order of the circuit court in 1957 and became a city by court order in 1975. Its area is 2.5 square miles. Population 6,734.

MARTINSVILLE, in Henry County, was named for Joseph Martin, an early settler and Revolutionary War soldier who represented Henry County in the General Assembly in 1791, when the town was established. Martinsville was incorporated as a town in 1873 and became a city by court order in 1928. Its area is 11.2 square miles. Population 16,162.

NEWPORT NEWS was located in Warwick County, which is now extinct. The origin of the name is uncertain but the phrase "Newportes News" appeared in documents as early as 1619 and probably commemorated Christopher Newport, who made five voyages to Virginia between 1607 and 1619. Newport News was a small settlement until late in the nineteenth century, when it became the eastern terminus of the Chesapeake and Ohio Railway. It was established as a town in 1880 and incorporated as a city by act of the General Assembly in 1896 without ever having been incorporated as a town. Newport News was enlarged by consolidation with the city of Warwick in 1958. Its area is 69.2 square miles. Population 170,045.

NORFOLK was located in Norfolk County, which is now extinct. The city took its name from the former home of an early settler, Adam Thoroughgood, who was a native of the county of Norfolk in England. Norfolk was established in 1680 by an act of assembly. It was incorporated as a borough in 1736 and as a city in 1845. Norfolk was enlarged in 1906 by the annexation of the town of Berkeley. Its area is 65.98 square miles. Population 261,229.

NORTON, in Wise County, was first known as Prince's Flats, probably for William Prince, who settled in the area about 1787. The present name honors Eckstein Norton, president of the Louisville and Nashville Railroad in 1891 when the Clinch Valley branch of the railway was finished. Norton was incorporated as a town in 1894 and became a city by court order in 1954. Its area is 6.83 square miles. Population 4,247.

PETERSBURG was formed from parts of Dinwiddie, Prince George, and Chesterfield Counties. A garrison and fur-trading post called Fort Henry was established there in 1645 on the site of the Indian village Appamattuck. The present name, suggested in 1733 by William Byrd II, honors Peter Jones, Byrd's companion on expeditions into the Virginia backcountry. Petersburg was established in 1748 and incorporated as a town in 1784. In the latter year the towns of Blandford, Pocahontas, and Ravenscroft were added to Petersburg. It was incorporated as a city in 1850. Petersburg was enlarged by annexation from both Prince George and Dinwiddie Counties in 1972. Its area is 23.09 square miles. Population 38,386.

POQUOSON, in York County, was established as a post office between 1885 and 1888. The word *pocosin*, as it is now spelled, is of Algonquian origin and means dismal, or swamp. Poquoson became a town in 1952 as the result of a referendum and became a city by court order in 1976. Its area is 14.7 square miles. Population 11,005.

PORTSMOUTH was located in Norfolk County, which is now extinct. It was named by its founder, William Crawford, for the English seaport and was established in 1752. Portsmouth was incorporated as a town in 1836 and as a city in 1858. Its area is 29.9 square miles. Population 103,907.

RADFORD, in Montgomery County, was at different times known as Lovely Mount, English Ferry, Ingles's Ferry, Central Depot, and Central City. The town of Central City was established in 1885 and incorporated in 1887. Its name was changed to Radford in 1890 to honor John Blair Radford, a prominent local citizen, and it was incorporated as a city in 1892. Its area is 9.63 square miles. Population 15,940.

RICHMOND, located between Henrico and Chesterfield Counties, was named by William Byrd II, who envisioned the development of a city at the falls of the James River and with the help of William Mayo laid out the town in 1737. The name probably came from the English borough of Richmond upon Thames, which Byrd visited on several occasions. Richmond was established in 1742 and in 1779 was designated the capital of Virginia effective April 1780. It was incorporated as a town, although "stiled the city of Richmond," in 1782 and was incorporated as a city in 1842. It was the capital of the Confederacy from 1861 to 1865. Richmond was enlarged by the annexation of Manchester (or South Richmond) in 1910, and by the addition of Barton Heights, Fairmount, and Highland Park in 1914. A further annexation from Chesterfield County occurred in 1970. Its area is 62.5 square miles. Population 203,056.

ROANOKE, in Roanoke County, was first known as Big Lick because of salt deposits found in the vicinity. The town of Big Lick was established in 1852 and was incorporated in 1874. Its name was changed to Roanoke in 1882, and it became a city in 1884. Roanoke was enlarged by annexation from Roanoke County in 1976. Its area is 44.5 square miles. Population 96,397.

SALEM, in Roanoke County, was laid out in 1802 on land owned by James Simpson. The town is said to have been named by a member of the Bryan family, of Salem, New Jersey. The General Assembly established Salem in 1806 and incorporated it as a town in 1836. Salem was incorporated as a city by court order in 1968. Its area is 14.31 square miles. Population 23,756.

SOUTH BOSTON, in Halifax County, was named for Boston, Massachusetts. The town originally was located on the south side of the Dan River and called Boyd's Ferry. It was established in 1796 but was destroyed by floods shortly thereafter. Reestablished on the north side of the Dan River, it was incorporated as a town in 1884 and as a city by court order in 1960. Its area is 5.09 square miles. Population 6,997.

STAUNTON, in Augusta County, was named, according to most authorities, for Rebecca Staunton, wife of Sir William Gooch, lieutenant governor of Virginia from 1727 to 1749. Staunton was laid out in 1748 at the site of the Augusta County courthouse and was established as a town in 1761. It was incorporated as a town in 1801 and as a city in 1871. Its area is 19.7 square miles. Population 24,461.

SUFFOLK was located in Nansemond County, which is now extinct. It probably was named for the county of Suffolk in England. Established in 1742 on the site of John Constant's warehouse, Suffolk was incorporated as a town in 1808 and as a city by court order in 1910. In 1974 the city was enlarged when it merged with the former county of Nansemond. Its area is 430 square miles. Population 52,141.

VIRGINIA BEACH was located in Princess Anne County, which is now extinct. The oceanside resort was incorporated as a town in 1906 and as a city by an act of the General Assembly in 1952. It was greatly enlarged in 1963 by consolidation with Princess Anne County, which thereby became extinct. Its area is 258 square miles. Population 393,069.

WAYNESBORO, in Augusta County, was named for Anthony Wayne, an American general during the Revolution. James Flack and Samuel Estill laid out the town in 1797. Waynesborough, as it was first known, was established as a town in 1801 and incorporated as a town in 1834. It was consolidated with Basic City in 1923 and became a city by an act of the General Assembly in 1948. Its area is 13.787 square miles. Population 18,549.

WILLIAMSBURG, in James City and York Counties, was established by the General Assembly as Middle Plantation in 1633. After the capitol building at Jamestown burned in 1698, the assembly decided to move the capital of the colony to Middle Plantation, which was renamed Williamsburg in 1699 in honor of William III. Williamsburg was established in 1699 and declared a "city Incorporate" in 1722, although its actual status was that of a borough. It served as the capital of Virginia from 1699 until 1780. Williamsburg was incorporated as a city in 1884. Its area is 9 square miles. Population 11,530.

WINCHESTER, in Frederick County, was known first as Opequon, then as Frederick's Town (or Fredericktown), and, finally, upon establishment as a town in 1752, as Winchester. According to tradition, one of the town's founders, James Wood, named the town in honor of his birthplace in England. Winchester was incorporated as a town in 1779 and as a city in 1874. It was enlarged by annexation from Frederick County in 1970. Its area is 9.3 square miles. Population 21,947.

View of Winchester ca. 1930

View of the James River, Richmond, below the Atlantic Coast Line Railroad bridge, by photographer Harry Bagby, ca. 1920

RIVERS OF VIRGINIA

Appomattox River is in the cities of Colonial Heights, Hopewell, and Petersburg and the counties of Amelia, Appomattox, Buckingham, Chesterfield, Cumberland, Dinwiddie, Powhatan, Prince Edward, and Prince George.

Ararat River is in Patrick County.

Back River is in the city of Hampton and the counties of James City and York.

Banister River is in Halifax and Pittsylvania Counties.

Big Otter River is in Bedford and Campbell Counties.

Blackwater River is in Franklin County.

Blackwater River in the cities of Franklin and Suffolk and the counties of Isle of Wight, Southampton, Surry, and Sussex.

Bluestone River is in Tazewell County.

Browns Dan River is in Patrick County.

Buffalo River is in Amherst and Nelson Counties.

Bullpasture River is in Bath and Highland Counties.

Bush River is in Prince Edward County.

Calfpasture River is in Augusta and Rockbridge Counties; Little Calfpasture River is in Augusta and Rockbridge Counties.

Chickahominy River is in Charles City, Hanover, Henrico, James City, and New Kent Counties.

Clinch River is in Russell, Scott, Tazewell, and Wise Counties; North Fork Clinch River is in Lee, Scott, and Tazewell Counties; South Fork Clinch River is in Tazewell County.

Coan River is in Northumberland County.

Cold Spring River is in Rockingham County.

Conway River is in Greene and Madison Counties.

Corrotoman River is in Lancaster County.

Covington River is in Rappahannock County.

Cowpasture River is in Alleghany, Bath, Botetourt, and Highland Counties.

Cranesnest River is in Dickenson and Wise Counties.

Dan River is in the cities of Danville and South Boston and the counties of Halifax, Mecklenburg, Patrick, and Pittsylvania; Browns Dan River is in Patrick County; Little Dan River is in Patrick County.

Doyles River is in Albemarle County.

Dry River is in Rockingham County; Little Dry River is in Rockingham County.

Eastern Branch Elizabeth River is in the cities of Chesapeake, Norfolk, and Virginia Beach.

East River is in Giles County.

East River is in Mathews County.

Elizabeth River is in the cities of Chesapeake, Norfolk, and Portsmouth; Eastern Branch Elizabeth River is in the cities of Chesapeake, Norfolk, and Virginia Beach; Southern Branch Elizabeth River is in the cities of Chesapeake, Norfolk, and Portsmouth; Western Branch Elizabeth River is in the cities of Chesapeake and Portsmouth.

Falling River is in Appomattox, Campbell, and Charlotte Counties; Little Falling River is in Appomattox and Campbell Counties.

German River is in Rockingham County.

Great Wicomico River is in Northumberland County.

Guest River is in the city of Norton and the counties of Scott and Wise.

Hampton River is in the city of Hampton.

Hardware River is in Albemarle and Fluvanna Counties.

Harris River is in the city of Hampton.

Hazel River is in Culpeper and Rappahannock Counties.

Holston River: Middle Fork Holston River is in Washington and Wythe Counties; North Fork Holston River is in Bland, Scott, Smyth, and Washington Counties; South Fork Holston River is in Smyth and Washington Counties.

Hughes River is in Culpeper, Madison, and Rappahannock Counties.

Hyco River is in Halifax County.

Indian River is in the city of Chesapeake.

Jackson River is in the cities of Clifton Forge and Covington and the counties of Alleghany, Bath, Botetourt, and Highland.

James River is in the cities of Lynchburg, Newport News, Richmond, and Suffolk and the counties of Albemarle, Amherst, Appomattox, Bedford, Botetourt, Buckingham, Campbell, Charles City, Chesterfield, Cumberland, Fluvanna, Goochland, Henrico, Isle of Wight, James City, Nelson, Powhatan, Prince George, Rockbridge, and Surry.

Jordan River is in Rappahannock County.

Lafayette River is in the city of Norfolk.

Little Calfpasture River is in Augusta and Rockbridge Counties.

Little Dan River is in Patrick County.

Little Dry River is in Rockingham County.

Little Falling River is in Appomattox and Campbell Counties.

Little Nottoway River is in Nottoway County.

Little Otter River is in the city of Bedford and Bedford County.

Little Piney River is in Amherst County.

Little River is in Arlington, Fauquier, and Loudoun Counties.

Little River is in Augusta County.

Little River is in Floyd, Grayson, Montgomery, Pulaski, Russell, and Tazewell Counties.

Little River is in Goochland, Hanover, and Louisa Counties.

Little Wicomico River is in Northumberland County.

Little Willis River is in Buckingham and Cumberland Counties.

Lynch River is in Albemarle and Greene Counties.

Lynnhaven River is in the city of Virginia Beach.

McClure River is in Dickenson County.

Machipongo River is in Accomack and Northampton Counties.

Mat River is in Spotsylvania County.

Mattaponi River is in Caroline, King and Queen, and King William Counties; Mat River is in Spotsylvania County; Matta River is in Caroline and Spotsylvania Counties; Ni River is in Caroline and Spotsylvania Counties; Poni River is in Caroline County; Po River is in Caroline and Spotsylvania Counties; Ta River is in Spotsylvania County.

Matta River is in Caroline and Spotsylvania Counties.

Maury River is in the cities of Buena Vista and Lexington and the county of Rockbridge.

Mayo River: North Mayo River is in Henry and Patrick Counties; South Mayo River is in Henry and Patrick Counties.

Mechums River is in Albemarle County.

Meherrin River is in the city of Emporia and the counties of Brunswick, Greensville, Lunenburg, Mecklenburg, and Southampton; Middle Meherrin River is in Charlotte and Lunenburg Counties; North Meherrin River is in Charlotte and Lunenburg Counties; South Meherrin River is in Charlotte, Lunenburg, and Mecklenburg Counties.

Middle Fork Holston River is in Smyth, Washington, and Wythe Counties.

Middle Meherrin River is in Charlotte and Lunenburg Counties.

Middle River is in Augusta County.

Moormans River is in Albemarle County.

Motto River is in Caroline and Spotsylvania Counties.

Nansemond River is in the city of Suffolk.

Newfound River is in Hanover and Louisa Counties.

New River is in the city of Radford and the counties of Carroll, Giles, Grayson, Montgomery, Pulaski, and Wythe.

Ni River is in Caroline and Spotsylvania Counties.

North Anna River is in Caroline, Hanover, Louisa, Orange, and Spotsylvania Counties.

North Fork Clinch River is in Lee, Scott, and Tazewell Counties.

North Fork Holston River is in Bland, Scott, Smyth, and Washington Counties.

North Fork Shenandoah River is in Rockingham, Shenandoah, and Warren Counties.

North Landing River is in the cities of Chesapeake and Virginia Beach.

North Mayo River is in Henry and Patrick Counties.

North Meherrin River is in Charlotte and Lunenburg Counties.

North River is in Augusta and Rockingham Counties.

North River is in Buckingham County.

North River is in Gloucester and Mathews Counties.

Northwest River is in the city of Chesapeake.

Northwest Yeocomico River is in Westmoreland County.

Nottoway River is in Brunswick, Dinwiddie, Greensville, Lunenburg, Nottoway, Prince Edward, Southampton, and Sussex Counties; Little Nottoway River is in Nottoway County.

Occoquan River is in Fairfax and Prince William Counties.

Otter River: Big Otter River is in Bedford and Campbell Counties; Little Otter River is in the city of Bedford and Bedford County.

Pagan River is in Isle of Wight County.

Pamunkey River is in Caroline, Hanover, King William, and New Kent Counties.

Pedlar River is in Amherst County.

Perrin River is in Gloucester County.

Piankatank River is in Gloucester, Mathews, and Middlesex Counties.

Pigg River is in Franklin and Pittsylvania Counties.

Piney River is in Amherst and Nelson Counties; Little Piney River is in Amherst County.

Piney River is in Rappahannock County.

Pocaty River is in the cities of Chesapeake and Virginia Beach.

Pocomoke River is in Accomack County.

Poni River is in Caroline County.

Poquoson River is in the city of Poquoson and York County.

Po River is in Caroline and Spotsylvania Counties.

Poropotank River is in Gloucester and King and Queen Counties.

Potomac River is in the city of Alexandria and the counties of Arlington, Fairfax, King George, Loudoun, Northumberland, Prince William, Stafford, and Westmoreland; South Branch Potomac River is in Highland County.

Pound River is in Dickenson and Wise Counties.

Powell River is in Lee and Wise Counties.

Rapidan River is in Culpeper, Greene, Madison, Orange, and Spotsylvania Counties.

Rappahannock River is in the city of Fredericksburg and the counties of Caroline, Culpeper, Essex, Fauquier, King George, Lancaster, Middlesex, Rappahannock, Richmond, Spotsylvania, Stafford, and Westmoreland.

Rivanna River is in Albemarle and Fluvanna Counties.

Roach River is in Greene County.

Roanoke (Staunton) River is in the cities of Roanoke and Salem and the counties of Bedford, Campbell, Charlotte, Franklin, Halifax, Mecklenburg, Montgomery, Pittsylvania, and Roanoke.

Robinson River is in Culpeper and Madison Counties.

Rockfish River is in Albemarle and Nelson Counties.

Rose River is in Madison County.

Rush River is in Rappahannock County.

Russell Fork River is in Buchanan and Dickenson Counties.

Saint Marys River is in Augusta County.

Sandy River is in the city of Danville and Pittsylvania County.

Sandy River is in Prince Edward County.

Severn River is in Gloucester County.

Shenandoah River is in Clarke and Warren Counties; North Fork Shenandoah River is in Rockingham, Shenandoah and Warren Counties; South Fork Shenandoah River is in Page, Rockingham, and Warren Counties.

Shoemaker River is in Rockingham County.

Slate River is in Buckingham County.

Smith River is in the city of Martinsville and the counties of Franklin, Henry, and Patrick.

South Anna River is in Hanover, Louisa, and Orange Counties.

South Branch Potomac River is in Highland County.

Southern Branch Elizabeth River is in the cities of Chesapeake, Norfolk, and Portsmouth.

South Fork Clinch River is in Tazewell County.

South Fork Holston River is in Smyth and Washington Counties.

South Fork Shenandoah River is in Page, Rockingham, and Warren Counties.

South Mayo River is in Henry and Patrick Counties.

South Meherrin River is in Charlotte, Lunenburg, and Mecklenburg Counties.

South River is in Caroline and Spotsylvania Counties.

South River is in the city of Waynesboro and the counties of Augusta, Greene, Rockbridge, and Rockingham.

South Yeocomico River is in Northumberland County.

Staunton River is in Madison County.

Staunton (Roanoke) River is in the cities of Roanoke and Salem and the counties of Bedford, Campbell, Charlotte, Franklin, Halifax, Mecklenburg, Montgomery, Pittsylvania, and Roanoke.

Stinking River is in Pittsylvania County.

Ta River is in Spotsylvania County.

Thornton River is in Culpeper and Rappahannock Counties.

Tye River is in Amherst and Nelson Counties.

Ware River is in Gloucester County.

Warwick River is in the city of Newport News.

Western Branch Elizabeth River is in the cities of Chesapeake and Portsmouth.

West Yeocomico River is in Northumberland and Westmoreland Counties.

Wicomico River: Great Wicomico River is in Northumberland County; Little Wicomico River is in Northumberland County.

Willis River is in Buckingham and Cumberland Counties; Little Willis River is in Buckingham and Cumberland Counties.

Yeocomico River is in Northumberland and Westmoreland Counties; Northwest Yeocomico River is in Westmoreland County; South Yeocomico River is in Northumberland County; West Yeocomico River is in Northumberland and Westmoreland Counties.

York River is in Gloucester, James City, King and Queen, King William, New Kent, and York Counties.

Appomattox Falls, Petersburg

Cowpasture River, Alleghany County

Nineteenth-century photograph of Aquia Church in Stafford County. The exterior brick walls of the church are highlighted by quoins and rusticated doorways made of stone quarried from the local Aquia Creek.

SOME HISTORIC PLACES OF WORSHIP

A mid-nineteenth-century photograph of Richmond's First African Baptist Church
(Valentine Museum, Richmond, Virginia)

The buildings in this list—which includes all of Virginia's surviving colonial churches as well as numerous places of worship built during the nineteenth and twentieth centuries that are of unusual historic importance—appear under the names by which they are currently known. Many of the churches are Episcopalian because the Church of England was the established church of the Virginia colony. At times the only denomination tolerated by civil authorities, the Anglican Church was supported throughout the colonial period by public taxation, and its church buildings were erected and maintained at public expense. Fewer churches of other colonial denominations, subject to legal disabilities and dependent solely on their own members for financial support, have survived. In 1786 the General Assembly formally disestablished the Church of England in Virginia.

ABINGDON CHURCH, in Gloucester County, was built about 1755 and was the parish church of Abingdon Parish. Major changes in the structure were made in 1868, as a result of damage to the church during the Civil War.

AQUIA CHURCH, in Stafford County, was first erected in 1751 and was rebuilt in 1757, after a fire gutted the earlier structure. The second building retained the original walls. It was the parish church of Overwharton Parish and was named for Aquia Creek. It is a National Historic Landmark.

AUGUSTA STONE PRESBYTERIAN CHURCH, in Augusta County, was built between 1747 and 1749 by a congregation of Scotch-Irish pioneers. Constructed of native limestone, it is the oldest surviving church in the Valley of Virginia.

BEDFORD HISTORIC MEETING HOUSE, in Bedford, was built in 1838 as a Methodist church and sold in 1886 to the Episcopal Church. There the church operated a school for African American children until a local public school for blacks could be established.

BETHLEHEM CHURCH, in Rockingham County, was built as a Quaker meetinghouse between 1844 and 1845 by a local stonemason, Jeremiah Clemens. The building served as a military hospital during the Civil War. After the war its membership merged with the local Christian Church. The building has not been used for religious services since 1952.

BETH SHALOME congregation, organized about August 1789 in the city of Richmond, is the sixth-oldest Jewish congregation in the United States. The congregation dedicated the first synagogue building in Virginia on Mayo Street in 1822. In 1898 Beth Shalome was absorbed by Beth Ahabah, which had been organized in 1841. The Beth Shalome synagogue building was sold and later razed in 1934. Beth Ahabah built its first synagogue on Eleventh Street in 1848. This building was replaced by a new synagogue in 1880, which was sold in 1905 soon after Beth Ahabah congregation had moved to its present location on West Franklin Street.

BLANDFORD CHURCH, in Petersburg, was built between 1736 and 1737 and was the parish church of Bristol Parish. It has at different times been known as Bristol Parish Church, as Saint Paul's Church, and as the Brick Church on Wells's Hill. The present name reflects the fact that the church stood in the town of Blandford, now a part of Petersburg. The building was abandoned after the American Revolution, but it was restored in 1901 and now is maintained as a memorial to soldiers of the Confederate army.

BREMO SLAVE CHAPEL, in Fluvanna County, was built in 1835 as a slave chapel for Bremo, the plantation of John Hartwell Cocke. The chapel was moved about 1883 from the chapel field of Lower Bremo to the village of Bremo Bluff to serve as the parish hall of Grace Episcopal Church.

BRIERY CHURCH, in Prince Edward County, was first built about 1760. The present Gothic Revival structure was erected on the site about 1855 by Robert Lewis Dabney, a noted theologian and later a major on Thomas J. ("Stonewall") Jackson's staff.

BRUTON PARISH CHURCH, in Williamsburg, was the church of Bruton Parish. The original part of the building was completed about 1715, and additions were made in 1721 and in 1752. The governors, councillors, and other officials of colonial Virginia worshiped regularly in Bruton Parish Church, now a National Historic Landmark.

BURKE'S GARDEN CENTRAL CHURCH, in Tazewell County, was built in 1875 and replaced a building dating from the 1820s. The church and its cemetery were established to serve several denominations of settlers of German origin that migrated from Pennsylvania to southwestern Virginia.

The original Temple Beth Shalome, Mayo Street, Richmond, was erected in 1822. After nearly sixty years, the congregation moved to a new location, and the building was occupied by a local business. It was demolished in 1934. *(Valentine Museum, Richmond, Virginia)*

CATHEDRAL OF THE SACRED HEART, in Richmond, was built between 1903 and 1906 from a design by Joseph H. McGuire, a New York architect. Funds for the construction were donated by New York financier Thomas Fortune Ryan, a Nelson County native. Since 1906 it has served as the cathedral of the Catholic Diocese of Richmond.

CHESTER PRESBYTERIAN CHURCH, in Chesterfield County, was built in 1880 by Martin T. Grove, one of several northerners drawn to the Chester area during the post–Civil War years in search of Union-army treasure. Beset by guilt, Grove almost singlehandedly built the church. He moved back to the North two days after the church was dedicated.

CHRIST CHURCH, in Albemarle County, was built between 1831 and 1832 by William B. Phillips, a master craftsman and designer of several houses and public buildings. The brick Episcopal church closely follows the architectural form refined by his mentor, Thomas Jefferson.

CHRIST CHURCH, in Alexandria, was begun in 1767 and completed in 1773. Built as the Lower Church of Fairfax Parish, it was given its present name in 1814. The pews used by George Washington and by Robert E. Lee are still preserved there. It is a National Historic Landmark.

CHRIST CHURCH, in Lancaster County, was built about 1732 as the parish church of Christ Church Parish. The church was the gift of Robert ("King") Carter, one of the colony's wealthiest planters. His elaborate tomb is located in the churchyard of this National Historic Landmark..

CHRIST CHURCH, in Middlesex County, was built about 1714 as the parish church of Christ Church Parish. It was abandoned after the American Revolution but was returned to use in the 1840s.

CONFEDERATE MEMORIAL CHAPEL, in Richmond, was built in 1887 as part of the adjacent R. E. Lee Camp Confederate Soldiers' Home. Paid for by the veterans themselves, the small wood-frame building was dedicated to the South's war dead. The chapel served the home's former soldiers until the last resident died in 1941.

COURT STREET BAPTIST CHURCH, in Lynchburg, was completed in 1880 and constructed by African American artisans and laborers for the city's principal black congregation.

EMMANUEL EPISCOPAL CHURCH, in Albemarle County, was founded in the mid-nineteenth century and included among its parishioners the Langhorne family of nearby Mirador. Nancy Langhorne, later Lady Astor, with her brothers and sisters commissioned a remodeling of the brick Episcopal church in 1911.

FALLS CHURCH, in Falls Church, was built between 1767 and 1769. Named for the Little Falls of the Potomac River a few miles away, it was the Upper Church of Fairfax Parish. It is believed to have been designed by James Wren, who drew the plans for Christ Church, in Alexandria, and Pohick Church, in Fairfax County.

FARNHAM CHURCH, in Richmond County, was built about 1737 and was the church of North Farnham Parish. The present structure retains the colonial brick walls, but was substantially rebuilt after a post-Revolution fire.

FIRST BAPTIST CHURCH, in Norfolk, was completed in 1906 on the same site as its parishioners' earlier church, built in 1830. It was also the parent church of several other Norfolk congregations. Constructed in a Romanesque Revival style, it serves a congregation first organized in 1800.

FIRST BAPTIST CHURCH, in Roanoke, was built between 1898 and 1900 to serve Roanoke's African American community. The congregation began in 1855 as a Bible class for slaves. The church, supplanted by a new structure in 1982, is now used as a performing-arts center.

FIRST CALVARY BAPTIST CHURCH, in Norfolk, was built in 1916 in the Georgian Revival style and remains a landmark of the city's African American community. The church is noted for its extensive terra-cotta ornamentation.

FORK CHURCH, in Hanover County, was named for its proximity to the confluence of the North Anna and South Anna Rivers, the major tributaries of the Pamunkey River. Built between 1736 and 1740, it was the Second Lower Church of Saint Martin's

Parish. Dolley Payne (who married James Madison), Patrick Henry, and novelist Thomas Nelson Page attended services there.

FOURTH BAPTIST CHURCH, in Richmond, was completed in 1884. The Greek Revival church was built to serve a congregation that began as a religious assembly of slaves.

FRYING PAN CHURCH, in Fairfax County, was completed by 1791. One of the oldest-surviving Baptist churches in Virginia, it served whites as well as both free blacks and slaves. Its name is derived from local lore: sometime before 1725 Indians camping along a nearby creek supposedly left behind a frying pan. In 1984 the building was deeded to the Fairfax County Park Authority.

GLEBE CHURCH, in Suffolk, was known originally as Bennett's Creek Church. It was built between 1737 and 1738 to serve Suffolk Parish, one of the few colonial parishes that maintained possession of its glebe lands after the American Revolution. A glebe was the land yielding a revenue or belonging to a parish church.

GOOSE CREEK FRIENDS MEETING HOUSE COMPLEX, in Loudoun County, includes the stone meetinghouse built in 1765, which replaced a log structure of 1738, and a brick building erected in 1817, as well as the cemetery and an early schoolhouse.

GRACE CHURCH, in Albemarle County, was designed in 1847 and built soon thereafter. The Episcopal church is the only known Virginia work of William Strickland, one of the period's leading architects. The original interior woodwork was destroyed by fire in 1895.

GRACE CHURCH, in Cumberland County, was built between 1840 and 1843 by Valentine Parrish, a local master builder. The Episcopal church is the only building remaining from a town established in 1787 and named Ca Ira, perhaps for a song first sung during the French Revolution by Parisians as they marched to Versailles in 1789. The town was later a milling and tobacco-warehouse center.

GRACE CHURCH, in Yorktown, was built about 1697 and served both York Parish and, after 1707, Yorkhampton Parish. It is the only surviving colonial structure in Virginia built of marl, a natural deposit of marine shells and clay. The church's communion silver, the second oldest preserved in Virginia, was made in 1649.

HEBRON EVANGELICAL LUTHERAN CHURCH, in Madison County, is the oldest Lutheran church in Virginia and also the oldest Lutheran church in continuous use in the United States. The central part of the frame building was constructed in 1740 by German settlers, many of whom were descendants of miners employed at Alexander Spotswood's ironworks in Spotsylvania County. The wing was added between 1790 and 1802.

HICKORY NECK CHURCH, in James City County, was built in 1734 as the Lower Church of Blisland Parish. A wing added about 1773 is the only part of the colonial building that has survived.

HOPEWELL FRIENDS MEETING HOUSE, in Frederick County, was built in 1759 and enlarged in 1789. The Hopewell meeting had been organized in 1734 by Quakers from Pennsylvania.

HUNGARS CHURCH, in Northampton County, was built between 1742 and 1751 as the third church of Hungars Parish. Abandoned after the disestablishment, it was returned to service in 1819. Major repairs were made to the building in 1840 and 1851, and subsequent alterations were made between 1892 and 1955. The church is one of two surviving colonial Episcopal churches on Virginia's Eastern Shore.

JAMESTOWN CHURCH, in James City County, is almost entirely a modern reconstruction of the brick church built between 1639 and 1644. The original foundations and the tower, which was added between 1647 and 1680, are all that remain of the seventeenth-century structure.

LAMB'S CREEK CHURCH, in King George County, was built about 1769 to serve Brunswick Parish and was named for a nearby creek.

LEE CHAPEL, in Lexington, was built in 1867 as the school chapel for what was then Washington College. There in 1870 the body of Robert E. Lee lay in state. In 1883 an addition was added to house the Lee family crypt as well as Virginia sculptor Edward V. Valentine's recumbent statue of the Confederate general. While president of the college from 1865 until his death, Lee maintained his office on the chapel's lower floor. It is a National Historic Landmark.

LEIGH STREET BAPTIST CHURCH, in Richmond, was designed by Philadelphia architect Samuel Sloan and completed in 1857. The congregation was organized in the early 1850s by Baptist missionary Reuben Ford. Under its members' auspices, seven other Richmond Baptist churches were established.

LEXINGTON PRESBYTERIAN CHURCH, in Lexington, was completed in 1845 from a design by Philadelphia architect Thomas U. Walter. Samuel McDowell Reid, clerk of the Rockbridge County Court and an amateur architect, secured the commission for Walter. Included among the church members was Thomas J. (later "Stonewall") Jackson.

LITTLE ENGLAND CHAPEL, in Hampton, was built between 1878 and 1880 under the sponsorship of the American Missionary Association. Constructed by students from Hampton Institute and used as a church and Sunday school by the African American residents of an area known as Cock's Newtown, the weatherboard building is the only known surviving black missionary chapel of its type in Virginia.

LITTLE FORK CHURCH, in Culpeper County, stands near the confluence of the Hazel and Rappahannock Rivers. Built between 1774 and 1776, it served Saint Mark's Parish and is one of the few colonial churches still extant in the piedmont section of the state.

LOWER CHAPEL, in Middlesex County, was built about 1717 as the Lower Chapel of Christ Church (Middlesex) Parish. It is one of the few colonial Virginia churches with brickwork laid completely in English bond. After the Episcopal disestablishment, Lower Chapel became a Methodist church.

MANGOHICK BAPTIST CHURCH, in King William County, was built between 1730 and 1732 near Mangohick Creek. It first served Saint Margaret's Parish as a chapel of ease, a house of worship used by Anglican parishioners who lived too far from their parish church to attend its services regularly. The building became the

Upper Church of Saint David's Parish in 1744. Abandoned after the Episcopal disestablishment, the building was returned to use by a black Baptist congregation after the Civil War.

MATTAPONY BAPTIST CHURCH, in King and Queen County, probably was built between 1730 and 1734, although some authorities assign a construction date of 1755. Originally built as the Lower Church of Saint Stephen's Parish, it became a Baptist church early in the nineteenth century and was named (with a slight change in spelling) for the nearby Mattaponi River.

MAUCK'S MEETING HOUSE, in Page County, dates from as early as 1798. The congregation of both Mennonites and Baptists was organized in about 1772 and included slaves and free blacks. Although eventually dominated by Baptists, the congregation attracted ministers of various denominations. The building, also known as the Mill Creek Meeting House, is maintained by the Page County Heritage Association.

MERCHANT'S HOPE CHURCH, in Prince George County, probably was completed about 1657. It was the Upper Church of Martin's Brandon Parish and seems to have been named for Martin's (or Merchant's) Hope, an early plantation on the Appomattox River.

MONUMENTAL CHURCH, in the city of Richmond, was built in 1814 on the site of the Richmond Theatre, which was destroyed by fire on 26 December 1811. Designed by architect Robert Mills, the church was erected as a memorial to the seventy-two victims of the disaster. Octagonal in shape, it is one of the earliest Greek Revival buildings in the country, and is now a National Historic Landmark.

MOUNT SINAI BAPTIST CHURCH, in King William County, known formerly as Cattail Church, was built in 1751 as the parish church of Saint David's Parish. Abandoned after the Episcopal disestablishment, it was eventually returned to use by its present African American congregation.

MOUNT ZION BAPTIST CHURCH, in Charlottesville, was organized in 1867 to provide the African American Baptist community with its own place of worship. The congregation's first church was enlarged several times, then demolished to make room for the present church, completed in 1884. Local tradition attributes the church's design to Charlottesville architect George Wallace Spooner, who later worked on the Univerity of Virginia Rotunda after it was damaged by fire in 1895.

NEW PROVIDENCE PRESBYTERIAN CHURCH, in Rockbridge County, was completed in 1859 and patterned after a design by Robert Lewis Dabney, a well-known Presbyterian minister and amateur architect. The congregation was organized in 1746 by John Blair, a noted Presbyterian minister. One of Virginia's earliest missionary organizations, the Female Benevolent Society, was founded at New Providence in 1819.

OAKLAND GROVE PRESBYTERIAN CHURCH, in Alleghany County, was built about 1847 as a mission of the Covington Presbyterian Church. It is the oldest-known ecclesiastical structure in the county and served the mountainous area's Scotch-Irish settlers. The building was used as a hospital during the Civil War.

OLD CHAPEL, in Clarke County, was built in 1793 and was one of the earliest Episcopal churches west of the Blue Ridge. Made of limestone rubble, it replaced a nearby log church dating from 1747. The Episcopal bishop William Meade in his early career served as a lay reader there. The church fell into disuse after 1834 but is still maintained by its parish.

OLD CHURCH, in King and Queen County, was built between 1724 and 1729 as the Upper Church of Stratton Major Parish. Abandoned in 1768, it was thereafter used by various denominations until a Methodist congregation acquired possession of the building in 1842.

OLD DONATION CHURCH, in Virginia Beach, was built in 1736 as the parish church of Lynnhaven Parish. The name, which came into use after the Episcopal disestablishment, derives from a gift of land to the parish in the colonial period. Although the building stood in ruins for years, it has been restored within its original walls.

OLD FIRST AFRICAN BAPTIST CHURCH, in Richmond, was built in 1876 on the site of an earlier Baptist church of 1802. The original parent congregation was white, but included slaves and free blacks. The black members purchased the church property in 1841 when white Baptists erected a new church a block away. No longer used for worship, the building since 1955 has been part of the Medical College of Virginia.

OLD FIRST BAPTIST CHURCH, in Richmond, was built between 1839 and 1841 and was designed by Thomas U. Walter, architect of the dome of the United States Capitol. The building replaced an earlier church, only a block away, built in 1802. The congregation's black members in 1841 established their own First African Baptist Church in the 1802 building. During the Civil War the church served as an emergency hospital for Confederate soldiers. The building since 1938 has been part of the Medical College of Virginia.

OLD PRESBYTERIAN MEETING HOUSE, in Alexandria, was built by a congregation organized in 1772. The original building, erected in 1774 and enlarged in 1790, burned in 1835; parts of the original walls were retained when the church was rebuilt. During most of the nineteenth century it was known as the First Presbyterian Church.

OLIVET PRESBYTERIAN CHURCH, in New Kent County, was built in 1857. The small, simple wooden church, known first as Mount Olivet, was constructed to provide local Presbyterians with their own place of worship; since 1800 they had conducted services at Saint Peter's, an abandoned Episcopal church. Although its congregation relocated in 1934, Olivet has remained an unaltered example of a rural, antebellum Virginia church.

POHICK CHURCH, in Fairfax County, begun in 1769 and completed in 1774, served Truro Parish. George Washington and George Mason, vestrymen of the parish, served on the building committee that planned and supervised the church's construction in the Georgian style.

PRESBYTERIAN CHURCH OF FREDERICKSBURG, in Fredericksburg, was built in 1833 and was the town's first temple-form public building. During the Civil War the building served as a hospital for both Union and Confederate soldiers, and it was there in 1862 that Clara Barton, founder of the American Red Cross, nursed casualties after the Battle of Fredericksburg.

Constructed in 1793 of limestone rubble, Old Stone Chapel, or Old Chapel, in Clarke County, was one of the earliest Episcopal churches west of the Blue Ridge.

PROVIDENCE PRESBYTERIAN CHURCH, in Louisa County, was completed about 1747 and was called Providence Meeting House before 1785. It is one of the few colonial frame churches still standing.

QUAKER MEETING HOUSE, in Lynchburg, completed in 1798, was first known as the South River Friends' Meeting House. The stone building replaced two earlier structures, the first constructed in 1757. Abandoned in the 1850s, the meetinghouse was restored in 1904 for use by Presbyterians. John Lynch, Lynchburg's founder, lies buried in the adjacent Quaker cemetery.

SAINT GEORGE'S CHURCH, in Accomack County, formerly known as Pungoteague Church, was completed in 1737. The parish church of Accomack Parish until 1762, when it became the church of the newly created Saint George's Parish, it is one of two surviving colonial Episcopal churches on Virginia's Eastern Shore.

SAINT JAMES'S CHURCH, in Accomack County, was built in 1838 and is known for its unusual architectural details, especially its rare trompe l'oeil interior arch. The Episcopal congregation constructed the building with bricks salvaged from a nearby eighteenth-century church.

SAINT JOHN'S AFRICAN METHODIST EPISCOPAL CHURCH, in Norfolk, was completed in 1887–1888 for a congregation first organized in 1800 and reorganized in 1864 as part of the African Methodist Episcopal Church. The Romanesque Revival church was designed by Norfolk architect Charles M. Cassell.

SAINT JOHN'S CHURCH, in Amelia County, was consecrated in 1852 and built on the site of a colonial church known as Grub Hill Church, a name derived from the Grub Hill slave quarters of the Tabb family, which donated the land for the building. Owned by the trustees of Christ Episcopal Church, the building is now used only occasionally for worship services.

SAINT JOHN'S CHURCH, in Hampton, was built in 1728 and was the parish church of Elizabeth City Parish. Its communion silver, made in 1619 for Charles City Parish, is believed to be the oldest still in use in Virginia.

SAINT JOHN'S CHURCH, also known as Old Saint John's, in King William County, was begun in 1734 and additions were made between 1755 and 1756. It was the parish church of Saint John's Parish, and its members included Carter Braxton, a signer of the Declaration of Independence.

SAINT JOHN'S CHURCH, in the city of Richmond, is the oldest place of worship in the capital. In 1775, when the Virginia's second revolutionary convention was meeting there, Patrick Henry made his celebrated "liberty or death" speech. The original frame building was erected in 1741, a wing was added in 1772, and other additions were made between 1830 and 1905. Saint John's Church was known by various names (such as Henrico Parish Church, the Town Church, and the Church on Richmond Hill) before its present name was conferred about 1829. It is a National Historic Landmark.

SAINT JOHN'S CHURCH, in Suffolk, formerly known as Chuckatuck Church, was built in 1756 and was the parish church of Suffolk Parish. The present name was adopted in 1828.

SAINT LUKE'S CHURCH, in Isle of Wight County, probably was erected in 1682 as the second building on the site. It was known as Newport Parish Church or the Old Brick Church before the present name was adopted in 1828. It is a National Historic Landmark.

SAINT MARY'S CATHOLIC CHURCH, in Alexandria, was built in 1826 by a congregation founded in 1796. It serves the oldest Catholic congregation in Virginia.

SAINT MARY'S CATHOLIC CHURCH, in Fairfax County, was built in 1858 to serve Irish immigrants hired to construct the Orange and Alexandria Railroad. Clara Barton, founder of the American Red Cross, established a hospital in the church during the Second Battle of Manassas in 1862. Many of the battle's Union dead are buried in the churchyard.

SAINT MARY'S WHITECHAPEL, in Lancaster County, formerly was the parish church of Saint Mary's Whitechapel Parish and was named for the London suburb of Whitechapel. The original structure was completed about 1669. An addition, the oldest surviving part of the present church, was built between 1739 and 1741. In 1832 the seventeenth-century portion of the building was demolished, leaving only the eighteenth-century additions. The family of Mary Ball, mother of George Washington, worshiped at Saint Mary's Whitechapel.

SAINT PAUL'S CHURCH, in King George County, was built between 1766 and 1767 and was the parish church of Saint Paul's (earlier Chotank) Parish. It is one of the few colonial churches built in the form of a Greek, rather than a Latin, cross.

SAINT PAUL'S CHURCH, in Norfolk, was built in 1739 as the parish church of Elizabeth River Parish. Known as the Borough Church until the present name came into use in 1832, it is the oldest building in the city of Norfolk. The south wall contains a British cannonball fired during Lord Dunmore's 1776 bombardment of Norfolk.

SAINT PAUL'S CHURCH, in Prince William County, was built about 1802 as a district courthouse. After a reorganization of the Virginia district court system in 1807, the building was sold to the Hygeia Academy, which later failed. In 1834, Bishop William Meade consecrated the building as Saint Paul's Episcopal Church.

SAINT PAUL'S CHURCH, in the city of Richmond, built in 1845, is sometimes known as the Church of the Confederacy. Robert E. Lee and Jefferson Davis both worshiped there during the Civil War. Davis was attending services at Saint Paul's on the morning of 2 April 1865 when he received word of the fall of Petersburg.

SAINT PETER'S CHURCH, in New Kent County, was completed about 1703 and first served as the Lower Church of Saint Peter's Parish. In 1704, Saint Peter's became the parish church. Martha Dandridge Custis, who married George Washington in 1759 was a member of the congregation.

SAINT PETER'S CATHOLIC CHURCH, in the city of Richmond, was built in 1834 and is the oldest Catholic church in the city. It was designated as the cathedral of the Diocese of Richmond in 1841 and continued as the diocesan cathedral until 1906 when the Cathedral of the Sacred Heart was consecrated.

SAINT THOMAS'S CHAPEL, in Frederick County, was built about 1835 for the Episcopal congregation of Middletown. The church served as both a Confederate hospital and a Union-army stable during the Civil War. The building was closed in 1930, donated to the Middletown community in 1966, and has been restored as an interdenominational chapel.

SAINT THOMAS'S EPISCOPAL CHURCH, in Orange County, was built between 1833 and 1834 and was modeled on Christ Church in Charlottesville (later demolished), Thomas Jefferson's only ecclesiastical work. The designer and builder was probably William B. Phillips, who worked for Jefferson in the construction of the University of Virginia. In the Civil War, the church served as a hospital during four different battles.

SAPPONY CHURCH, in Dinwiddie County, was built between 1725 and 1726 as one of the two chapels of Bristol Parish. Devereux Jarrett, a proponent of the Great Awakening and of the Methodist movement within the Episcopal Church, served as its rector from 1763 to 1801.

SHARON LUTHERAN CHURCH, in Bland County, was built about 1883 to replace an 1821 building. Lutheran and Presbyterian congregations shared both structures until 1911 when the latter group built its own church. The cemetery is noted for its many headstone-carvings reflecting the area's German folk culture.

SIXTH MOUNT ZION BAPTIST CHURCH, in Richmond, was first organized in 1867 by the Reverend John Jasper. The African American congregation moved several times before establishing its church in a small brick chapel at the corner of Duval and Saint John Streets in the city's Jackson Ward neighborhood. In 1887 the chapel and a later addition were razed and a larger Romanesque Revival structure was erected. Jasper gained a national reputation for his famous sermon "The Sun Do Move."

SLASH CHRISTIAN CHURCH, in Hanover County, was built about 1729 and served as the Upper Church of Saint Paul's Parish. Abandoned by its congregation after the Episcopal disestablishment, the church was shared by Methodists and Disciples of Christ until 1842, when the Disciples took sole possession. Slash Church, the oldest-known frame church building in Virginia, takes its name from a nearby swamp called The Slashes.

SOMERSET CHRISTIAN CHURCH, in Orange County, was built about 1857 to serve the small rural community of Somerset. It is a rare unaltered example of a mid-nineteenth-century, wood-frame country church.

THIRD STREET BETHEL AFRICAN METHODIST EPISCOPAL CHURCH, in Richmond, was built about 1857 to serve the city's large free black population. The Virginia Conference of the African Methodist Episcopal denomination was organized there in 1867. The building remains one of the nation's few surviving antebellum black churches.

TIMBER RIDGE PRESBYTERIAN CHURCH, in Rockbridge County, was built in 1755. This structure of native limestone replaced a log meetinghouse, built about 1746, that stood approximately two miles to the north. For several years after it was built, the church housed the Augusta Academy, the forerunner of Washington and Lee University.

TINKLING SPRING PRESBYTERIAN CHURCH, in Augusta County, was built in 1850 under the direction of Robert Lewis Dabney, who designed several churches in Virginia. First organized in the late 1730s, it served the second-oldest Presbyterian congregation in the Shenandoah Valley.

VAUTER'S CHURCH, in Essex County, was built about 1719; the south wing was added in 1731. It served as the Upper Church of Saint Anne's Parish and was named for a family that owned land adjoining the church's site.

WADDELL MEMORIAL PRESBYTERIAN CHURCH, in Orange County, was built in 1874 and named for James Waddell, a blind local preacher. The Presbyterian church was designed by J. B. Danforth, an amateur architect and a faculty member at Union Theological Seminary in Richmond.

WARE CHURCH, in Gloucester County, was first built about 1660 and is believed to have been rebuilt between 1710 and 1715 after a fire destroyed the earlier structure. The new church was constructed on a site across the river from the original church. It was the parish church of Ware Parish, which was named for the Ware River.

WESTOVER PARISH CHURCH, in Charles City County, built about 1731, served as the parish church of Westover Parish. William Byrd II, William Henry Harrison, and John Tyler were among those who worshiped there.

YEOCOMICO CHURCH, in Westmoreland County, was built about 1706. It was the Lower Church of Cople (formerly Nomini) Parish and was named for a nearby creek. It is a National Historic Landmark.

A ca. 1935 photograph in Saluda, Middlesex County. White, frame churches dot Virginia's countryside.

Poet Anne Spencer (1882–1975), of Lynchburg, did much of her writing in this small detached office, built by her husband, looking out on the garden behind the main house. *(Courtesy of Historic American Buildings Survey. Photo by Richard Cheek.)*

SOME HISTORIC HOUSES

The following list, by no means exhaustive, includes houses that have important connections with major figures or events of Virginia history or that have exceptional architectural interest.

ADAM THOROUGHGOOD HOUSE, in Virginia Beach, may have been built as early as 1636 by Adam Thoroughgood and is one of the oldest-surviving dwellings in North America. A National Historic Landmark, the house is maintained by the Adam Thoroughgood House Foundation.

AGECROFT HALL, in Richmond, is a fifteenth-century, half-timbered manor house brought from Manchester, England, in 1926 by Elizabeth Booker Williams and Thomas C. Williams Jr. It is maintained by the Agecroft Association.

AMPTHILL, formerly in Chesterfield County, was built sometime before 1732 by Henry Cary II. His son Archibald Cary was a distinguished Virginia leader during the Revolution. The house was moved to the city of Richmond in 1929. It is privately owned.

ANNE SPENCER HOUSE, in Lynchburg, was built in 1903 and was the home of African American poet and Civil Rights activist Anne Spencer (1881–1975). Visitors to her house included W. E. B. Du Bois, Martin Luther King Jr., and Thurgood Marshall. The site is owned by the Friends of Anne Spencer Memorial Foundation.

ARLINGTON HOUSE, in Arlington County, also known as the Custis-Lee Mansion, was built between 1802 and 1817 by George Washington Parke Custis, grandson of Martha Custis Washington and father-in-law of Robert E. Lee. Lee and Mary Ann Randolph Custis were married there in 1831. The United States government took possession of the house in 1861, and Arlington National Cemetery was established there. The house is maintained by the National Park Service.

ASH LAWN–HIGHLAND, in Albemarle County, was a residence of James Monroe, who called it Highland. He built the western section of the present building between 1796 and 1799 and maintained possession of the house until 1827. The remainder of the house was added by subsequent owners. The house is owned by the College of William and Mary in Virginia.

AZUREST SOUTH, in Ettrick, Chesterfield County, was designed by Amaza Lee Meredith (1895–1984), one of the nation's first black female architects and founder in 1930 of the fine arts department at Virginia State University. Completed in 1939, the house is one of the state's few examples of the International Style and is now owned by Virginia State University.

BACON'S CASTLE, in Surry County, is one of the oldest-surviving houses in Virginia. The brick Jacobean mansion was built about 1655 by Arthur Allen. During Bacon's Rebellion in 1676 the house was occupied by followers of Nathaniel Bacon Jr., but the rebel leader himself probably never saw it. It is owned by the Association for the Preservation of Virginia Antiquities and is a National Historic Landmark.

Nationally acclaimed architect Alexander Jackson Davis designed Belmead, in Powhatan County, for Philip St. George Cocke in 1845. It served as the home of Saint Emma's Industrial and Agricultural School for African American students from 1897 until the early 1970s.

BELMEAD, in Powhatan County, was designed by Alexander Jackson Davis for Philip St. George Cooke. Built in 1845 as a Gothic Revival villa, the house in 1897 was donated to the Catholic Church. There the church established Saint Emma's Industrial and Agricultural School to assist African American students. The property is maintained by the Sisters of the Blessed Sacrament, a Philadelphia-based Catholic order.

BELMONT, in Stafford County, was built about 1761 and enlarged after 1825. The house was purchased in 1916 by Gari Melchers (1860–1932), a renowned artist of genre scenes, portraits, and religious works. The house and artist's studio, as well as much of Melcher's artwork, were bequeathed by his wife to Mary Washington College, which maintains the National Historic Landmark.

BERKELEY, in Charles City County, was built in 1726 by Benjamin Harrison (ca. 1700–1745). It was the birthplace of his son Benjamin Harrison (1726–1791), a signer of the Declaration of Independence and governor of Virginia, and of the latter's son, William Henry Harrison, ninth president of the United States. It is privately owned and a National Historic Landmark.

BERRY HILL, in Halifax County, was built between 1842 and 1844 by James Coles Bruce and designed by John Evans Johnson. Modeled on the Parthenon, Berry Hill is one of the finest Greek Revival mansions in the nation. The house is privately owned and a National Historic Landmark.

BOOKER T. WASHINGTON NATIONAL MONUMENT, in Franklin County, is the birthplace of the distinguished educator who founded Tuskegee Institute. Washington was born in 1856 in a slave cabin on the plantation of James Burroughs. The house is maintained by the National Park Service.

BRANDON, in Prince George County, was built in seven sections about 1765 by Nathaniel Harrison. Two earlier houses formed the wings of the mansion, which followed the Palladian forms popular in mid-eighteenth-century England and Virginia. The house is privately owned and a National Historic Landmark.

BREMO, in Fluvanna County, was built by John Hartwell Cocke, a soldier, planter, and reformer, and was completed in 1820. It is a five-section brick house constructed by master builder John Neilson, who apparently gave the house its Palladian proportions. It is privately owned. An opponent of slavery, Cocke was a vice president of the American Colonization Society and in defiance of both law and custom taught his slaves to read and write. It is a National Historic Landmark.

CARLYLE HOUSE, in Alexandria, was completed in 1753 for John Carlyle, a Scottish merchant. There in 1755 British general Edward Braddock met with the governors of five colonies to devise the strategies for the French and Indian War. The house has been restored as a museum by the Northern Virginia Regional Park Authority.

CARTER'S GROVE, in James City County, was built in the 1750s on land purchased by Robert ("King") Carter for his daughter Elizabeth. Her son Carter Burwell built the house. The property is maintained by the Colonial Williamsburg Foundation, Inc., and is a National Historic Landmark.

CASTLE HILL, in Albemarle County, was built in 1764 by Thomas Walker, colonial physician and explorer. His granddaughter Judith Page Walker, and her husband, William Cabell Rives, made a brick addition to the house about 1825, so that the structure is actually two houses, one a colonial farmhouse and the other a piedmont plantation house. It is privately owned.

CENTRE HILL, in Petersburg, was built in 1823 for Robert Bolling and remodeled in the 1850s. Few other Virginia antebellum houses approach its scale and detail. During the siege of Petersburg, Union general George Lucas Hartsuff established his headquarters there. Abraham Lincoln visited the house on 7 April 1865, a week before his death. The house has been restored by the city of Petersburg and is now a museum.

CHARLES RICHARD DREW HOUSE, in Arlington, was from 1920 to 1939 the home of Dr. Charles R. Drew (1904–1950), an African American surgeon who pioneered research in the use of blood plasma and helped lead the Plasma for Britain program during World War II. Drew was also the first black American to receive the doctor of science degree. The house is a National Historic Landmark.

ELSING GREEN, in King William County, was built in the 1750s by Carter Braxton. It is a large, two-story, Gothic U-shaped building done in Flemish bond. It is said to have been burned twice—once before completion and again about 1800—but it was rebuilt within its original walls. An earlier, one-and-a-half story structure built in the 1690s survives as the east dependency of the main house. It is privately owned and a National Historic Landmark.

ESTOUTEVILLE, in Albemarle County, was built between 1827 and 1830 for John Coles III by James Dinsmore, a Philadelphia master builder who had worked for Thomas Jefferson at both Monticello and the University of Virginia. Drawing upon ancient Roman architectural precedents as well as from the work of Italian designer Andrea Palladio, Dinsmore created perhaps the first structure in what might be categorized as a native academic style.

EXECUTIVE MANSION, in Richmond, was authorized in 1810 by the General Assembly and was designed by Boston architect Alexander Parris. First occupied in 1813, it continues to be the residence of Virginia's governor. The mansion was enlarged in 1908 by Richmond architect Duncan Lee and additional changes were made in 1958. A detailed exterior restoration was completed in 1989. It is a National Historic Landmark.

GEORGE WASHINGTON BIRTHPLACE NATIONAL MONUMENT, in Westmoreland County, is a four-hundred-acre national park commemorating the birth site of the first president of the United States. The house in which Washington was born, formerly known as Popes Creek plantation and also as Wakefield, was completed in 1726 but burned in 1779. The present house on the site is a reconstruction of a typical eighteenth-century tidewater plantation house. The property is maintained by the National Park Service.

GUNSTON HALL, in Fairfax County, the residence of George Mason, revolutionary statesman and author of the Virginia Declaration of Rights, was completed in 1758. A National Historic Landmark, the house is now owned by the commonwealth of Virginia and administered by the National Society of the Colonial Dames of America.

HOLLY KNOLL, in Gloucester County, was the retirement home of African American educator Robert R. Moton (1867–1940), a founder of the National Urban League, a former president of Tuskegee Institute, and an adviser on black affairs to five U.S. presidents. The house is a National Historic Landmark.

JOHN MARSHALL HOUSE, in Richmond, was the residence of the famous chief justice of the U. S. Supreme Court. Now a National Historic Landmark, the house was built for Marshall between 1788 and 1791, and he lived there from about 1791 until his death in 1835. The house is the only surviving eighteenth-century brick house in Richmond and is maintained by the Association for the Preservation of Virginia Antiquities.

KENMORE, in Fredericksburg, was formerly known as Millbrook and was the residence of George Washington's sister Betty and her husband, Fielding Lewis. It was begun about 1752 and completed about 1756. It is maintained by the Kenmore Association and is a National Historic Landmark.

KERR PLACE, in Accomack County, was built between 1799 and 1806 for John Shepherd Ker (later Kerr), an Onancock merchant. The residence is perhaps the Eastern Shore's best example of Federal architecture. Since 1960 the house has been owned by, and served as the headquarters of, the Eastern Shore of Virginia Historical Society. The grounds have been restored by the Garden Club of Virginia.

LEE-FENDALL HOUSE, in Alexandria, was built in 1785 and remodeled between 1850 and 1852. Built as the home of Philip Richard Fendall and Elizabeth Lee Fendall, it is the earliest of several Old Town Alexandria houses occupied by the Lee family. John L. Lewis, influential labor leader and famed head of the United Mine Workers, lived in the house from 1937 until his death in 1969. It is maintained by the Virginia Trust for Historic Preservation.

LONG BRANCH, in Clarke County, is one of four surviving houses in America designed at least in part by Benjamin Henry Latrobe, the first professional architect in the United States. The house was begun in 1811 for Robert Burwell. It is a notable example of the American Classic Revival style of architecture and is privately owned.

LYNNHAVEN HOUSE, in Virginia Beach, was built about 1724 and is representative of the small, brick houses constructed by many prosperous Virginia farmers in the early eighteenth century. After falling into disrepair, the house was donated in 1971 to the Association for the Preservation of Virginia Antiquities, which has meticulously restored the dwelling.

McCORMICK FARM AND WORKSHOP, in Rockbridge County, was the birthplace and early residence of Cyrus Hall McCormick. In 1832 McCormick designed and built the first successful model of his mechanical reaper in the log shop on the property. The farm, also known as Walnut Grove, is maintained by Virginia Polytechnic Institute and State University and is a National Historic Landmark.

MAGGIE L. WALKER HOUSE, in Richmond, was built about 1883 and purchased in 1904 by Maggie L. Walker (1867–1934), chief executive of the Saint Luke Penny Savings Bank and the nation's first woman bank president. Maggie Walker was also a founder of the Richmond Council of Colored Women and active in numerous other African American causes. The house is maintained by the National Park Service and is a National Historic Landmark.

MARY WASHINGTON HOUSE, in Fredericksburg, was built about 1754. It was purchased in 1772 by George Washington for his mother, who lived there until her death in 1789. It is maintained by the Association for the Preservation of Virginia Antiquities.

MONTICELLO, in Albemarle County, was the residence of Thomas Jefferson, who designed it and began its construction in 1770. After making alterations, he completed it in 1809. He and members of his family are buried in the nearby graveyard. The house and grounds are maintained by the Thomas Jefferson Memorial Foundation. Monticello is a National Historic Landmark and is on the World Heritage List.

MONTPELIER, in Orange County, was the residence of James Madison, fourth president of the United States. The central portion was built about 1760 by Madison's father, and Madison himself made additions between 1793 and 1800 (the portico was built in 1809 following instructions given by Thomas Jefferson). Since 1984, the house has been owned by the National Trust for Historic Preservation. It is a National Historic Landmark.

MOORE HOUSE, in Yorktown, was built by Lawrence Smith about 1725. It was purchased by Augustine Moore in 1768. On 18 October 1781, English, French, and American officers met at the Moore House to draft the terms of surrender that Lord Cornwallis and the British troops at Yorktown accepted the following day. The house is maintained by the National Park Service.

MORVEN PARK, in Loudoun County, was the home of two governors, one of Virginia and the other of Maryland. Built about 1780, it was greatly enlarged in the 1850s by Thomas Swann Jr., later a governor of Maryland. Westmoreland Davis, governor of Virginia, made further additions while he lived there from 1903 to 1942. The house was renovated and opened to the public as a museum in 1967. It is maintained by the Westmoreland Davis Memorial Foundation, Inc.

MOSES MYERS HOUSE, in Norfolk, was built about 1792 and was one of the first brick buildings in Norfolk constructed after fire destroyed most of the town in 1776. The home of Moses Myers, a prominent nineteenth-century Norfolk merchant, it is now maintained by the Chrysler Museum.

MOUNT AIRY, in Richmond County, was built between 1748 and 1758 by John Tayloe II to replace an earlier house on the site that burned in 1740. The second house burned in 1844, and the interiors and roof were reconstructed. Francis Lightfoot Lee, one of the signers of the Declaration of Independence, is buried there. A National Historic Landmark, it is considered to be one of the finest Georgian mansions in North America and is privately owned.

MOUNT VERNON, in Fairfax County, was the residence of George Washington, who inherited it from his half brother Lawrence Washington. The central portion of the house, which may have been built as early as 1740, was already complete when George Washington took possession of it after his half brother's death in 1752. Washington made major additions to the mansion in 1759 and in 1773, and had completed it in its present form by 1787. He and his wife are buried in a tomb near the house. The house and grounds are maintained by the Mount Vernon Ladies' Association of the Union and are a National Historic Landmark.

NELSON HOUSE, in Yorktown, was built between 1725 and 1740, either by Thomas Nelson or his son William. It was later occupied by Thomas Nelson Jr., a signer of the Declaration of Independence, governor of Virginia, and commander of the Virginia militia at Yorktown. Lafayette planted a tree near the house in 1824 during his return visit to the United States. The house, which is also called York Hall, is owned by the National Park Service.

NEWSOME HOUSE, in Newport News, was built in 1899 and from 1906 to 1942 was the residence of J. Thomas Newsome (1869–1942), editor of the *Newport News Star* and among the first African American attorneys certified to practice before the Virginia Supreme Court of Appeals. The house now serves as the Newsome House Museum and Cultural Center, founded in 1991.

OAK HILL, in Fauquier County, was a residence of Chief Justice John Marshall. The original part of the house was begun by his father, Thomas Marshall, about 1773, and extensive additions were made by the chief justice between 1815 and 1820. It is privately owned.

OAK HILL, in Loudoun County, the last Virginia residence of James Monroe, was built between 1820 and 1823. Monroe lived there after his retirement from the presidency in 1825 until his wife's death in 1830, when he moved to New York. It is privately owned and is a National Historic Landmark.

OATLANDS, in Loudoun County, was begun in 1804 and considerably altered during the ensuing twenty years. The house was developed by George Carter, the son of Robert Carter of Nomini, and remained in the Carter family until 1897. In 1903 the house was purchased by William Corcoran Eustis, grandson of the philanthropist William Wilson Corcoran. A National Historic Landmark, the house and its surrounding acreage were donated in 1965 to the National Trust for Historic Preservation.

POMPEY CALLAWAY HOUSE, in Elliston, Montgomery County, was completed in 1910. A former slave, Pompey Callaway may have modeled his late-nineteenth-century-style house on the antebellum home of his former owner. Callaway made his own bricks and, working weekends, took many years to construct his home. Except for a small addition, the house survives with few alterations.

POPE-LEIGHEY HOUSE, in Fairfax County, was built in 1940 by Frank Lloyd Wright. It is an example of his "Usonian" dwellings, which were designed to be practical, economical, and organically related to their sites. It was moved from its original Falls Church site in 1964 to accommodate a new roadway, and is presently owned and maintained by the National Trust for Historic Preservation.

POPLAR FOREST, in Bedford County, was designed and built by Thomas Jefferson as his rural retreat. Jefferson began work on the house in 1809 and in 1823, at age eighty, was still supervising interior work. The walls, chimneys, and columns are original, but the octagonal house was gutted by fire in 1845. A National Historic Landmark, it is owned by the Corporation for Jefferson's Poplar Forest.

PRESTWOULD, in Mecklenburg County, was built about 1795 by Sir Peyton Skipwith, one of colonial Virginia's few baronets. Unlike most colonial mansions, which were built of brick, the house is constructed of hewn limestone. The site also includes a wood-frame slave house, one of the earliest-surviving such houses in the South. The property is maintained by the Prestwould House Foundation.

RED HILL, in Charlotte County, was the last residence of Patrick Henry. He lived there from 1793 until his death in 1799 and is buried there. The frame house is maintained by the Patrick Henry Memorial Foundation.

SABINE HALL, in Richmond County, was built about 1730 and was the residence of Landon Carter, a son of Robert ("King") Carter. Additions and alterations were made in 1764, the 1830s, 1929, and the 1960s. It is privately owned and a National Historic Landmark.

SARATOGA, in Clarke County, was the residence of American Revolutionary War general Daniel Morgan. It was built in 1781 by Hessian prisoners and was named for the Battle of Saratoga, in which Morgan took a distinguished part. It was later the home of Virginia writers Philip Pendleton Cooke and his brother John Esten Cooke. The house is privately owned and a National Historic Landmark.

Montgomery County's Smithfield, completed in 1774 and photographed ca. 1935 prior to extensive restoration, is an example of an early western Virginia plantation house.

SCOTCHTOWN, in Hanover County, was built about 1719 and was the residence of Patrick Henry from 1771 to 1778. Dolley Payne (the future wife of James Madison), whose father purchased the house about 1781, lived there as a child. A National Historic Landmark, the house is maintained by the Association for the Preservation of Virginia Antiquities.

SHERWOOD FOREST, in Charles City County, was the home of John Tyler, tenth president of the United States. Tyler purchased the house in 1842 and lived there from 1845 until his death in 1862. The house is privately owned and a National Historic Landmark.

SHIRLEY, in Charles City County, was built about 1769 by Charles Carter on land patented in 1660 by his great-grandfather Edward Hill. Anne Carter Lee, mother of Robert E. Lee, was born there. It is privately owned and a National Historic Landmark.

SMITHFIELD, in Montgomery County, was built in 1773–1774 by William Preston and is an early example of a western Virginia plantation house. James Patton Preston and his grandson John Buchanan Floyd were both born in the house and both served as governor of Virginia. The house is owned by the Association for the Preservation of Virginia Antiquities.

STAUNTON HILL, in Charlotte County, was designed in 1848 by architect John E. Johnson and completed two years later while its owner, Charles Bruce, was traveling in Europe. It is one of the finest Gothic Revival houses in the United States and is privately owned.

STONEWALL JACKSON HOUSE, in Lexington, was purchased in 1858 by the future Confederate general Thomas J. ("Stonewall") Jackson, then a professor at the Virginia Military Institute. The Jacksons moved there early in 1859 and remained until the spring of 1861; it is the only house the general ever owned. It is maintained by the Historic Lexington Foundation.

STRATFORD HALL, in Westmoreland County, was completed by Thomas Lee about 1730. It was the birthplace of Richard Henry Lee and his brother Francis Lightfoot Lee, signers of the Declaration of Independence, and of Robert E. Lee. A National Historic Landmark, the house and adjacent buildings are maintained by the Robert E. Lee Memorial Association.

SUTHERLIN HOUSE, in Danville, was built between 1857 and 1858 for Major William T. Sutherlin, a member of the Virginia Convention of 1861 and later a Confederate quartermaster. In April 1865, after the fall of Richmond, Danville was chosen as the South's temporary capital. For two weeks Jefferson Davis resided in the house and there signed his last proclamation as Confederate president. For many years the house served as the Danville Public Library. Later restored, the Sutherlin House now serves as the Danville Museum of Fine Arts and History.

TUCKAHOE, in Goochland County, was built about 1712 by Thomas Randolph, a son of William Randolph, of Turkey Island. Thomas Jefferson lived there as a boy, and Thomas Mann Randolph, who married Jefferson's daughter Martha, was born there. Among the property's many surviving outbuildings are two double-pen slave quarters. The house is privately owned and a National Historic Landmark.

VIRGINIA HOUSE, in Richmond, was designed by Henry Grant Morse. The house incorporates major portions of the sixteenth-century English house Warwick Priory, including much of the stone from the exterior walls and parts of the interior woodwork. The house was erected at its present site between 1925 and 1928. In 1929, the owners, Alexander W. Weddell and Virginia Chase Weddell, gave the house and gardens to the Virginia Historical Society, which maintains them.

VIRGINIA RANDOLPH COTTAGE, in Glen Allen, Henrico County, was built in 1937 and served as a classroom and home for pioneer educator Virginia Randolph (1874–1958). A daughter of slaves, Randolph was especially instrumental as an early supervisor for what later became the Negro Rural School Fund, a program utilizing African American supervisors to upgrade public-school vocational training for southern black students. A National Historic Landmark, the house in 1969 became the Virginia Randolph Education Center and is now a museum.

WALTER REED BIRTHPLACE, in Gloucester County, is a small, white, frame house in which Walter Reed was born in 1851. As an army physician in Cuba, Reed proved that yellow fever is transmitted by mosquitoes. The house was restored by the Medical Society of Virginia and the Association for the Preservation of Virginia Antiquities and is maintained by the APVA.

WESTOVER, in Charles City County, was built about 1730 by William Byrd II, planter, author, and colonial official. It remained in the possession of the Byrd family until 1814. A renowned example of Georgian architecture in the United States, it is privately owned and a National Historic Landmark.

WHITE HOUSE OF THE CONFEDERACY, in Richmond, was designed by Robert Mills for Richmond physician John Brockenbrough. The residence was completed in 1818 and enlarged several times by subsequent owners. During the Civil War it served as the Executive Mansion of the Confederate States of America, and thus the official residence of Jefferson Davis and his family. Since 1894, the house has been owned by the Confederate Memorial Literary Society and maintained by the Museum of the Confederacy. It is a National Historic Landmark.

WICKHAM HOUSE, in Richmond, was built in 1812 for John Wickham, defense attorney for Aaron Burr, and was designed by Alexander Parris. While owned by the Valentine family, the house included sculptor Edward Virginius Valentine's extensive studio. It is now part of the Valentine Museum and is a National Historic Landmark.

WILTON, formerly in Henrico County, was built in 1753 by William Randolph II. In 1933 it was taken down and rebuilt in the city of Richmond. It is maintained by the National Society of the Colonial Dames of America.

WOODLAWN PLANTATION, in Fairfax County, was completed in 1805 on land that George Washington gave to his adopted daughter, Nelly Parke Custis, on the occasion of her marriage to Washington's nephew Lawrence Lewis. It was designed by William Thornton, first architect of the United States Capitol. The house is maintained by the National Trust for Historic Preservation.

WOODROW WILSON BIRTHPLACE, in Staunton, was completed about 1847 and served for more than eighty years as the manse of the First Presbyterian Church. The Reverend Joseph Wilson was pastor of the church from 1855 to 1857, and his son, the future president, was born in the house on 28 December 1856. A National Historic Landmark, the manse is maintained by the Woodrow Wilson Birthplace Foundation, Inc.

WYTHE HOUSE, in Williamsburg, was built and probably was designed by Richard Taliaferro at the time that he was repairing the Governor's Palace and adding its ballroom wing. His daughter Elizabeth married George Wythe, an American statesman and a signer of the Declaration of Independence, and this house was their home for many years. A National Historic Landmark, it is maintained by the Colonial Williamsburg Foundation, Inc.

A ca. 1930 view of Kerr Place in Onancock, built on a fifteen-hundred-acre tract that extended from Onancock Creek to the town of Tasley. Set deep in a large, wooded lawn with a circular drive, the house retains its original opulent yet pastoral setting much like an English country manor house.

Smithfield in Isle of Wight County is perhaps the best preserved of Virginia's early seaports.

SOME OTHER PLACES OF
HISTORICAL SIGNIFICANCE

In addition to houses and churches, a number of public and commercial buildings, monuments, battlefields, communities, and other places in Virginia have interesting and important historical associations.

ABERDEEN GARDENS HISTORIC DISTRICT, in Hampton, was built between 1934 and 1937 to replace local African American workers' substandard housing. The project was initiated by Hampton Institute (now Hampton University) and funded by the U.S. Department of the Interior's Division of Subsistence Housing. It was designed and built by an all-black labor force. Eleanor Roosevelt visited the 440-acre model community in 1938. The area was expanded in the 1940s and 1950s.

ABINGDON HISTORIC DISTRICT, in Washington County, comprises the best-preserved example of the many eighteenth-century communities established along the route of the Valley Turnpike. Founded in 1778, the town of Abingdon includes an unusually large number of brick Federal and antebellum buildings. It is also the home of the Barter Theatre, a repertory theater founded in 1933 by Robert Porterfield.

ACCOMAC HISTORIC DISTRICT, in Accomack County, consists of approximately one hundred and fifty varied examples of eighteenth- and nineteenth-century public buildings and dwellings, both vernacular and formal. The town, first called Matopkin, was an active court center as early as the 1670s and was formally established as the county seat in 1690. It was later known as Drummond or Drummondtown until renamed Accomac in 1893.

ALBEMARLE COUNTY COURTHOUSE HISTORIC DISTRICT, in Charlottesville, includes a courthouse, town hall, and the Swan and Eagle Taverns. Among the surviving law offices, perhaps the most notable is No. O ("No. Nothing") Court Square, a circa 1823 Federal-style building. The 1803 courthouse also served as a community church, or "Common temple." Thomas Jefferson occasionally attended services there.

ALEXANDRIA HISTORIC DISTRICT covers an area of almost one hundred blocks and contains the largest number and concentration of late-eighteenth and early-nineteenth-century urban buildings in Virginia. Among them are the Bank of Alexandria, completed in 1807; the Carlyle House, finished in 1752 for John Carlyle, a well-to-do merchant; Christ Church, built between 1767 and 1773, which George Washington often attended; the Friendship Fire Company, organized in 1774, to which Washington donated its first engine in 1775; Gadsby's Tavern, built in 1752 and now a National Historic Landmark, where Washington recruited volunteers in 1754 for the French and Indian War; and Robert E. Lee's boyhood home, which was built in 1795. Light-Horse Harry Lee, Robert E. Lee's father, brought his family there in 1812, and young R. E. Lee lived there intermittently until 1825.

ALMSHOUSE ANNEX, in Richmond, was completed circa 1908 as a separate, adjunct building for the city's African American poor. The main almshouse, completed in 1860–1861, was intended to care solely for Richmond's indigent white population. The annex building has been restored as low-income housing.

APPOMATTOX COURT HOUSE, in Appomattox County, was the scene of General Robert E. Lee's surrender to Union general Ulysses S. Grant on 9 April 1865. The village includes the old county courthouse, the home of Wilmer McLean where the surrender negotiations took place, and other period buildings. Maintained with an 1860s atmosphere by the National Park Service, the village is now a National Historical Park.

ATTUCKS THEATER, in Norfolk, was completed in 1919 and designed by African American architect Harvey M. Johnson. Named for Crispus Attucks, a black man killed in the "Boston Massacre" of 1770 and perhaps the first casualty of the American Revolution, the theater was built and operated exclusively by blacks during the era of segregation.

BANNEKER SW-9 INTERMEDIATE BOUNDARY STONE, in Arlington County, at the intersection of Eighteenth and Van Buren Streets, was placed in 1792 to mark the westernmost point of the District of Columbia. The district's boundaries were surveyed by Major Andrew Ellicott (1754–1820), assisted by Benjamin Banneker (1731–1806), an African American mathematician, scientist, and surveyor. It is a National Historic Landmark.

BEN VENUE, in Rappahannock County, was built between 1844 and 1846 and is attributed to James Leake Powers, a local builder. The plantation site includes three brick slave-houses, unique Virginia examples of African American plantation housing constructed with such conscious and detailed architectural features.

BLUEMONT HISTORIC DISTRICT, in Loudoun County, includes turn-of-the-century as well as earlier stone and log structures. Located on the eastern slope of the Blue Ridge, the town was originally known as Snickers Gap and by 1824 as Snickersville. The community straddled one of the major routes between the Shenandoah Valley and tidewater ports along the Potomac River. Renamed Bluemont, the former trading center by the 1920s had become a resort community.

CAPE HENRY, in Virginia Beach, was the site of the first landing of the English settlers in Virginia in 1607. The site is commemorated with a granite cross as the Cape Henry Memorial. It is located within the Fort Story military reservation and is maintained by the National Park Service as part of the Colonial National Historical Park. Also situated near the memorial is the Cape Henry Lighthouse, which is believed to be the first lighthouse built in the United States and is now a National Historic Landmark. Constructed by the federal government, it was completed about October 1792 and was used until it was replaced by a cast-iron lighthouse completed in 1881. The 1792 structure was deeded to the Association for the Preservation of Virginia Antiquities in 1930. The 1881 lighthouse has been under the command of the Fifth Coast Guard District since 1939.

CAPITOL OF VIRGINIA, in Richmond, is the meeting place of the Virginia General Assembly, the oldest legislative body in the Western Hemisphere. It also served as the capitol for the Confederate States of America. The central portion was

Cape Henry Lighthouses at Fort Story, Virginia Beach

built from plans provided by Thomas Jefferson and was completed in 1792. The wings were added in 1906, and further changes were completed in 1964. It is a National Historic Landmark.

CHIPPOKES PLANTATION, in Surry County, was settled as early as 1619. The older of the two houses there may have been built between 1805 and 1824 by Lucy Ludwell Paradise. The larger house was constructed in a somewhat Italianate style in 1854 by Albert Carroll Jones. In 1969 the houses and farm were given to the commonwealth of Virginia, and the plantation is now maintained as an exhibition farm by the Virginia Division of State Parks.

CITY POINT HISTORIC DISTRICT, in Hopewell, was settled as early as 1613. First called Bermuda City, the village was later known as Charles City Point and still later as City Point. Incorporated in 1826, it was annexed to Hopewell in 1923. During the 1864 Union campaign to capture Richmond, City Point served as the Federal army's headquarters and supply depot. During World War I, the town became the center of an extensive munitions industry.

CUMBERLAND GAP NATIONAL HISTORICAL PARK lies partly in Lee County, Virginia, and partly in adjacent areas of Kentucky and Tennessee. It includes the pass through the Cumberland Mountains by which thousands of pioneers traveled to Kentucky and the Ohio country during the late eighteenth century. The park is maintained by the National Park Service.

EGYPTIAN BUILDING, in Richmond, was the first building erected for the Medical College of Virginia. Completed in 1845, it was designed by Thomas Stewart, of Philadelphia, and is perhaps the finest example of Egyptian Revival architecture in the United States. It is a National Historic Landmark.

EXCHANGE HOTEL, in Orange County, was built in 1860 as a hostelry serving the railroad junction of Gordonsville. Because of its location, the building during the Civil War became part of the Gordonsville Receiving Hospital, which admitted more than twenty-three thousand Confederate casualties within only a year. A hotel again after the war, the building has been restored and is maintained by Historic Gordonsville, Inc.

FALMOUTH HISTORIC DISTRICT, in Stafford County, was established in 1727 at the farthest navigable point of the Rappahannock River. It remained a major trading center until 1850. Surviving buildings include a small Federal-period customhouse, an early-nineteenth-century brick warehouse, a large commercial building, as well as rare examples of vernacular workers' housing. Also within the district are the Federal-period Union Church and three eighteenth-century houses: Belmont, Carlton, and Clearview.

FINCASTLE HISTORIC DISTRICT, in Botetourt County, was named in honor of George, Lord Fincastle, son of John Murray, fourth earl of Dunmore, the last royal governor of Virginia. Founded in 1772, Fincastle served as one of the last outposts for settlers crossing the Shenandoah Valley toward the west. Several streets retain early weatherboarded log houses as well as various antebellum churches and a reconstructed Greek Revival county courthouse.

FORT MONROE, in Hampton, was built between 1819 and 1834 to protect the Hampton Roads area. It was designed by General Simon Bernard, a former military engineer under Napoleon Bonaparte. The largest enclosed fortification in the United States, it has never been captured by an enemy. Inside the fort is the Casemate Museum and the cell where Jefferson Davis was imprisoned in 1865. It remains an active United States Army installation and is a National Historic Landmark.

FRANKLIN AND ARMFIELD OFFICE, in Alexandria, served from 1828 to 1836 as one of the largest slave-trading companies in the South. At its height, the business traded in thousands of slaves each year. The building served other slave-trading businesses until 1861, when Union authorities converted it to use as a prison. The building is a National Historic Landmark.

FREDERICKSBURG HISTORIC DISTRICT contains an important concentration of colonial and antebellum buildings. Among the most interesting buildings are the James Monroe Museum and Memorial Library (now a National Historic Landmark), originally Monroe's law office, built in the 1750s; the Hugh Mercer Apothecary Shop, built in 1761; the Rising Sun Tavern (now a National Historic Landmark), built about 1760 by Charles Washington, youngest brother of George

Washington, and the site of the organization of the Virginia Society of the Cincinnati in 1783; and Stoner's Store Museum, founded in 1957, which contains items that would have been found in country stores from the revolutionary period to the 1890s.

FREDERICKSBURG AND SPOTSYLVANIA NATIONAL MILITARY PARK consists of terrain and landmarks involved in the Battles of Fredericksburg (13 December 1862), Chancellorsville (1–4 May 1863), the Wilderness (5–7 May 1864), and Spotsylvania Courthouse (8–18 May 1864). Also included in this area is the restored building near Guinea Station where Thomas J. ("Stonewall") Jackson died on 10 May 1863 from wounds received at Chancellorsville. The military park is maintained by the National Park Service.

GENERAL DOUGLAS MacARTHUR MEMORIAL, in Norfolk, was formerly Norfolk's city hall and courthouse building. Built between 1847 and 1850, it was remodeled in 1960–1961 to serve as a memorial to General MacArthur, whose remains are buried under the rotunda.

GOOSE CREEK RURAL HISTORIC DISTRICT, in Loudoun County, consists of an area of approximately ten thousand acres and was home to Virginia's largest concentration of Quaker settlers, primarily English Friends who emigrated from Maryland, New Jersey, and Pennsylvania beginning in the 1730s. The district includes more examples of stone architecture than any other area of the state, while the central village of Lincoln encompasses a wide variety of eighteenth-, nineteenth-, and twentieth-century rural vernacular architecture. The Quaker farms were worked without slave labor and thus tended to be small enough to sustain a single family; many of the farm boundaries as originally patented still survive.

HANOVER COUNTY COURTHOUSE HISTORIC DISTRICT includes the courthouse that was built about 1733. It was the scene in 1763 of the famous Parsons' Cause trial, which brought young Patrick Henry to prominence. The courthouse is still in use and is a National Historic Landmark. Across the street is a rambling, two-story frame building that was Hanover Tavern. Construction began in 1723, and in 1760 the tavern was purchased by Patrick Henry's father-in-law. For many years the former tavern has housed the Barksdale Theatre. Since 1990, the building has been owned by the Hanover Tavern Foundation.

HARRISON SCHOOL, in Roanoke, was built in 1916 through the efforts of Lucy Addison and other African American educators to provide southwestern Virginia students with a secondary, academic education rather than the industrial, vocational curriculum usually mandated for black pupils. The former school building has been renovated for housing.

HOLLEY GRADED SCHOOL, in Northumberland County, was completed in 1933 and built with funds and labor donated solely by the county's African American citizens. The wood-frame schoolhouse now serves as a community center.

HOLLYWOOD CEMETERY, in Richmond, was dedicated in 1849. It is the burial place of James Monroe and John Tyler, presidents of the United States, and of many other distinguished Virginians, including John Randolph of Roanoke and oceanographer Matthew Fontaine Maury. Jefferson Davis, president of the Confederate States of America, is also buried there. The Monroe Tomb is a National Historic Landmark.

A late-nineteenth-century Memorial Day scene at the Confederate Monument in Richmond's Hollywood Cemetery, photographed by Huestis P. Cook *(Valentine Museum, Richmond, Virginia)*

HOWARD'S NECK, in Goochland County, was completed about 1825 for Edward Cunningham, a Richmond businessman, and was perhaps designed by Robert Mills. The property includes an assemblage of three double-pen, log slave-quarters, a common type of African American housing of which few examples survive in Virginia.

HOWLAND CHAPEL SCHOOL, in Northumberland County, was built in 1867 to educate the children of former slaves. Its construction was funded by New York philanthropist and reformer Emily Howland. It is currently owned by the First Baptist Church of Heathsville and is being used as a museum.

JACKSON WARD HISTORIC DISTRICT, in Richmond, was by the turn of the century among the foremost African American communities in the United States. It remains the nation's largest historic district related principally to black enterprise and culture. Among its noted residents were publisher John Mitchell Jr., banker Maggie L. Walker, clergymen W. W. Browne and John Jasper, entertainer Bill ("Bojangles") Robinson, and attorney Giles B. Jackson, the first black admitted to practice before the Supreme Court of Virginia. The district is a National Historic Landmark.

JAMESTOWN, in James City County, is the site of the first permanent English settlement in North America. It was the capital of the Virginia colony from 1607 to 1699. The site, which includes a reconstruction of the church and the excavated foundations of several seventeenth-century buildings, is maintained by the National Park Service and the Association for the Preservation of Virginia Antiquities.

LEE CHAPEL, in Lexington, is the burial place of Robert E. Lee, who served as president of Washington College (now Washington and Lee University) from 1865 until his death in 1870. The chapel, which contains the recumbent statue of Lee by Virginia-born sculptor Edward Virginius Valentine, is on the campus of Washington and Lee University and is a National Historic Landmark.

LOTT CARY BIRTH SITE, in Charles City County, a late-eighteenth-century vernacular dwelling, marks the sole remaining vestige of the plantation birth site of Lott Cary (1780–1829), the first African American missionary to Africa and a founder of the republic of Liberia.

MADDEN'S TAVERN, in Culpeper County, was designed and built about 1840 by Willis Madden, a free black. The rural vernacular building is perhaps the only example of an antebellum Virginia tavern owned and operated by an African American.

MANASSAS NATIONAL BATTLEFIELD PARK, near Bull Run Creek in Prince William County, includes sites connected with both the First Battle of Manassas on 21 July 1861 and the Second Battle of Manassas on 29 to 30 August 1862 and a large statue of General Thomas Jonathan Jackson, who gained the nickname Stonewall from his conduct in the first battle. The park is maintained by the National Park Service.

MEADOW FARM, in Henrico County, played a role in Gabriel's Rebellion, an 1800 slave revolt. Gabriel was owned by Thomas Prosser of a nearby farm. It was Mosby Sheppard, of Meadow Farm, who after being warned of the impending revolt by one of his own slaves informed Governor James Monroe in time to suppress the uprising. The site is administered by the Henrico County Division of Recreation and Parks.

MIDDLEBURG HISTORIC DISTRICT, in Loudoun County, encompasses a varied assemblage of eighteenth- to twentieth-century rural-Virginia structures. The town, founded in 1787, first grew as a way station on the Ashby's Gap Turnpike. During the Civil War the community was often the site of cavalry raids but throughout the conflict maintained a staunch loyalty to the Confederacy. Since about 1920 the Middleburg area has become internationally renowned as a horse-breeding and sporting center.

NEW MARKET BATTLEFIELD PARK, in Shenandoah County, is the site of the Battle of New Market, which took place on 15 May 1864. Virginia Military Institute cadets joined General John C. Breckinridge's Confederate brigades to defeat Union forces there. The Bushong House, a museum located in the center of the battle site, and the Hall of Valor Museum are maintained by the Virginia Military Institute.

NEWTOWN HISTORIC DISTRICT, in King and Queen County, during the late colonial period served as a tidewater crossroads village on the Great Post Road extending from Williamsburg to Philadelphia. The town was later the site of several private academies and during the Civil War was often traversed by Union and Confederate armies.

NORTHAMPTON COUNTY COURTHOUSE SQUARE HISTORIC DISTRICT, in the town of Eastville, has served as the seat of county government since 1690. The district's buildings include the 1731 courthouse (moved to its present site in 1913) and clerk's office as well as a debtors' prison (circa 1814). The three structures are maintained by the Association for the Preservation of Virginia Antiquities. The Eastern Shore court square also includes the present (and fifth) courthouse, completed in 1899, and the circa 1780 Eastville Inn.

OLD CHRISTIANSBURG INDUSTRIAL INSTITUTE AND SCHAEFFER MEMORIAL BAPTIST CHURCH, in Montgomery County, were built in 1885. The church is named for Captain Charles S. Schaeffer, an agent of the Freedmen's Bureau who helped establish a county education program in 1866. The buildings were used to provide schooling for the area's African American community.

OLD STONE HOUSE, in Richmond, built about 1737, is believed to be the oldest house in the city. Constructed of stone, a material seldom used in colonial architecture in eastern Virginia, the house is owned by the Association for the Preservation of Virginia Antiquities and serves as part of the Edgar Allan Poe Museum.

PETERSBURG NATIONAL MILITARY PARK, in Prince George County, includes fortifications and entrenchments constructed by both the Union and the Confederate armies during the siege of Petersburg, which lasted from June 1864 until April 1865. The military park is maintained by the National Park Service.

PHOENIX BANK OF NANSEMOND, in Suffolk, was founded in 1919 and built in 1921 as a solely African American institution dedicated to serving Suffolk and Nansemond County's black laborers and farmers. The bank closed in 1931 and the building has since been used for various businesses; its exterior stone name-plaque survives.

PITTSYLVANIA COUNTY COURTHOUSE, in Chatham, was built in 1853. There in 1878 local African American citizens were denied the right to serve as grand

and petit jurors. As a result, the United States Supreme Court ruled that the county had violated the Civil Rights Act of 1875 and that the Fourteenth and Fifteenth Amendments empowered the federal government to extend its authority further in behalf of black citizens. The courthouse is a National Historic Landmark.

POCAHONTAS EXHIBITION MINE, in Tazewell County, is one section of a larger mine opened in 1882 by the Pocahontas Collieries Company. The exhibition mine was opened to the public in 1938.

PORT ROYAL HISTORIC DISTRICT, in Caroline County, was established in 1744 as a tobacco port along the banks of the Rappahannock River. Bypassed by railroad development in the early nineteenth century, once-thriving Port Royal survives within its original boundaries and with much of its original appearance intact. Its historic buildings include Saint Peter's Episcopal Church and its colonial-era rectory. Confederate nurse Sally Tompkins and writer George Fitzhugh were natives of Port Royal.

RICHMOND NATIONAL BATTLEFIELD PARK, in Henrico and Hanover Counties, includes the sites of the Seven Days' Battle (26 June–1 July 1862), Cold Harbor (1–3 June 1864), and other engagements in the vicinity of the Confederate capital, as well as fortifications used by both sides during the sieges of Richmond. The park is maintained by the National Park Service.

SAINT LUKE BUILDING, in Richmond, was constructed in 1903 and is the oldest African American–affiliated office building in the city. The structure served as the national headquarters of the Independent Order of Saint Luke, a black benevolent society formed after the Civil War to encourage savings, to provide financial aid as well as health and insurance benefits, and to bolster business enterprises. The organization for many years was under the leadership of Maggie Lena Walker, the first woman in the United States to establish and direct a bank.

SAYLERS CREEK BATTLEFIELD PARK, in Amelia and Prince Edward Counties, encompasses the site of the last major battle (6 April 1865) fought by the Army of Northern Virginia. The park is maintained by the commonwealth of Virginia and is a National Historic Landmark.

SCOTTSVILLE HISTORIC DISTRICT, in Albemarle County, includes approximately one hundred period buildings, many of them of the antebellum period. Scott's Landing, later Scottsville, originated after settler Edward Scott patented the land in 1732. The small settlement at the large horseshoe bend of the James River grew to become one of Virginia's largest flour markets during the heyday of the James River and Kanawha Canal. The town was severely damaged during a Union raid in 1865 and thereafter steadily declined as a commercial center. Its abrupt decline, however, left its surviving vernacular houses and Classical Revival churches essentially unchanged.

SMITHFIELD HISTORIC DISTRICT, in Isle of Wight County, consists of approximately fifty period buildings, including a 1752 courthouse. Founded in 1749 on the banks of the Pagan River, Smithfield remains perhaps the best preserved of Virginia's eighteenth-century seaports. The community is also internationally known for the production of Smithfield hams.

TREDEGAR IRON WORKS, in Richmond, served as the Confederacy's foremost iron manufacturer. The company flourished from the 1840s until after the Civil War and its fortunes corresponded with Richmond's rise and decline as a center of southern industry. The site is a National Historic Landmark and currently part of the Valentine Riverside museum complex.

TRUXTON HISTORIC DISTRICT, in Portsmouth, includes 250 houses within a forty-two-acre neighborhood. Named for Thomas Truxton, an early naval hero, the community was built in 1918 by the U.S. Housing Corporation, a federal agency, to house wartime workers employed at the Norfolk Naval Shipyard in Portsmouth. The development was the first wartime government housing project built exclusively for African Americans.

UPPERVILLE HISTORIC DISTRICT, in Fauquier County, includes numerous nineteenth-century brick, wood, and log structures. Laid out as a township in 1797 along the route of the Alexandria-Winchester Turnpike, the small community was divided into a commercial and a residential sector, the latter at the hamlet's upper end, for which the community is named. Upperville is among Virginia's best-preserved linear villages, those early communities that grew with the regional commerce that traversed their primary thoroughfare.

WARRENTON HISTORIC DISTRICT, in Fauquier County, began as a small crossroads village that by 1759 had become the county seat. Until its incorporation in 1810, the town was known as Fauquier Court House. It was renamed for Warren Academy, the first of many private academies and seminaries located there, and still includes an extraordinary number of nineteenth-century commercial, residential, and governmental structures.

WASHINGTON HISTORIC DISTRICT, in Rappahannock County, was named for George Washington, who as a young surveyor platted the town's grid plan in 1749. Incorporated in 1796, the town in 1833 became the county seat when Rappahannock County was formed from Culpeper County. The 1833 courthouse was built by Malcolm F. Crawford, one of Thomas Jefferson's craftsmen in the construction of the University of Virginia.

WATERFORD HISTORIC DISTRICT, in Loudoun County, began as a circa 1733 Quaker village. By the 1830s the Quakers had established a thriving milling community that included seventy houses as well as numerous commercial buildings constructed in the regional vernacular style. Many of the town's original structures survive. The district is a National Historic Landmark.

WEYANOKE PLANTATION, in Charles City County, was first settled perhaps as early as 6500 B.C. By the early 1600s the area was inhabited by the Weyanoke Indians, one of the larger groups of the Powhatan chiefdom. English colonists settled the site in 1619 and evidence suggests that the first African Americans brought to North America also lived there. The property fell into disuse after the Indian raids of 1622. A small settlement was again established there in the 1650s. The present plantation house was built in 1798.

WILLIAMSBURG, in James City and York Counties, was the capital of Virginia from 1699 until 1780. The center of the city has been restored to its eighteenth-century appearance through the initial efforts of John D. Rockefeller Jr. and William Archer Rutherfoord Goodwin, rector of Bruton Parish Church, and the continuing work of the Colonial Williamsburg Foundation, Inc. The restored or reconstructed buildings in Williamsburg include the Capitol, the Governor's Palace, the Wren Building (a National Historic Landmark) at the College of William and Mary, Bruton Parish Church, Raleigh Tavern, and the Wythe House, as well as many other structures including two National Historic Landmarks, the Peyton Randolph and James Semple Houses. The Williamsburg Historic District itself is a National Historic Landmark.

YORKTOWN, in York County, was the scene of the final campaign of the Revolutionary War and of the surrender of General Charles Cornwallis's British army to French and American forces under General George Washington on 19 October 1781. The battlefield and the Moore House, where the surrender negotiations took place, are maintained by the National Park Service as part of Colonial National Historical Park.

"Lover's Leap" in Natural Tunnel State Park, Scott County

STATE PARKS, PRESERVES, FORESTS, AND WILDLIFE MANAGEMENT AREAS

On 1 July 1983, the Virginia Commission of Outdoor Recreation was merged with the Division of Parks to form the Division of Parks and Recreation, in 1988 renamed the Division of State Parks. The merger expanded the division's administrative functions and also assigned to it responsibility for the Old Dominion's more than three dozen recreational, historic, and natural-area parks. The division also manages 29.5 miles (795 acres) of the otherwise federally owned 543-mile-long Virginia section of the Appalachian National Scenic Trail.

The Old Dominion's system of state parks originated during the Great Depression. Of the fifteen Virginia state parks established during the 1930s and early 1940s, eleven were first developed as work projects of the federal government's Civilian Conservation Corps and soon thereafter transferred to the state's care and use. Four of the parks were further developed by the Virginia Division of Forestry and transferred to the state park system through the Cooperative Use Agreement of 1939. Two of the original parks—the George Washington Grist Mill and the Southwest Virginia Museum—were received by donation. One, the Saylers Creek park, the state acquired by both donation and purchase.

Virginia added two parks to the state system in the 1950s, and another nine during the 1960s. Two more were acquired in the 1970s. Three have been opened since. Still another, Belle Isle State Park encompassing 700 acres in Lancaster County, was acquired in 1993 and is under development. It is one of four state parks purchased since the 1992 Parks and Recreational Facilities bond issue; the other three are as yet unnamed.

As part of Virginia's Department of Conservation and Recreation, the Division of State Parks also manages six sites designated as protected natural areas: five were established in the 1960s and another in 1974. Although many state parks offer multiple attractions within a single site—historic attractions, lakes, picnic areas, or hiking trails, for example—Virginia state parks are divided into three broad categories as defined by each one's primary emphasis. Six are currently designated as historical parks, six as natural areas, and twenty-five as recreational parks.

In addition to its Division of State Parks, the Department of Conservation and Recreation also includes the Division of Natural Heritage, which manages another nine sites. Each is open to the public and is part of the Virginia Natural Area Preserve System. Authorized by the General Assembly in 1989 and in contrast to the more traditional system of state park–land acquisition, the program is designed to acquire through Conservation Easements only those ownership rights necessary to protect a site's environmental diversity.

Together, the Department of Conservation and Recreation's Divisions of State Parks and Natural Heritage administer forty-six sites. In addition, Virginia's Departments of Forestry and of Game and Inland Fisheries maintain eleven state forests and twenty-nine wildlife management areas with varying degrees of public access. Five of the state forests were established in the 1930s: one was acquired by donation, while four were first developed as federal woodlands. Twenty of the Wildlife Management Areas were established in the 1960s and 1970s.

Whether park, forest, or other protected area, many of Virginia's public lands have been enlarged tract by tract over many years, thus each entry's date of acquisition refers only to the initial purchase or donation of acreage. Collectively, the Old Dominion's eighty-six state parks, forests, preserves, and natural and wildlife management areas encompass more than 268,000 acres.

AMELIA WILDLIFE MANAGEMENT AREA, in Amelia County, encompasses 2,217 acres and includes the 105-acre Amelia Lake, completed in 1969 and opened for fishing in 1971. Adjacent to the area is an additional 1,000 acres of forest managed by the Westvaco and Chesapeake Corporations.

APPOMATTOX-BUCKINGHAM STATE FOREST, in Appomattox and Buckingham Counties, encompasses 19,705 acres near the headwaters of the Willis River. The land was acquired in the mid-1930s by the federal government under the Bankhead-Jones Farm Tenant Act, in 1939 leased to the commonwealth of Virginia, and in 1954 deeded to the state. Also acquired under the federal program were lands later incorporated as part of the Cumberland, Prince Edward–Gallion, and Pocahontas State Forests.

BEAR CREEK LAKE STATE PARK, in Cumberland County, was acquired in 1939 and was one of four recreation areas established in Virginia by the federal government's depression-era Civilian Conservation Corps. The park encompasses 150 acres amid the Cumberland State Forest, which includes a designated hiking path, the Willis River Trail. The land was previously controlled by the U.S. Department of Agriculture as part of its depression-era resettlement program.

BETHEL BEACH NATURAL AREA PRESERVE, in Mathews County, encompasses 50 acres and was acquired by The Nature Conservancy on behalf of the commonwealth under the Partners in Conservation Project. Dedicated in 1991, the preserve includes sandy-beach, low-dune, and salt-marsh habitats for several rare marsh- and nesting-bird species.

BIG SPRING BOG NATURAL AREA PRESERVE, in Grayson County, encompasses 50 acres and was acquired by The Nature Conservancy on behalf of the commonwealth under the Partners in Conservation Project. Dedicated in 1990, the preserve includes a rare wetland area known as a cranberry glade.

BOURASSA STATE FOREST, in the southern portion of Bedford County, adjoins Smith Mountain Lake at two points and encompasses 288 acres. The forestland was donated to the state in 1968 by J. Leo Bourassa and Hester R. Bourassa.

BREAKS INTERSTATE PARK, in Dickenson County, near Breaks, Virginia, encompasses 4,500 acres spanning the Virginia-Kentucky border and was created in 1956 by joint action of the two state legislatures. The park includes a deep gorge shaped over many centuries by a mountain stream, Russell Fork.

BRIERY CREEK WILDLIFE MANAGEMENT AREA, in Prince Edward County, encompasses 2,968 acres. Opened in 1989, the area also includes the 845-acre Briery Creek Lake, completed in 1986. The south-central piedmont area includes both waterfowl and small game habitats.

BUSH MILL STREAM NATURAL AREA PRESERVE, in Northumberland County, encompasses 110 acres. The preserve was acquired in 1992 with the assistance of The Nature Conservancy, the Northern Neck Audubon Society, the Open Space Recreation and Conservation income tax check-off fund, and individual citizens. Located at the juncture of the Bush Mill Stream and Great Wicomico River, the preserve includes fresh-to-brackish tidal marshes and numerous waterfowl and wading birds.

C. F. PHELPS WILDLIFE MANAGEMENT AREA, in Fauquier and Culpeper Counties along the Rappahannock River, was acquired in 1975 and encompasses 4,540 acres. The area was named for Chester F. Phelps, longtime director of the Commission of Game and Inland Fisheries. Prior to the commission's purchase of the land, it was used primarily for farming. The area includes portions of the Rappahannock River, designated officially as one of Virginia's scenic waterways. The area also includes a small museum featuring memorabilia associated with C. F. Phelps.

CALEDON NATURAL AREA, in King George County, was established in 1974 and encompasses 2,529 acres along the Potomac River. The park serves as summer home for one of the most extensive concentrations of American bald eagles on the East Coast.

CHARLES C. STEIRLY HERON ROOKERY NATURAL AREA, near Waverly, in Sussex County, was established in 1964 and encompasses 19 acres of swampland donated to the commonwealth of Virginia in order to preserve one of the state's few remaining heron rookeries.

CHICKAHOMINY WILDLIFE MANAGEMENT AREA, on the eastern edge of Charles City County, encompasses 6,000 acres. Acquired in 1972, it is unique among Virginia's tidewater wildlife management areas in that it includes mostly woodland and is managed for upland game rather than wetland species. The wildlife habitat includes beaver and turkey.

CHIPPOKES PLANTATION STATE PARK, in Surry County, was acquired by donation and established in 1967. The park encompasses 1,683 acres on the south shore of the James River. The site is named for Choupocke (or Choapoke), an early-seventeenth-century Native American chief, and has been farmed continuously for more than three and a half centuries. The park is operated as a farm and museum and includes the Historic Chippokes Plantation.

CLAYTOR LAKE STATE PARK, near Dublin, in Pulaski County, was acquired by donation in 1946 and established in 1951. The park encompasses 472 acres and overlooks the 5,000-acre Claytor Lake. The site includes the circa 1876 Italianate-style Howe House, currently used as the park's visitor center.

CLINCH MOUNTAIN WILDLIFE MANAGEMENT AREA, in Russell, Smyth, Tazewell, and Washington Counties, encompasses 25,477 acres, including the Black Cherry Natural Area. Acquired in 1961, the wildlife management area along the Appalachian Mountain Range also includes thirty-five miles of hiking trails and the 300-acre Laurel Bed Lake and several trout streams, including Big Tumbling Creek. The park is jointly administered by Virginia's Department of Conservation and Recreation and the Department of Game and Inland Fisheries.

CONWAY-ROBINSON MEMORIAL STATE FOREST, in Prince William County near Gainesville, encompasses 400 acres astride U.S. Route 29. Administered by the Virginia Department of Forestry, the forestland was donated to the state in 1938 by the Conway-Robinson Park Memorial Association. The area includes a Civil War–era railroad bed. Both the Virginia Federation of Garden Clubs and the Daughters of the American Revolution maintain monuments adjacent to Route 29.

CROOKED CREEK WILDLIFE MANAGEMENT AREA, in the mountainous region of Carroll County near Galax, is primarily a trout-fishing area. Acquired in 1972, the area encompasses 1,785 acres. Six miles of Crooked Creek and the East Fork Crooked Creek are used for trout fishing.

CUMBERLAND STATE FOREST, in Cumberland County, encompasses 16,779 acres. The land was acquired in the mid-1930s by the federal government under the Bankhead-Jones Farm Tenant Act, in 1939 leased to the commonwealth of Virginia, and in 1954 deeded to the state. The forest's eleven-mile-long Willis River Trail traverses the Rock Quarry Natural Area and overlooks Winston Lake and Horn Quarter Creek.

DICK CROSS WILDLIFE MANAGEMENT AREA, on the north bank of the Roanoke River in Mecklenburg County, was established in 1963 and encompasses 1,372 acres. Formerly known as the Elm Hill Wildlife Management Area, it was rededicated in 1991 in honor of Richard Hunter Cross Jr., a forty-five-year staff member of the Department of Game and Inland Fisheries. The site is unusual among Virginia's wildlife management areas in that it is used extensively for sanctioned hunting-dog field trials. The site also includes Elm Hill, built circa 1769 and once home to Sir Peyton Skipwith.

DOUTHAT STATE PARK, in Alleghany and Bath Counties, near Clifton Forge, was acquired in 1933 and established in 1936. The park encompasses 4,493 acres within the Allegheny Mountains and is traversed by 45 miles of trails. A federal project of the New Deal, the park was completed between 1933 and 1942 and includes a 50-acre lake as well as more than forty structures completed by the Civilian Conservation Corps.

FAIRY STONE FARMS WILDLIFE MANAGEMENT AREA, in Henry and Patrick Counties northwest of Martinsville, was acquired in 1963. The area encompasses 5,343 acres and encircles Fairy Stone State Park. An additional 7,000 acres are accessible through cooperative agreements with the Division of State Parks and the U.S. Army Corps of Engineers.

FAIRY STONE STATE PARK, in Henry and Patrick Counties, was acquired in 1933 and established in 1936 and encompasses 4,570 acres amid the foothills of the Blue Ridge Mountains. The park is named for the intricate cross-shaped crystals often found in the area. The park includes more than twenty depression-era structures built between 1933 and 1938 by the Civilian Conservation Corps and a 168-acre lake adjoining the Philpott Reservoir.

FALSE CAPE STATE PARK, southwest of Virginia Beach, was established in 1968 and encompasses 4,321 acres. Inaccessible to vehicles, the park preserves an undeveloped area of the Atlantic coastline's Outer Banks. Located adjacent to the Back Bay National Wildlife Refuge and along the Atlantic Flyway, the park annually hosts an extensive migratory bird population.

Civilian Conservation Corps at work on the dam and lake site for Douthat State Park near Clifton Forge (*above*). The lake shortly after completion (*below*).

G. RICHARD THOMPSON WILDLIFE MANAGEMENT AREA, in Fauquier County with portions in Warren and Clarke Counties, was acquired in 1971 and encompasses 4,160 acres along the slopes of the Blue Ridge Mountains. The area also includes Thompson Lake and is traversed by the Appalachian National Scenic Trail. Sky Meadows State Park adjoins the wildlife management area on its northeastern edge.

GATHRIGHT WILDLIFE MANAGEMENT AREA, in Bath County west of Warm Springs, is located atop three mountains—the Allegheny, Bolar, and Coles—and was purchased by the Department of Game and Inland Fisheries in 1958. It encompasses 13,428 acres, including the 2,500-acre Lake Moomaw formed by the Gathright Dam at the Jackson River Gorge.

GEORGE WASHINGTON GRIST MILL HISTORICAL PARK, in Fairfax County, was acquired and established in 1932 as part of the Washington Bicentennial celebration and encompasses 7 acres. It is the commonwealth's first state park and first historical park. While the original eighteenth-century mill on Dogue Run no longer exists, the site includes buildings reconstructed by the Civilian Conservation Corps using materials and machinery from a similar mill of the period.

GOSHEN PASS NATURAL AREA, in Rockbridge County, near Goshen, was acquired by donation in 1961 and encompasses 936 acres on the southwest face of Little North Mountain. The slope is divided into three ridges extending from the peak's highest point at 3,600 feet. The Department of Highways and Transportation maintains a wayside area at the pass.

GOSHEN WILDLIFE MANAGEMENT AREA, in Rockbridge County, was acquired in 1960. The area encompasses 16,128 acres and includes three major mountains: Bratton, Forge, and Hogback, the last peak reaching 3,451 feet. Adjacent to the area is the Deerfield Ranger District of the George Washington National Forest.

GRAYSON HIGHLANDS STATE PARK, in Grayson County, was established in 1965 and encompasses 4,754 acres. Several depression-era farm buildings as well as a circa 1880 family graveyard are adjacent to the park area. Located near Mount Rogers, the Old Dominion's highest point above sea level, the park provides views of 5,000-foot-high peaks.

HARDWARE RIVER WILDLIFE MANAGEMENT AREA, in the southwestern corner of Fluvanna County near Scottsville, was purchased in 1972 and encompasses 1,034 acres. Subject to frequent flooding, the area borders a one-and-a-half-mile stretch of the James River and is drained by two waterways, the Hardware River and Doby Creek.

HAVENS WILDLIFE MANAGEMENT AREA, in Roanoke County near Salem, encompasses 7,160 acres on Lewis Mountain. The Department of Game and Inland Fisheries purchased most of the tract in 1930. The area's steep terrain includes several small streams and is generally inaccessible except to the hike-in nature enthusiast.

HIDDEN VALLEY WILDLIFE MANAGEMENT AREA, in Washington County, was acquired in 1961 and encompasses 6,400 acres on Brumley Mountain. Sixteen miles of hiking trails traverse the area, which includes Brumley Creek and the 60-acre Hidden Valley Lake.

HIGHLAND WILDLIFE MANAGEMENT AREA, in Highland County near Monterey, was acquired in 1962 and encompasses 13,993 acres in three separate forest tracts. Seventeen miles of hiking trails traverse an area that includes Jack and Bullpasture Mountains and the 4,200-foot-high Sounding Knob. The Bullpasture and Cowpasture Rivers flow through the area and a cable suspension footbridge crosses the Bullpasture at Bullpasture Gorge just north of Williamsville.

HOG ISLAND WILDLIFE MANAGEMENT AREA, in Surry County near the town of Surry and across Lawnes Creek in Isle of Wight County, was acquired in 1950 and encompasses 3,908 acres divided among several tracts. The name is derived from the seventeenth-century practice of leaving hogs on islands where they could forage unfettered but still restricted. The site is managed primarily as a wintering area for waterfowl.

HOLLIDAY LAKE STATE PARK, in Appomattox County, was established in 1939 and encompasses 250 acres, including a 150-acre lake, within the 19,705-acre Appomattox-Buckingham State Forest. The park was one of four recreation areas established in Virginia by the federal government's depression-era Civilian Conservation Corps. The land was previously controlled by the U.S. Department of Agriculture as part of its depression-era resettlement program.

HORSEPEN LAKE WILDLIFE MANAGEMENT AREA, near the geographic center of Virginia (Mount Rush) in Buckingham County, was acquired in 1974 and encompasses 3,000 acres of rolling hills and the 18-acre Horsepen Lake. Formerly one of the U.S. Forest Service's woodland research sites, the area includes mink, muskrat, otter, and wood duck.

HUNGRY MOTHER STATE PARK, in Smyth County near Marion, was acquired in 1933 and established in 1936 and encompasses 2,180 acres. Completed between 1935 and 1940 by the Civilian Conservation Corps, the park includes a 108-acre lake as well as the Hemlock Haven Conference Center. Mollys Knob, at 3,270 feet, forms the park's highest elevation.

JAMES RIVER WILDLIFE MANAGEMENT AREA, on the northwest bank of the James River in Nelson County near Wingina, was acquired in 1968 and encompasses 671 acres including 3,300 feet fronting the river. The area also includes 200 acres of open land once used for pasture and cropland.

JOHNSON CREEK NATURAL AREA PRESERVE, in Alleghany County, encompasses 105 acres and was acquired by The Nature Conservancy on behalf of the commonwealth under the Partners in Conservation Project. Dedicated in 1990, the preserve ranks among Virginia's finest shale-barren habitats and includes numerous rare plant species.

KIPTOPEKE STATE PARK, in Northampton County, was established in 1992 and encompasses 375 acres along a major flyway for migratory birds. The park's coastal dune environment on the Chesapeake Bay side of the Eastern Shore also provides a habitat for several rare animal species.

LAKE ANNA STATE PARK, in Spotsylvania County, was established in 1972 and encompasses 2,058 acres, including eight and a half miles of shoreline along the Lake Anna Reservoir. The park also includes remnants of a former gold-mining enterprise.

LEESYLVANIA STATE PARK, in Prince William County, was established in 1975 and encompasses 505 acres, including river bluffs, beach area, and a forest of holly trees. Listed on the National Register of Historic Places in 1984, Leesylvania was once the site of the Lee family home.

LESESNE STATE FOREST, in Nelson County, was established in 1968 and encompasses 421 acres. The land was donated by Anne du Pont Valk and Dr. Arthur de T. Valk Jr. The forest includes one of the world's largest stands of hybrid chestnut trees.

LICK CREEK NATURAL AREA, in Smyth and Bland Counties, was established in 1961 and encompasses 836 acres between the southern slope of Carter Mountain and the northern slope of Brush Mountain. Between the slopes converge valleys formed by Lick and Lynn Camp Creeks. Ridges rising to approximately 3,200 feet tower above the waterways.

LITTLE NORTH MOUNTAIN WILDLIFE MANAGEMENT AREA, in Augusta and Rockbridge Counties, was acquired in 1958. The area extends along a thirty-mile-long strip of Little North Mountain, encompassing 17,538 acres and joining the Goshen Wildlife Management Area at the latter's northern end. The area is criss-crossed by thirty-seven miles of access roads.

MASON NECK STATE PARK, in Fairfax County, near Woodbridge, was acquired by donation and established in 1967. Encompassing 1,804 acres, the recreational area is adjacent to the Mason Neck National Wildlife Refuge.

MOCKHORN ISLAND WILDLIFE MANAGEMENT AREA, in Northampton County, was acquired in 1959 and encompasses 9,452 acres. The 342-acre Gatr Tract, also on the ocean side of Northampton County, was acquired in 1981 and is administered as part of the Mockhorn Island area. One of the Atlantic coastline's endangered barrier islands, the Eastern Shore area is accessible only by boat. Predominantly a tidal marsh, the island is home to a wide variety of waterfowl, including heron, egret, clapper rail, black duck, bufflehead, and goldeneye.

NATURAL TUNNEL STATE PARK, in Scott County, was acquired and established in 1967 and encompasses 603 acres. The park includes a 850-foot-long, ten-story-high natural tunnel carved from a limestone ridge over a period of thousands of centuries. The passage was first used as a railway tunnel in the 1880s by the South Atlantic and Ohio Railway.

NEW RIVER TRAIL STATE PARK, in Grayson and Wythe Counties, was established in 1987 and encompasses 399 acres spread along a fifty-seven-mile-long linear greenway that follows the course of an abandoned railroad right-of-way from Galax to Pulaski. Twenty-nine miles of the trail follow the course of the New River.

NIDAY PLACE STATE FOREST, in the southeastern part of Craig County on Johns Creek Mountain, encompasses 218.75 acres. The first state forest established west of Roanoke, the land was donated in 1988 by Anne H. Cutler.

NORTH LANDING RIVER NATURAL AREA PRESERVE, in Virginia Beach, encompasses 1,886 acres and was acquired by The Nature Conservancy on behalf of the commonwealth and with the cooperation of the National Fish and Wildlife Foundation and Ducks Unlimited. Dedicated in 1990, the preserve includes forested swampland and freshwater tidal marshes supporting as many as twenty-seven rare species of wildlife.

OCCONEECHEE STATE PARK, in Mecklenburg County, was established in 1968 and encompasses 2,690 acres. The park is named for the Occaneechi Indians who lived in the area from circa 1250 to the late 1600s. The park is located on a wooded peninsula on the north shore of the John H. Kerr Reservoir, popularly known as Buggs Island Lake.

PARKERS MARSH NATURAL AREA, in Accomack County, was established by donation in 1960 and encompasses 758 acres. The area is bordered by Onancock Creek to the south, Back Creek on the north, and the Chesapeake Bay to the west. Parkers Marsh is accessible only by boat or by wading across the "Thorofare," a canal connecting Back and Onancock Creeks.

PAUL STATE FOREST, known locally as "Paul's Woods," is located in "the heart of the Shenandoah Valley" southwest of Harrisonburg in Rockingham County and encompasses 173 acres. It was donated to the Virginia Department of Forestry in 1963 by Judge John Paul for "such purposes as experimentation in or demonstration of approved forestry practices."

PETTIGREW WILDLIFE MANAGEMENT AREA, in Caroline County, encompasses 934 acres and was acquired from Fort A. P. Hill in 1979. At one time sea bottom, the tract includes Mount and Ware Creeks, the former containing many beaver impoundments. The habitat also supports muskrat and otter.

PINNACLE NATURAL AREA PRESERVE, in Russell County, encompasses 90 acres. Acquired by Russell County in 1946 and long known as Big Cedar Creek Park, the site was conveyed by the county in 1989 to The Nature Conservancy for transfer to the commonwealth. The preserve includes a 600-foot-high rock formation, the Pinnacle, from which the site derives its name.

POCAHONTAS STATE FOREST, in Chesterfield County, encompasses 5,873 acres. The land was acquired in the mid-1930s by the federal government under the Bankhead-Jones Farm Tenant Act, in 1939 leased to the commonwealth of Virginia, and in 1954 deeded to the state.

POCAHONTAS STATE PARK, in Chesterfield County, was established in 1939 and deeded to Virginia in 1946. The park encompasses 1,783 acres within the 5,873-acre Pocahontas State Forest. The park includes two lakes, Swift Creek and Beaver, and three hiking trails: Beaver Lake Nature Trail, the Awareness Trail, and the Grist Mill Bicycle Trail. Formerly known as the Swift Creek Recreation Area and completed between 1935 and 1940, the park was one of only two Recreation Demonstration Areas in Virginia developed by the National Park Service under the Federal Emergency Relief Land Program of 1934. The Civilian Conservation Corps completed more than forty structures for the park. It is the only Virginia state park designed specifically for utilization by large groups.

POOR MOUNTAIN NATURAL AREA PRESERVE, in Roanoke County, encompasses 1,000 acres and was acquired by The Nature Conservancy on behalf of the commonwealth. Dedicated in 1990, the preserve includes the world's largest assemblage of the piratebush, a rare shrub. The area is named for its impoverished soil, derived from shale and sandstone bedrock.

POWHATAN WILDLIFE MANAGEMENT AREA, in Powhatan County, was acquired in 1963 and encompasses 4,415 acres and a thirty-mile network of hiking trails. The area remains one of the few Virginia wildlife-management sites with an extensive trail system; the area also includes two lakes and four ponds.

PRINCE EDWARD–GALLION STATE FOREST, in eastern Prince Edward County, encompasses 6,964 acres. The forest provides a habitat for deer and turkey and surrounds Twin Lakes State Park. The land was acquired in the mid-1930s by the federal government under the Bankhead-Jones Farm Tenant Act, in 1939 leased to the commonwealth of Virginia, and in 1954 deeded to the state.

PRINCESS ANNE WILDLIFE MANAGEMENT AREA, in Virginia Beach, is located in and around Back Bay. Acquired in 1963 and formerly known as the Trojan-Pocahontas and Barbours Hill Wildlife Management Area, the multiple-tract site was renamed in 1993. Barbours Hill is part of False Cape State Park and contains a group of marshy coves and points along the cape, with some high ground and dunes. Trojan, with 406 acres, is made of up marshy shoreline; Pocahontas encompasses 737 acres of marsh islands. All three areas are part of a large, coastal freshwater bay separated from the Atlantic Ocean by the narrow barrier beach, False Cape. Among the area's attractions are many varieties of migratory and resident birds. The north-central section of the bay includes the Back Bay National Wildlife Refuge.

RAGGED ISLAND WILDLIFE MANAGEMENT AREA, in Isle of Wight County on the James River at the southern end of the James River Bridge, was acquired in 1977 and encompasses 1,537 acres of brackish-water marsh and small pine-covered islands. Financed through the Nongame Wildlife and Endangered Species Program, a long boardwalk and trail provide access to the marsh area.

RAPIDAN WILDLIFE MANAGEMENT AREA, in Madison and Greene Counties, was acquired in 1963 and encompasses ten tracts totaling 9,525 acres. Traversed by the Conway and Rapidan Rivers as well as Devils Ditch, the area offers steep terrain rising from 900 to 3,000 feet. The area also includes remnants of long-abandoned mountain cabins and of rock piles where small fields were cleared. Black bear and brook trout abound in the area.

SAXIS WILDLIFE MANAGEMENT AREA, on Pocomoke Sound in northwestern Accomack County, appears much like an island but is actually a peninsula encompassing 5,775 acres of tidal marsh interspersed with points of forested high-ground called hammocks. Acquired in 1957, the habitat includes loon, heron, and egret in abundance as well as muskrat, red fox, gray fox, mink, and river otter.

SAYLERS CREEK BATTLEFIELD HISTORICAL PARK, in Amelia County, was acquired and established by donation in 1937. The park encompasses 221 acres. There on 6 April 1865, thereafter known by Confederate veterans as Black Thursday, the Army of Northern Virginia on its retreat from Petersburg sustained a crippling defeat, losing at least a quarter of what remained of Robert E. Lee's army. It was the last major battle before the surrender at Appomattox Courthouse.

SEASHORE STATE PARK AND NATURAL AREA, in Virginia Beach, was acquired in 1933 and established in 1936. Together, the park and natural area encompass 2,670 acres. Built between 1935 and 1940, the park despite its susceptibility to weather damage retains a number of its original structures. The site faces two waterfronts: the Chesapeake Bay on one side and on the other a collection of creeks and lakes known as Broad Bay, Crystal Lake, Linkhorn Bay, and Lynnhaven Inlet. As of 1991, it was the most-visited Virginia state park. Most of the park is made up of the Seashore Natural Area, established in 1960 and encompassing 2,570 acres of dunes and other natural elements of a beach environment. The park's twenty-five miles of trails, including the Baldcypress Nature Trail, are designated part of the National Recreation Trails System. The seashore was designated a National Natural Landmark in 1965.

SHOT TOWER HISTORICAL STATE PARK, in Wythe County, was acquired and established in 1964 and opened to the pubic in 1968. The park encompasses 7 acres. Built in 1807 and located on a bluff overlooking the New River, the park's seventy-five-foot-high tower was used in the manufacture of munitions for area settlers. The site is a National Historic Landmark.

SKY MEADOWS STATE PARK, in Clarke and Fauquier Counties, was established in 1975 and encompasses 1,132 acres in the Blue Ridge Mountains. The park area includes two mid-nineteenth-century farmsteads, the Mount Bleak and Turner farms, and a circa 1830 log slave-dwelling. The park also serves as an access to the Appalachian National Scenic Trail.

SMITH MOUNTAIN LAKE STATE PARK, in Bedford County, was established in 1967 with the purchase of the antebellum Five Oaks Plantation and other acreage. The park encompasses 1,506 acres along the north shore of Smith Mountain Lake, the second-largest freshwater lake in the Old Dominion.

SOUTHWEST VIRGINIA MUSEUM, in Big Stone Gap, Wise County, was donated to the commonwealth of Virginia in 1943 and encompasses 8 acres. The site includes the house of Rufus Ayers (1849–1926), attorney general of Virginia from 1886 to 1890, and is representative of the many imposing mansions built in the Big Stone Gap area in the late nineteenth century. The four-story house was first preserved by former Virginia Congressman C. Bascom Slemp (1870–1943), who bequeathed it to the citizens of Virginia. The house was opened as a museum in 1948.

STAUNTON RIVER BRIDGE BATTLEFIELD HISTORICAL STATE PARK, in Halifax County, was acquired in 1957 and encompasses 7 acres. There, on 25 June 1864, a Confederate force of less than one thousand old men and boys defended a railroad bridge from an attacking force of more than two thousand Federals. The site commemorates the area's sole Civil War engagement.

STAUNTON RIVER STATE PARK, in Halifax County, was acquired in 1933 and established in 1936. The park encompasses 1,414 acres on a peninsula extending out into Buggs Island Lake. It was the only one of eleven Virginia parks constructed by the Civilian Conservation Corps to include a swimming-pool complex.

STEWARTS CREEK WILDLIFE MANAGEMENT AREA, in Carroll County, was acquired in 1988 and opened in 1989. The area encompasses 1,100 acres along the North and South Forks of Stewarts Creek. The mountainous wildlife habitat includes brook trout, grouse, and turkey.

TABB MONUMENT HISTORICAL PARK, in Amelia County, was established in 1936 and encompasses a 1-acre tract, on which is erected a marker to the memory of noted Virginia poet and philosopher John Banister Tabb (1845-1909), a Catholic priest.

TURKEYCOCK MOUNTAIN WILDLIFE MANAGEMENT AREA, in the southeast corner of Franklin County, was acquired in 1981 and encompasses 2,679 acres in a rugged mountainous terrain drained by numerous small streams. Established in the late 1980s, the area supports a variety of wildlife including turkey.

TWIN LAKES STATE PARK, in Prince Edward County, was established by the federal government and transferred to the commonwealth of Virginia in 1939. The park encompasses 470 acres within the Prince Edward–Gallion State Forest. Twin Lakes combines two previously separate recreational facilities: Goodwin Lake State Park and Prince Edward Lake State Park, the latter redeveloped in the 1950s as a separate park for blacks. During the segregation era, Prince Edward Lake State Park was Virginia's only state park open to African Americans. The parks were two of the four recreational areas established in Virginia by the federal government's depression-era Civilian Conservation Corps.

WESTMORELAND STATE PARK, near Montross, in Westmoreland County, was acquired in 1933 and established in 1936 and encompasses 1,295 acres along the south shore of the Potomac River. Along the park's shoreline are cliffs among which can be seen fossils exposed by tidal erosion. Most of the original Civilian Conservation Corps buildings completed between 1935 and 1940 survive.

WHITE OAK MOUNTAIN WILDLIFE MANAGEMENT AREA, in Pittsylvania County, was acquired in 1967 and encompasses 2,712 acres of rolling, hilly terrain on the north and south slopes of the White Oak Mountain Range. The Bannister River forms the northern boundary of the area, which includes twelve ponds.

WHITE OAK SWAMP NATURAL AREA PRESERVE, in Henrico County, encompasses 800 acres. The site was acquired by the federal government in the 1940s for use as a decoy airdrome to protect Byrd Field in the event of German invasion. The land was transferred to the commonwealth after World War II. A preserve since 1990, the land includes swamp, bottomland hardwood forest, and diverse wildlife.

WHITNEY STATE FOREST, located south of Warrenton in Fauquier County, encompasses 147.5 acres. Formerly known as Hooewood, the woodland was donated by Helen Whitney Gibson to the Virginia Department of Forestry in 1972. A portion of the tract's original homesite survives.

WRECK ISLAND NATURAL AREA PRESERVE, in Northampton County, encompasses 1,380 acres. An offshore preserve located seven miles east of Oyster, Virginia, the area is made up of two offshore islands, Wreck and Bone, most commonly known collectively as Wreck Island. Acquired in 1961 and managed as the Wreck and Bone Islands Natural Area by the Division of State Parks, the site in 1991 was transferred to the Division of Natural Heritage. Approximately three miles long and one-half mile wide, the island area provides refuge for otter, mink, raccoon, and numerous shorebirds. Wreck Island is included in the Maryland-Virginia Barrier Islands International Shorebird Reserve, established in 1990 as part of the Western Hemisphere Shorebird Reserve Network.

YORK RIVER STATE PARK, in James City County, was established in 1969 and encompasses 2,491 acres along the south shore of the York River between Richmond and Hampton Roads. The park is especially noted for its estuarine environment, formed by the York River, Taskinas Creek, and a saltwater marsh.

ZOAR STATE FOREST, near Aylett in King William County, encompasses 378 acres and is the first state forest established east of Richmond. The woodland was donated to the Virginia Department of Forestry by Albert H. Stoddard in 1987. The forest includes approximately a mile of Mattaponi River frontage as well as a turn-of-the-century home and outbuildings and 49 acres of open land.

Athlete at State Teachers College at Harrisonburg ca. 1928

EDUCATIONAL INSTITUTIONS

Virginians have been interested in education since the early days of the colony. In 1618 the Virginia Company of London authorized the establishment of a college at Henrico for the education of colonists' sons as well as Native Americans. The institution was abandoned after the English-Powhatan War of 1622. In 1693 the College of William and Mary, the second-oldest college in the United States, was established by royal charter.

Precollegiate education in the colonial period was almost completely a matter of private responsibility. Free schools, such as those endowed by Benjamin Syms and Thomas Eaton in Hampton, appeared in some places during the seventeenth century, but these were supported by private contributions rather than by taxation. The typical school of colonial Virginia was conducted on a plantation by a clergyman or by a private tutor hired by the planter. Pupils at these schools were the planter's children and, sometimes, the children of his nearest white neighbors.

In 1779 Thomas Jefferson's "Bill for the More General Diffusion of Knowledge" called for the free education of all white male youths, regardless of their social or economic status. Jefferson proposed an educational system composed of county elementary schools for the first three years of a boy's training, district schools for the abler boys to prepare for college, and a state-supported college in which the most talented students could complete their educations. The General Assembly rejected Jefferson's proposal, but in 1796 it authorized the counties to create and finance public schools to provide white males with instruction in "reading, writing and common arithmetic." Because establishment of these schools was not required, however, many counties did not create them, and those that did often provided meager financial support. Virginia did not attain a genuine state-supported system of public elementary and secondary schools until after the Civil War.

In 1819, forty years after he had proposed his comprehensive scheme for public education, Jefferson secured passage of a charter for the University of Virginia. Private institutions also sprang up throughout Virginia late in the eighteenth and early in the nineteenth centuries. In antebellum academies and seminaries pupils learned the classics, modern languages, science, and history. Preparatory institutions such as these were the forerunners of Hampden-Sydney College, Washington College (now Washington and Lee University), Hollins College, and Mary Baldwin College—all of which began offering collegiate instruction before the Civil War. New postsecondary institutions established before the Civil War included the Virginia Military Institute, the Medical College of Virginia, and four church-related colleges: Richmond College (now part of the University of Richmond), Randolph-Macon College, Emory & Henry College, and Roanoke College.

The Civil War slowed the advance of public education in Virginia, but the Constitution of 1869 provided for a state-supported system of public elementary schools. William Henry Ruffner, the commonwealth's first superintendent of public instruction, organized Virginia's first real statewide system of public schools, establishing separate schools for white and black children. After its discouraging beginning, Virginia gradually had begun to provide all of its children—white and black, male and female—with basic educational opportunities.

Higher education also advanced after the Civil War. Virginia State College, the commonwealth's first state-supported college for African Americans, was established near Petersburg, and Virginia's first training school for white teachers was created by expanding the program of the Farmville Female Seminary. Virginia's first land-grant college, the Virginia Agricultural and Mechanical College (now Virginia Polytechnic Institute and State University) was founded at Blacksburg, and two private black institutions were established during the second half of the nineteenth century, Hampton Institute and Virginia Union University. At the close of the century, Randolph-Macon Woman's College, at Lynchburg, became the first accredited woman's college in the state. Although some Virginia cities had high schools, until 1906 the state did not have a publicly supported system of secondary education. Soon after the General Assembly had created a statewide system of high schools, it also established normal schools at Fredericksburg, Harrisonburg, and Radford to train white high-school teachers. In 1954, the United States Supreme Court ruled in the *Brown* v. *Board of Education of Topeka, Kansas*, decision that "separate but equal" public educational facilities were unconstitutional. By the mid-1960s, state-supported educational institutions in Virginia had abandoned the earlier policy of active racial segregation.

During the twentieth century, some academies and seminaries became junior colleges, some of which, in turn, became four-year institutions. Prior to 1966, many of Virginia's four-year colleges augmented their programs by establishing affiliated two-year junior colleges: the University of Virginia maintained branches on the Eastern Shore and at Wise, Baileys Crossroads, Martinsville, and Roanoke; Virginia Polytechnic Institute at Clifton Forge, Danville, Roanoke, and Wytheville; the College of William and Mary at Newport News and Petersburg; and Virginia State College at Norfolk.

As the state's economy became increasingly industrialized, the General Assembly expanded postsecondary educational opportunities early in the 1960s. First, in 1962, it created a commission on vocational education. Then, on 6 April 1966, it established a department of community colleges to bring the state-supported branch colleges into one system. Only Richard Bland College of the College of William and Mary, Clinch Valley College of the University of Virginia (which became a four-year institution in 1968), and the Danville Division of Virginia Polytechnic Institute (which entered the community college system in 1968) were exempt. Thus, the first members of the Virginia Community College System were the University of Virginia's Patrick Henry College and Eastern Shore and Lynchburg branches, and the Virginia Polytechnic Institute's Roanoke Technical Institute, its Roanoke Center, and its Clifton Forge–Covington and Wytheville branches. Between 1966 and 1972, eleven existing technical schools and branch colleges and fourteen new institutions were placed in the system. By 1994, Virginia had twenty-three community colleges with thirty-four campuses.

Since the creation of the Virginia Community College System in 1966, other institutional changes also have occurred in Virginia's system of higher education. In 1965, Virginia had twenty-nine senior colleges and universities and eighteen junior colleges. By 1994, Virginia had five junior and two-year colleges, twenty-three community colleges, and forty-four senior colleges, universities, and postgraduate institutions. The descriptive sketches that follow are divided into three sections: institutions offering baccalaureate or graduate degrees, two-year and junior colleges, and community colleges.

Four-Year Colleges and Universities and Postgraduate Institutions

AVERETT COLLEGE, in Danville, is a private, coeducational, Baptist college founded in 1859 as Union Female College. Affiliated with the Baptist General Association of Virginia in 1910, it has been known as Averett College since its accreditation in 1917 as a junior college. In 1969 Averett College became coeducational and added a four-year baccalaureate degree program. A master's degree program was added in 1978.

BLUEFIELD COLLEGE, in Bluefield, is a coeducational Baptist-affiliated college chartered in 1920 and opened as a junior college for men in 1922. Although women attended the school as day students, the college did not become formally coeducational until 1951. Bluefield College was accredited as a four-year institution in 1977.

BRIDGEWATER COLLEGE, in Bridgewater, near Harrisonburg, is a four-year, coeducational, liberal arts college affiliated with the Church of the Brethren. It was founded in 1880 as the Spring Creek Normal and Collegiate Institute, on Spring Creek, in Rockingham County. Moved from its original site to Bridgewater in 1882, it was renamed the Virginia Normal School; it was given its present name in 1889. Daleville College at Daleville, Virginia, and Blue Ridge College at New Windsor, Maryland, were consolidated with Bridgewater College in 1923 and 1930, respectively.

CHRISTENDOM COLLEGE, in Front Royal, was founded in 1977 by Warren H. Carroll to educate students for the lay apostolate of the Catholic Church. A four-year, coeducational, liberal arts college offering associate and baccalaureate degrees, the school was begun with a donation of one thousand dollars and opened with twenty-six students.

CHRISTOPHER NEWPORT UNIVERSITY, in Newport News, was established by the General Assembly in 1960 as a two-year, coeducational college and a branch of the College of William and Mary. In 1971 it became a four-year baccalaureate institution, Christopher Newport College, and on 1 July 1977 was made independent of the College of William and Mary. The school first offered graduate programs in 1991 and in 1992 was renamed Christopher Newport University.

CLINCH VALLEY COLLEGE OF THE UNIVERSITY OF VIRGINIA, in Wise, was established in 1954 by the Extension Division of the University of Virginia and became a branch of the university in 1957. A two-year, coeducational institution until 1968, it was granted four-year status by the 1968–1969 session of the General Assembly, and it awarded its first bachelor of arts degrees in June 1970 and bachelor of science degrees in 1973. Clinch Valley College is the only branch institution still affiliated with the University of Virginia.

THE COLLEGE OF WILLIAM AND MARY IN VIRGINIA, in Williamsburg, is the second-oldest college within the present limits of the United States. It was chartered in 1693 by the reigning king and queen of England, William III and Mary II, for whom it was named. The original building, the reconstruction of which is known as the Wren Building, was completed in 1697. Included among its distinguished alumni are Thomas Jefferson, James Monroe, John Marshall, and John Tyler. The Phi Beta Kappa Society was founded there in 1776. The college became a state institution in 1906 and coeducational in 1918. It includes under its jurisdiction Richard Bland

College, in Petersburg; the Virginia Institute of Marine Science, at Gloucester Point; and Ash Lawn–Highland, in Albemarle County.

EASTERN MENNONITE COLLEGE AND SEMINARY, in Harrisonburg, is a coeducational college founded by the Mennonite Church in 1917 as a junior college. First called Eastern Mennonite School, it became a four-year college in 1947, when the name Eastern Mennonite College was adopted. Eastern Mennonite Seminary, a graduate school of theological studies formally established in 1965, and Eastern Mennonite High School are also located on the campus.

EASTERN VIRGINIA MEDICAL SCHOOL OF THE MEDICAL COLLEGE OF HAMPTON ROADS, in Norfolk, was established in 1973. The only privately funded medical school in Virginia, the institution also receives support from the commonwealth of Virginia and the seven cities of Hampton Roads. Eastern Virginia Medical School does not operate a teaching hospital but is instead affiliated with more than thirty health-care facilities in the eastern Virginia region.

EMORY & HENRY COLLEGE, in Emory, is a four-year, coeducational college affiliated with the United Methodist Church. Chartered in 1838, the college was named for Methodist bishop John Emory and Virginia statesman Patrick Henry. It was the first college established in southwestern Virginia and is designated a National Historic Landmark.

FERRUM COLLEGE, in Ferrum, a coeducational, four-year, Methodist-affiliated institution, was founded in 1913 as Ferrum Training School and in 1926 offered junior-college courses. It initiated a baccalaureate program in 1974 and in 1976 was accredited as a four-year institution.

GEORGE MASON UNIVERSITY, in the city of Fairfax, began in 1948 as an extension center of the University of Virginia. In 1956 it became a two-year, coeducational, branch college of the university. When it opened temporary quarters at Baileys Crossroads in September 1957 it was called University College. In 1959 the city of Fairfax donated land for the college, and in 1960 it was renamed for Virginia statesman George Mason. In March 1966 the General Assembly authorized expansion to a four-year program. On 1 March 1972 it was separated from the University of Virginia and renamed George Mason University.

HAMPDEN-SYDNEY COLLEGE, in Prince Edward County, is a liberal arts college for men founded by the Presbyterians in 1776 on the model of Princeton University. Incorporated in 1783, James Madison and Patrick Henry served on its first board of trustees. William Henry Harrison was a member of the class of 1793. The college is named for John Hampden and Algernon Sydney, seventeenth-century English republicans known as martyrs in the cause of liberty.

HAMPTON UNIVERSITY, in Hampton, was founded in 1868 by General Samuel Chapman Armstrong, an agent of the Freedmen's Bureau. A private, coeducational, predominantly black institution, the school was first known as the Hampton Normal and Agricultural Institute and later as Hampton Institute. It was supported by funds from philanthropic and religious groups and by federal land-grant funds (1872-1920). From 1878 until 1912 federal funding also supported a program for Native American students, who continued to attend Hampton until 1923. Hampton first offered a bachelor's degree program in 1922 and graduate courses in 1928.

Hampton Institute, early 1900s, by Norfolk photographer Harry C. Mann. The Châteauesque main building, Virginia Hall, was designed by Richard Morris Hunt and built by students at the school.

Among the school's most famous graduates is Booker T. Washington. The school was renamed Hampton University in 1984 and is a National Historic Landmark.

HOLLINS COLLEGE, near Roanoke, is a private liberal arts college for women founded in 1842 on the site of the former Roanoke Female Seminary. First known as the Valley Union Seminary, it was originally a coeducational institution. It became the Female Seminary at Botetourt Springs in 1852 and in 1855 was renamed Hollins Institute in honor of benefactors John Hollins and Ann Halsey Hollins. The institute awarded its first baccalaureate degree in 1903 and became Hollins College in 1910. It was the first chartered women's college in Virginia, and its president from 1901 to 1933, Matty Cocke, was the first woman college president in the commonwealth. Hollins College began a coeducational master's degree program in 1958.

JAMES MADISON UNIVERSITY, in Harrisonburg, was founded as the State Normal and Industrial School for Women at Harrisonburg in 1908. Its name has changed four times: to the State Normal School for Women at Harrisonburg in 1914, State Teachers College at Harrisonburg in 1924, Madison College (in honor of the fourth president of the United States) in 1938, and James Madison University in 1977. The school admitted men to summer sessions in 1910, to regular sessions in 1946, and became coeducational in 1966.

LIBERTY UNIVERSITY, in Lynchburg, was founded in 1971 by the Reverend Jerry Laymon Falwell. First named Liberty Baptist College, it became a university in 1985. A coeducational school, Liberty University is affiliated with Thomas Road Baptist Church, of Lynchburg.

LONGWOOD COLLEGE, in Farmville, is a coeducational, state-supported college developed from the Farmville Female Seminary, which was incorporated in 1839. Renamed the State Female Normal School in 1884, it was the first publicly supported institution for teacher education in Virginia. After various name changes, the institution became Longwood College in 1949, taking the name from an estate that is now part of the college property. In 1976 the college became coeducational.

LYNCHBURG COLLEGE, in Lynchburg, is a coeducational college of liberal arts and sciences founded by the Disciples of Christ in 1903 as Virginia Christian College. The name was changed in 1919 to Lynchburg College.

MARY BALDWIN COLLEGE, in Staunton, was founded as the Augusta Female Seminary in 1842 by Rufus Bailey, a minister and teacher from Maine. Woodrow Wilson's father, the Reverend Joseph Ruggles Wilson, served as chaplain of the seminary during the 1850s, when the younger Wilson was born. In 1895 the seminary was renamed to honor Mary Julia Baldwin, who served as principal from 1863 until 1897 and without whose guidance the school might not have survived the Civil War. In 1916, Mary Baldwin Seminary became a junior college, and in 1923 it became a four-year institution, Mary Baldwin College. In 1976 the college acquired the buildings and grounds of the former Staunton Military Academy.

MARYMOUNT UNIVERSITY, in Arlington, is an independent, coeducational institution affiliated with the Catholic Church. Founded by the Religious of the Sacred Heart of Mary in 1950 as a two-year college for women, the school was known as Marymount College of Virginia. Marymount received accreditation in 1975 to offer bachelor's degrees, and in the fall of 1979 began a master's degree program. It became a university in 1986.

MARY WASHINGTON COLLEGE, in Fredericksburg, is a coeducational, state-supported college founded in 1908 as the State Normal School for Women at Fredericksburg. The name was changed in 1938 to Mary Washington College. In 1944 it was made a branch of the University of Virginia, and it became an independent member of the state system in 1972. In 1970 the college began accepting male students.

NORFOLK STATE UNIVERSITY, in Norfolk, was founded in 1935 as a junior college affiliated with Virginia Union University, in Richmond. By city and state legislative enactment it became Norfolk Polytechnic College in 1942, Norfolk Division of Virginia State College in 1944, Norfolk State College in 1969, and Norfolk State University in 1979. The coeducational university is one of Virginia's two predominantly black, state-supported institutions.

OLD DOMINION UNIVERSITY, in Norfolk, was founded in 1930 as the Norfolk Division of the College of William and Mary. In 1954 the institution was authorized to offer baccalaureate programs and in 1962 became an independent four-year institution named Old Dominion College. Authorization to offer the master's degree was granted to the college in 1964. The first doctoral programs were offered in 1969. The school was granted university status in 1970.

Randolph-Macon Woman's College, in Lynchburg, was founded in 1891.

PROTESTANT EPISCOPAL THEOLOGICAL SEMINARY IN VIRGINIA, in Alexandria, was founded in 1823. Also generally known as Virginia Theological Seminary or as Virginia Seminary, the Episcopal school offers four degree programs: a two-year master's degree in theological studies, a two-year master of arts in Christian education, a three-year master's degree in divinity, and a postordination doctorate in ministry.

RADFORD UNIVERSITY, in Radford, was established in 1910 by the General Assembly as the State Normal and Industrial School for Women. It opened in 1913, became Radford State Teachers College in 1924, and began to award the baccalaureate degree in 1936. In 1944 it became the women's division of Virginia Polytechnic Institute and was renamed Radford College. In 1964, Radford College was separated from its parent institution and was authorized to grant the master of arts degree. Radford became coeducational in 1972 and was given the name Radford University in 1979.

RANDOLPH-MACON COLLEGE, in Ashland, was founded in 1830 and is the oldest Methodist-affiliated college in continuous operation in the United States. Originally located at Boydton, in Mecklenburg County, it was moved to its present location in 1868. The name honors statesmen John Randolph of Roanoke and Nathaniel Macon, of North Carolina. The national honorary science fraternity, Chi Beta Phi, was founded at the college in 1916. Originally an all-male college, Randolph-Macon College became coeducational in 1971.

RANDOLPH-MACON WOMAN'S COLLEGE, in Lynchburg, is a women's private liberal arts college affiliated with the United Methodist Church. Founded in 1891 under the 1830 charter granted to Randolph-Macon College for men, it was the first college for women to be admitted to membership in the Southern Association of Colleges and Secondary Schools and the first southern college for women to receive a charter for a Phi Beta Kappa chapter. Pearl Buck, the first American woman to win the Nobel Prize for Literature, graduated from Randolph-Macon Woman's College in 1914.

REGENT UNIVERSITY, in Virginia Beach, was founded by the Reverend Marion Gordon ("Pat") Robertson and incorporated in 1977 as a postgraduate institution and educational adjunct of the Christian Broadcasting Network. Known from its inception as CBN University, it became Regent University in 1990. The school offers master's degree programs in business, communication and the arts, counseling, divinity, education, government, and law.

ROANOKE COLLEGE, in Salem, a coeducational, liberal arts college, was established as the Virginia Institute in 1842 by two Lutheran pastors, the Reverends David Frederick Bittle and Christopher C. Baughman. Chartered in 1845, it was first located near Staunton and moved to Salem in 1847. The name was changed to Roanoke College in 1853. The school is Virginia's only, and the nation's second-oldest, Lutheran college.

SAINT PAUL'S COLLEGE, in Lawrenceville, was founded in 1883 by the Reverend James Solomon Russell, rector of Saint Paul's Church. It was chartered in 1888 and incorporated as Saint Paul's Normal and Industrial School in 1890. In 1922 a collegiate department of teacher training was established. In 1941 the school began to grant baccalaureate degrees and became Saint Paul's Polytechnic Institute. Its name was changed to Saint Paul's College in 1957. The four-year, coeducational institution is one of three predominantly black colleges in the United States affiliated with the Episcopal Church.

SHENANDOAH UNIVERSITY, in Winchester, is a private, coeducational, liberal arts school affiliated with the United Methodist Church. Founded at Dayton, Virginia, in 1875 and chartered in 1884, it was known originally as Shenandoah Seminary. The school later added postsecondary courses and became known as Shenandoah Collegiate Institute and School of Music. In 1924 the name was changed to Shenandoah College, and the music department became the Conservatory of Music within the college. In 1937 the conservatory was separately incorporated, and it began offering a four-year program of study. The campus was moved in 1960 from Dayton to Winchester. In 1974 the college became a four-year institution and was rejoined with the conservatory under one charter as Shenandoah College & Conservatory of Music. In 1991 the school was renamed Shenandoah University.

SWEET BRIAR COLLEGE, in Amherst County, a four-year, liberal arts college for women, was created by the bequest of Indiana Fletcher Williams, who provided in her will that a college be founded in memory of her only daughter, Daisy, who had died in 1884 at the age of sixteen. The college was chartered in 1901 as Sweet Briar Institute, and its first classes met in 1906. Sweet Briar was named for the Williams family plantation on which it was built; the plantation's main house, an eighteenth-century Tuscan-style villa, is used as the college president's residence. Much of the campus was designed by noted architect Ralph Adams Cram.

UNION THEOLOGICAL SEMINARY IN VIRGINIA, in Richmond, was founded in 1812. A Presbyterian institution, the seminary offers master's degrees in divinity and theology, as well as doctor of ministry and doctor of philosophy degrees. Union Theological Seminary is one of three member schools of the Richmond Theological Center, an education consortium organized in 1961 that includes the Presbyterian School of Christian Education and the School of Theology of Virginia Union University.

UNIVERSITY OF RICHMOND, in Richmond, is a private liberal arts institution, developed from Dunlora Academy, a school for Baptist ministers established in 1830 at Dunlora, an estate in Powhatan County. The school became the Virginia Baptist Seminary in 1832. Eight years later the Baptists reorganized it as a men's school and obtained its charter as Richmond College. A law school was added in 1870. The college's first Richmond location was at present-day Grace and Lombardy Streets, and in 1914 it was moved to its current location in Richmond's west end. Also in 1914, a women's liberal arts undergraduate institution, Westhampton College, was added to Richmond College. The college became the University of Richmond in 1920 when Richmond College, Westhampton College for Women, the T. C. Williams School of Law, and the School of Business were combined.

UNIVERSITY OF VIRGINIA, in Charlottesville, was chartered by the General Assembly in 1819 and was opened for instruction in 1825. Thomas Jefferson, the founder of the university, drafted the first curriculum, helped select the first faculty, designed the original buildings, and served as the first rector of its board of visitors. The university's honor system was established in 1842. Its alumni include Edgar Allan Poe and Woodrow Wilson. The institution became fully coeducational in 1970. The university consists of ten schools, including law and medical schools and a college of arts and sciences. The Rotunda and the University of Virginia Historic District are both National Historic Landmarks.

VIRGINIA COMMONWEALTH UNIVERSITY, in Richmond, was created in 1968 by the General Assembly through the merger of the Medical College of Virginia and Richmond Professional Institute. The Medical College had been established in 1838 as the medical department of Hampden-Sydney College. It became an independent institution in 1854 and came under state control in 1860. In 1913 the Medical College of Virginia was merged with its rival, the University College of Medicine, founded in 1893. The Richmond Professional Institute had been founded in 1917 as the Richmond School of Social Work and Public Health, and it became the Richmond Division of the College of William and Mary in 1925 and the Richmond Professional Institute of the College of William and Mary in 1939. Prior to 1946 few men attended the institution, but RPI became fully coeducational after World War II, and in 1962 it became an independent college. Virginia Commonwealth University is the third-largest employer in the commonwealth.

VIRGINIA INTERMONT COLLEGE, in Bristol, is a four-year, coeducational, Baptist-affiliated college established in 1884 at Glade Spring, in Washington County. As a two-year college for women, it was first known as Southwest Virginia Institute. It was moved to Bristol in 1891, and soon thereafter the name was changed to Virginia Institute. In 1910 it became the first junior college to be accredited by the Southern

Association of Colleges and Secondary Schools. The name was changed again in 1922 to Virginia Intermont College. In September 1970 a baccalaureate program was begun, and in 1972 the college became coeducational.

VIRGINIA MILITARY INSTITUTE, in Lexington, is often called the West Point of the South. Established in 1839, it is the nation's oldest state-supported military college. Thomas Jonathan ("Stonewall") Jackson and oceanographer Matthew Fontaine Maury (known as the "Pathfinder of the Seas") were among its early faculty members. Its alumni include distinguished soldier and statesman George Catlett Marshall, recipient of the Nobel Prize for Peace for his plan to restore Europe after World War II. The institute's corps of cadets participated as a unit in the Battle of New Market on 15 May 1864. The Barracks and VMI Historic District are both National Historic Landmarks.

VIRGINIA POLYTECHNIC INSTITUTE AND STATE UNIVERSITY, in Blacksburg, was established by the General Assembly in 1872 under the terms of the 1862 Morrill Land Grant Act, which provided that income from the sale of public land in each state be used to establish colleges for the teaching of agricultural and mechanical arts. Founded as the Virginia Agricultural and Mechanical College, the new school took over the buildings and other property of the Preston and Olin Institute, a small Methodist school established in 1854. The new college's name was lengthened in 1895 to the Virginia Agricultural and Mechanical College and Polytechnic Institute and in 1944 shortened to Virginia Polytechnic Institute. Radford College served as its women's division from 1944 until 1964, when it was made an independent college. Popularly known as Virginia Tech, Virginia Polytechnic Institute became a state university in 1970.

VIRGINIA STATE UNIVERSITY, in Ettrick, near Petersburg, was founded in 1882 as a result of a campaign promise to Virginia's African American population made by William Mahone's Readjuster Party. Named the Virginia Normal and Collegiate Institute, the school is the nation's first fully state-supported four-year institution of higher learning for blacks and has been coeducational from its founding. The bill to establish the school was sponsored by black attorney Alfred W. Harris, a member of the House of Delegates from Dinwiddie County. In 1902 the General Assembly revised the school's charter to curtail its collegiate program and changed its name to Virginia Normal and Industrial Institute; the collegiate program was not restored until 1923. In 1920 the college superseded Hampton Institute as Virginia's land-grant college for African American youth. Its name was changed again in 1922, to Virginia State College. Renamed Virginia State University in 1979, it is one of Virginia's two predominantly black, state-supported schools as well as one of the commonwealth's two land-grant institutions.

VIRGINIA UNION UNIVERSITY, in Richmond, is a coeducational, four-year, predominantly black, liberal arts college. It developed from the Richmond Theological School for Freedmen, founded in 1865, and was incorporated as the Richmond Theological Institute in 1876. Incorporated in 1896 as Virginia Union University, the school was reincorporated in 1900 after its merger in 1899 with Wayland Seminary, of Washington, D.C. In 1932 the university also merged with Hartshorn Memorial College, a Richmond school founded in 1883 for black women, and in 1964 with Storer College, of Harpers Ferry, West Virginia.

VIRGINIA WESLEYAN COLLEGE, astride the Norfolk–Virginia Beach municipal line, was chartered in 1961 and opened in 1966. A small, private, coeducational, four-year, liberal arts college, it is affiliated with the United Methodist Church.

WASHINGTON AND LEE UNIVERSITY, in Lexington, a private, four-year, liberal arts school was founded as Augusta Academy in 1749 by Scotch-Irish pioneers and was located near Greenville, in Augusta County. The name was changed to Liberty Hall in 1776 and in 1782 chartered under the name Liberty Hall Academy. Renamed Washington Academy in 1798 in honor of George Washington, who had donated fifty thousand dollars to the school, the academy moved to Lexington in 1804 and was incorporated as Washington College in 1813. A year after the death of Robert E. Lee, the college's president from 1865 to 1870, the name was changed to Washington and Lee University. The Washington and Lee Law School became a division of the college in 1870 and became coeducational in 1972. The undergraduate division became coeducational in 1985. Both the Washington and Lee Historic District and its Lee Chapel are National Historic Landmarks.

Two-Year and Junior Colleges

COMMONWEALTH COLLEGE, in Virginia Beach, is one of the nation's oldest junior colleges. The private, coeducational school began as the Norfolk Ladies Seminary, founded in 1845, and the Norfolk Commercial Institute, founded in 1859. The institute ceased operation during the Civil War. In 1879, the Norfolk College for Young Ladies replaced the earlier women's school, and in 1889 its board of directors by separate charter established the Norfolk Business College for men. The latter college first admitted women as fulltime students in 1932. Known as Norfolk College by the mid-1940s, the general-business school ceased operation during World War II and did not reopen until 1952. Campuses were added in Virginia Beach in 1966, Hampton in 1981, Richmond in 1982, and Portsmouth in 1989. The school was renamed Commonwealth College in 1982.

COMMUNITY HOSPITAL OF ROANOKE VALLEY COLLEGE OF HEALTH SCIENCES, in Roanoke, was founded in 1982 as a private, two-year college offering degree and certificate programs in health-care disciplines. The college dates back to the formation of the Community Hospital of Roanoke Valley School of Nursing, which evolved from the 1965 merger of the Jefferson Hospital School of Nursing, founded in 1914, and the Lewis-Gale Hospital School of Nursing, founded in 1911.

RICHARD BLAND COLLEGE OF THE COLLEGE OF WILLIAM AND MARY, near Petersburg, was established in 1960 by the General Assembly as a branch of the College of William and Mary. It accepted its first students in the autumn of 1961. The college's primary mission is to offer transfer, associate degrees in the liberal arts and sciences. It remains the only two-year junior-college branch in the Virginia state system; all other state-supported institutions are either four-year institutions or members of the community college system.

SOUTHERN VIRGINIA COLLEGE FOR WOMEN, in Buena Vista, a private, nondenominational school, was established in 1867 as the Home School for Girls at Bowling Green, in Caroline County. The name was changed to Bowling Green Female

Seminary in 1872 and to Southern Seminary in 1900. The boarding school was moved to the former Buena Vista Hotel in Buena Vista in 1901. A college curriculum was added in 1926 when the school was renamed Southern Seminary and Junior College. In 1961 the school was renamed Southern Seminary College and in 1992 Southern Virginia College for Women.

VIRGINIA SEMINARY AND COLLEGE, in Lynchburg, is a private, coeducational, interdenominational institution founded in 1886 as the Lynchburg Baptist Seminary by the black Virginia Baptist State Convention. John Mitchell Jr., editor of the *Richmond Planet*, served on its inaugural board of managers. Renamed Virginia Seminary, the college first offered classes in 1890. In 1900 the school was reincorporated as Virginia Theological Seminary and College. In 1964 it became Virginia Seminary and College. The school was divided administratively in 1972 under a joint board of trustees: the college serves as a two-year institution, while the seminary offers a religion curriculum. Among its alumni are noted writer Anne Spencer, who graduated in 1899, and civil rights activist Vernon Johns, who also served as the school's president from 1929 to 1934.

Community Colleges

BLUE RIDGE COMMUNITY COLLEGE, in Weyers Cave, was established as Shenandoah Technical College in 1965. The name was changed in 1966 when it became part of the newly established community college system. Blue Ridge began operation in the autumn of 1967 and serves the cities of Harrisonburg, Staunton, and Waynesboro and the counties of Augusta, Highland, and Rockingham.

CENTRAL VIRGINIA COMMUNITY COLLEGE, in Lynchburg, was created in 1966 and opened in the autumn of 1967. It moved into its permanent facility in August 1968 and serves the residents of the cities of Bedford and Lynchburg and the counties of Amherst, Appomattox, Bedford, and Campbell.

DABNEY S. LANCASTER COMMUNITY COLLEGE, in Clifton Forge, opened in September 1964 as the Clifton Forge–Covington Division of Virginia Polytechnic Institute. In 1966 it was joined to the Virginia Community College System, and in the summer of 1967 its name was changed to honor a prominent Virginia educator and local resident, Dabney Stewart Lancaster (1889–1975). The college serves the cities of Buena Vista, Clifton Forge, Covington, and Lexington and the counties of Alleghany, Bath, Highland, and Rockbridge, as well as the northern half of Botetourt County.

DANVILLE COMMUNITY COLLEGE, in Danville, was formed by the merger of two institutions, the Danville Technical Institute (founded in 1936) and the Danville Division of Virginia Polytechnic Institute (founded in 1946). In the summer of 1967 the Danville Technical Institute became part of the Virginia Community College System, and on 1 July 1968 the Danville Division of Virginia Polytechnic Institute was joined to the existing community college to form the present comprehensive institution. Danville Community College serves the cities of Danville and South Boston and both Pittsylvania and Halifax Counties.

EASTERN SHORE COMMUNITY COLLEGE, in Melfa, opened in September 1964 as the Eastern Shore Branch of the University of Virginia. Serving the counties of

Accomack and Northampton, it became part of the community college system in 1971. First located at Wallops Island, the college moved into permanent facilities at Melfa in 1974.

GERMANNA COMMUNITY COLLEGE, in Locust Grove, eighteen miles west of Fredericksburg, was opened in October 1970. It serves the city of Fredericksburg and the counties of Caroline, Culpeper, Fauquier, King George, Madison, Orange, Spotsylvania, and Stafford.

J. SARGEANT REYNOLDS COMMUNITY COLLEGE, in Richmond, was created by the General Assembly on 8 July 1971 and named for former lieutenant governor Julian Sargeant Reynolds (1936–1971). The college opened in 1972 and has three campuses: the Parham Road campus, in northern Henrico County; the downtown campus, in Richmond; and the western campus, near the Goochland County courthouse. J. Sargeant Reynolds Community College serves the city of Richmond and the counties of Goochland, Hanover, Henrico, Louisa, and Powhatan.

JOHN TYLER COMMUNITY COLLEGE, in Chester, was named for the tenth president of the United States, a native of the area served by the college. Opened on 2 October 1967, John Tyler Community College serves the counties of Amelia, Charles City, Chesterfield, Dinwiddie, Prince George, Surry, and Sussex and the cities of Colonial Heights, Hopewell, Petersburg, and that portion of Richmond lying south of the James River. In addition to its main campus in Chester, the college offers an extension site in Midlothian.

LORD FAIRFAX COMMUNITY COLLEGE, in Middletown, was authorized in 1969 and opened in 1970. The college, named for the English nobleman who was the colonial proprietor for vast stretches of the Valley of Virginia, serves residents of the counties of Clarke, Frederick, Page, Rappahannock, Shenandoah, Warren, and a portion of Fauquier, as well as the city of Winchester.

MOUNTAIN EMPIRE COMMUNITY COLLEGE, in Big Stone Gap, was established in 1971 and serves the city of Norton and the counties of Lee, Scott, Wise, and the western portion of Dickenson.

NEW RIVER COMMUNITY COLLEGE, in Dublin, was established in 1959 as the New River Vocational and Technical School, in Radford. It was one of five such schools taken into the Virginia Community College System when the system was created in 1966. New River Community College serves the residents of the city of Radford and the counties of Floyd, Giles, Montgomery, and Pulaski.

NORTHERN VIRGINIA COMMUNITY COLLEGE, in northern Virginia, was established in 1965 as the Northern Virginia Technical College. Northern Virginia Community College became a member of the community college system and received its present name in 1966. In addition to the original campus at Baileys Crossroads, the college has an Annandale campus, which opened in 1967; Loudoun, Manassas, and Woodbridge campuses, which opened in 1972; an Alexandria campus, which opened in 1973; and the Extended Learning Institute, which opened in Annandale in 1975. These campuses serve the communities of Alexandria, Fairfax, Falls Church, Manassas, and Manassas Park, and the counties of Arlington, Fairfax, Loudoun, and Prince William.

PATRICK HENRY COMMUNITY COLLEGE, in Martinsville, was founded in 1962 as a two-year branch of the University of Virginia School of General Studies. It became an autonomous college of the university in 1964, when its name was changed to Patrick Henry College of the University of Virginia. The college moved to its present campus in the autumn of 1969 and became part of the Virginia Community College System in 1971. It serves the city of Martinsville and the counties of Henry and Patrick, as well as portions of Franklin County.

PAUL D. CAMP COMMUNITY COLLEGE, in the city of Franklin, was established in 1970 and opened its doors in the autumn of 1971 as part of the Virginia Community College System. The college was named for Paul Douglas Camp (1843–1924), a prominent local businessman. It serves the city of Franklin and both Southampton and Isle of Wight Counties; a branch campus serves part of the city of Suffolk.

PIEDMONT VIRGINIA COMMUNITY COLLEGE, in Charlottesville, was created in 1970 and opened in the autumn of 1972. It moved to its permanent facility in the summer of 1973 and serves Charlottesville and the counties of Albemarle, Fluvanna, Greene, Louisa, Nelson, and the northern portion of Buckingham.

RAPPAHANNOCK COMMUNITY COLLEGE, created in 1970, consists of two campuses: the north campus, opened in Warsaw in 1973, and the south campus, opened in Glenns in 1971. The college serves the counties of Essex, Gloucester, King and Queen, King William, Lancaster, Mathews, Middlesex, New Kent, Northumberland, Richmond, and Westmoreland, as well as portions of Caroline and King George Counties.

SOUTHSIDE VIRGINIA COMMUNITY COLLEGE has three campuses: the Christanna campus, opened at Cochran near Alberta in 1970; the John H. Daniel campus, opened in Keysville in 1971; and the Campus Without Walls, opened in Emporia in 1985. The Christanna campus was named for the eighteenth-century Fort Christanna. The Keysville campus honors John Hannah Daniel (1896–1972), member of the House of Delegates and a prominent local businessman who donated the land for that campus. The college serves the largest geographical service region within the Virginia Community College System (4,200 square miles), including the cities of Emporia and South Boston and the counties of Brunswick, Buckingham, Charlotte, Cumberland, Greensville, Halifax, Lunenburg, Mecklenburg, Nottoway, and Prince Edward.

SOUTHWEST VIRGINIA COMMUNITY COLLEGE, near Richlands, was opened in the autumn of 1968. It serves the residents of the counties of Buchanan, Russell, Tazewell, and part of Dickenson.

THOMAS NELSON COMMUNITY COLLEGE, in Hampton, was named in honor of Thomas Nelson Jr., a signer of the Declaration of Independence and governor of Virginia. Construction was begun in August 1967, and the first classes met on 30 September 1968. The college serves residents of the cities of Hampton, Newport News, Poquoson, and Williamsburg and the counties of James City and York.

TIDEWATER COMMUNITY COLLEGE, established in 1968, consists of three campuses, two full-time centers, and numerous off-campus sites in Chesapeake, Norfolk, Portsmouth, Suffolk, and Virginia Beach. It is the second-largest institution in the Virginia Community College System and serves parts of Isle of Wight County and the city of Suffolk, as well as the cities of Chesapeake, Norfolk, Portsmouth, and Virginia Beach.

VIRGINIA HIGHLANDS COMMUNITY COLLEGE, in Abingdon, was established on 30 November 1967 and serves Washington County, the western portion of Smyth County, and the city of Bristol, Virginia.

VIRGINIA WESTERN COMMUNITY COLLEGE, in Roanoke, was formed in February 1966 by the merger of the Extension Division of the University of Virginia, founded in 1927, and the Roanoke Technical Institute, founded in 1960. The college serves the cities of Roanoke and Salem, the southern portion of Botetourt County, the northern portion of Franklin County, and the counties of Craig and Roanoke.

WYTHEVILLE COMMUNITY COLLEGE, in Wytheville, was created in 1962 and opened in 1963 as a two-year branch college of Virginia Polytechnic Institute. It became a member of the Virginia Community College System on 1 July 1967 and serves the residents of the city of Galax and the counties of Bland, Carroll, Grayson, Wythe, and a portion of Smyth.

"Push Ball" at Radford State Teachers College ca 1933

A ca. 1920s library poster by Jon O. Brubaker

SOME SUGGESTIONS FOR FURTHER READING

Reference

Barden, Thomas E., ed. *Virginia Folk Legends*. Charlottesville, 1991.

Berman, Myron. *Richmond's Jewry, 1769–1976: Shabbat in Shockoe*. Charlottesville, 1979.

Biggs, Thomas H., ed. *Geographic and Cultural Names in Virginia*. Charlottesville, 1974.

Brownell, Charles E., Calder Loth, William M. S. Rasmussen, and Richard Guy Wilson. *The Making of Virginia Architecture*. Richmond, 1992.

Dabney, Virginius. *Virginia: The New Dominion, A History from 1607 to the Present*. 1971. Reprint. Charlottesville, 1983.

Duncan, Richard R., comp. *Theses and Dissertations in Virginia History: A Bibliography*. Richmond, 1986.

Hall, Virginius Cornick, Jr. *Portraits in the Collection of the Virginia Historical Society: A Catalogue*. Charlottesville, 1981.

_____. "Virginia Post Offices, 1798–1859." *Virginia Magazine of History and Biography* 81 (1973): 49–97.

Haynes, Donald, ed. *Virginiana in the Printed Book Collections of the Virginia State Library*. 2 vols. Richmond, 1975.

Herbener, Elizabeth R., and Jon Kukla, eds. *The General Assembly of Virginia, 11 January 1978–27 April 1989: A Register of Members*. Richmond, 1990.

Hiden, Martha W. *How Justice Grew, Virginia Counties: An Abstract of Their Formation*. 1957. Reprint. Baltimore, 1992.

Hogg, Anne M., and Dennis A. Tosh, eds. *Virginia Cemeteries: A Guide to Resources*. Charlottesville, 1986.

Howard, A. E. Dick. *Commentaries on the Constitution of Virginia*. 2 vols. Charlottesville, 1974.

Hummel, Ray O., ed. *A List of Places Included in 19th Century Virginia Directories*. 1960. Reprint. Richmond, 1981.

Kimball, Fiske. *The Capitol of Virginia: A Landmark of American Architecture*. Edited by Jon Kukla. Richmond, 1989.

Kirby, Jack Temple. "Virginia's Environmental History: A Prospectus." *Virginia Magazine of History and Biography* 99 (1991): 449–488.

Lebsock, Suzanne. *Virginia Women, 1600–1945: "A Share of Honour."* Rev. ed. Richmond, 1987.

Leonard, Cynthia Miller. *The General Assembly of Virginia, July 30, 1619–January 11, 1978: A Bicentennial Register of Members.* Richmond, 1978.

Loth, Calder. *The Virginia Landmarks Register.* 3d ed. Charlottesville, 1986.

Morgan, Philip, ed. *"Don't Grieve After Me": The Black Experience in Virginia, 1619–1986.* Hampton, Va., 1986.

Parramore, Thomas C., with Peter C. Stewart and Tommy L. Bogger. *Norfolk: The First Four Centuries.* Charlottesville, 1994.

Rubin, Louis D. *Virginia: A History.* 1977. Reprint. New York and Nashville, 1984.

Salmon, John S., comp. *A Guidebook to Virginia's Historical Markers.* 8th ed. Charlottesville, 1994.

Seale, William. *Virginia's Executive Mansion: A History of the Governor's House.* Richmond, 1988.

Swem, Earl G., comp. *Maps Relating to Virginia in the Virginia State Library and Other Departments of the Commonwealth: With the 17th and 18th Century Atlas-Maps in the Library of Congress.* 1914. Reprint. Richmond, 1989.

_____. *Virginia Historical Index.* 2 vols. 1934. Reprint. Gloucester, Mass., 1965.

Treadway, Sandra Gioia. "New Directions in Virginia Women's History." *Virginia Magazine of History and Biography* 100 (1992): 5–28.

Tyler-McGraw, Marie. *At the Falls: Richmond, Virginia, and Its People.* Chapel Hill, 1994.

Virginia Writers' Program, Work Projects Administration. *Virginia: A Guide to the Old Dominion.* 1940. Reprint. Richmond, 1992.

Watson, Ritchie Devon, Jr. *The Cavalier in Virginia Fiction.* Baton Rouge, 1985.

Wright, R. Lewis. *Artists in Virginia before 1900.* Charlottesville, 1983.

Younger, Edward, and James Tice Moore, eds. *The Governors of Virginia, 1860–1978.* Charlottesville, 1982.

Native Americans

Barbour, Philip L. *Pocahontas and Her World*. Boston, 1969.

Craven, Wesley Frank. *White, Red, and Black: The Seventeenth-Century Virginian*. Charlottesville, 1971.

Egloff, Keith, and Deborah Woodward. *First People: The Early Indians of Virginia*. Richmond, 1992.

Fausz, J. Frederick. "The Invasion of Virginia: Indians, Colonialism, and the Conquest of Cant, A Review Essay on Anglo-Indian Relations in the Chesapeake." *Virginia Magazine of History and Biography* 95 (1987): 133–156.

McCary, Ben C. *Indians in Seventeenth-Century Virginia*. Williamsburg, 1957.

Nash, Gary B. *Red, White, and Black: The Peoples of Early America*. Englewood Cliffs, N.J., 1974.

Rountree, Helen C. *Pocahontas's People: The Powhatan Indians of Virginia Through Four Centuries*. Norman, Okla., 1990.

_____. *The Powhatan Indians of Virginia: Their Traditional Culture*. Norman, Okla., 1989.

Colonial Virginia

Alvord, Clarence Walworth, and Lee Bidgood. *The First Explorations of the Trans-Allegheny Region by the Virginians, 1650–1674*. Cleveland, 1912.

Barbour, Philip L. *The Three Worlds of Captain John Smith*. Boston, 1964.

Beverley, Robert. *The History and Present State of Virginia*. Edited by Louis B. Wright. Chapel Hill, 1947. First published in London in 1705.

Billings, Warren M., Thad Tate, and John E. Selby. *Colonial Virginia: A History*. White Plains, N.Y., 1986.

Billings, Warren M., ed. *The Old Dominion in the Seventeenth Century: A Documentary History of Virginia, 1606–1689*. Chapel Hill, 1975.

Bockstruck, Lloyd DeWitt, comp. *Virginia's Colonial Soldiers*. Baltimore, 1988.

Breen, T. H. *Tobacco Culture: The Mentality of the Great Tidewater Planters on the Eve of Revolution*. Princeton, 1985.

Breen, T. H., and Stephen Innes. *"Myne Owne Ground": Race and Freedom on Virginia's Eastern Shore, 1640–1676*. New York, 1980.

Briceland, Alan Vance. *Westward from Virginia: The Exploration of the Virginia-Carolina Frontier, 1650–1710*. Charlottesville, 1987.

Carr, Lois Green, Philip D. Morgan, and Jean B. Russo. *Colonial Chesapeake Society*. Chapel Hill, 1988.

Craven, Wesley Frank. *Dissolution of the Virginia Company: The Failure of a Colonial Experiment*. New York, 1932.

Davis, Richard Beale. *Intellectual Life in the Colonial South, 1585–1763*. 3 vols. Knoxville, Tenn., 1978.

Hood, Graham. *The Governor's Palace in Williamsburg: A Cultural Study*. Williamsburg, 1991.

Kukla, Jon. "Order and Chaos in Early America: Political and Social Stability in Pre-Restoration Virginia." *American Historical Review* 90 (1985): 275–298.

_____. *Political Institutions in Virginia, 1619–1660*. New York, 1989.

Kulikoff, Allan. *Tobacco and Slaves: The Development of Southern Cultures in the Chesapeake, 1680–1800*. Chapel Hill, 1986.

Kupperman, Karen O., ed. *Captain John Smith: A Select Edition of His Writings*. Chapel Hill, 1988.

Menard, Russell R. "The Tobacco Industry in the Chesapeake Colonies, 1617–1730: An Interpretation." In *Research in Economic History: A Research Annual*, vol. 5, edited by Paul Uselding, 109–177. Greenwich, Conn., 1980.

Meyer, Virginia M., and John Frederick Dorman, eds. *Adventurers of Purse and Person: Virginia, 1607–1624/25*. 3d ed. Richmond, 1987.

Middleton, Arthur Pierce. *Tobacco Coast: A Maritime History of the Chesapeake Bay in the Colonial Era*. 1953. Reprint. Baltimore, 1984.

Morgan, Edmund S. *American Slavery, American Freedom: The Ordeal of Colonial Virginia*. New York, 1975.

Nugent, Nell Marion. *Cavaliers and Pioneers: Abstracts of Virginia's Land Patents and Grants, 1623–1732*. 3 vols. and supp. Richmond, 1934–1980.

Perry, James R. *The Formation of a Society on Virginia's Eastern Shore, 1615–1655*. Chapel Hill, 1990.

Quinn, David B., and Alison M. Quinn, eds. *Virginia Voyages from Hakluyt*. London and New York, 1973.

Rutman, Anita H. "Still Planting the Seeds of Hope: The Recent Literature of the Early Chesapeake Region." *Virginia Magazine of History and Biography* 95 (1987): 3–24.

Rutman, Darrett B., and Anita H. Rutman. *A Place in Time: Middlesex County, Virginia, 1650–1750*. New York, 1984.

Shea, William L. *The Virginia Militia in the Seventeenth Century*. Baton Rouge, 1983.

Smith, Daniel Blake. *Inside the Great House: Planter Family Life in Eighteenth-Century Chesapeake Society*. Ithaca, N.Y., 1980.

Sobel, Mechal. *The World They Made Together: Black and White Values in Eighteenth-Century Virginia*. Princeton, 1987.

Sydnor, Charles Sackett. *Gentlemen Freeholders: Political Practices in Washington's Virginia*. Chapel Hill, 1952.

Tate, Thad W., and David L. Ammerman, eds. *The Chesapeake in the Seventeenth Century: Essays on Anglo-American Society and Politics*. Chapel Hill, 1979.

Titus, James. *The Old Dominion at War: Society, Politics, and Warfare in Late Colonial Virginia*. Columbia, S.C., 1991.

Vaughan, Alden T. *American Genesis: Captain John Smith and the Founding of Virginia*. Boston, 1975.

Washburn, Wilcomb E. "Virginia's First Families and the First Families of Virginia." In *Exploring Virginia's Human Resources*, edited by Roscoe D. Hughes and Henry Leidheiser Jr., 7–18. Charlottesville, 1965.

_____. *The Governor and the Rebel: A History of Bacon's Rebellion in Virginia*. Chapel Hill, 1959.

Revolutionary Virginia

Brant, Irving. *James Madison*. 6 vols. Indianapolis, 1941–1961.

Buckley, Thomas E. *Church and State in Revolutionary Virginia, 1776–1787*. Charlottesville, 1977.

Eckenrode, Hamilton J., comp. *Virginia Soldiers of the American Revolution*. 2 vols. Reprint. Richmond, 1989.

Freeman, Douglas Southall. *George Washington*. 7 vols. New York: 1948–1957. Vol. 7 was completed after the author's death in 1953 by John A. Carroll and Mary W. Ashworth. A one-volume abridgement of this work, entitled *Washington* and prepared by Richard Harwell, was published in New York in 1968.

Gewehr, Wesley Marsh. *The Great Awakening in Virginia, 1740–1790*. Durham, N.C., 1930.

Isaac, Rhys. *The Transformation of Virginia, 1740–1790*. Chapel Hill, 1982.

Jefferson, Thomas. *Notes on the State of Virginia*. Edited by William Peden. Chapel Hill, 1957. First published in Paris in 1785, it has been published in many editions since.

_____. *The Papers of Thomas Jefferson*. Edited by Julian P. Boyd et al. 25 vols. to date. Princeton, 1950– .

Madison, James. *The Papers of James Madison*. Edited by William T. Hutchinson et al. 21 vols. to date. Chicago, 1962– .

Malone, Dumas. *Jefferson and His Times*. 6 vols. Boston, 1948–1981.

Mayer, Henry. *A Son of Thunder: Patrick Henry and the American Republic*. New York, 1986.

Mays, John David. *Edmund Pendleton, 1721–1803: A Biography*. 2 vols. 1952. Reprint. Richmond, 1984.

Miller, Helen Hill. *George Mason: Gentleman Revolutionary*. Chapel Hill, 1975.

Peterson, Merrill D. *Thomas Jefferson and the New Nation*. New York, 1970.

Sanchez-Saavedra, E. M. *A Guide to Virginia Military Organizations in the American Revolution, 1774–1787*. Richmond, 1978.

Selby, John E. *The Revolution in Virginia, 1775–1783*. Charlottesville, 1988.

Tate, Thad W. "The Coming of the Revolution in Virginia: Britain's Challenge to Virginia's Ruling Class, 1763–1776." *William and Mary Quarterly*, 3d ser., 19 (1962): 323–343.

Van Schreeven, William J., Robert L. Scribner, and Brent Tarter, eds. *Revolutionary Virginia, The Road to Independence*. 7 vols. Charlottesville, 1973–1983.

Washington, George. *The Papers of George Washington*. Edited by W. W. Abbot et al. 22 vols. to date. Charlottesville, 1976– .

Early-National and Antebellum Virginia

Beeman, Richard R. *The Old Dominion and the New Nation, 1788–1801*. Lexington, Ky., 1972.

Butler, Stuart Lee. *A Guide to Virginia Militia Units in the War of 1812*. Athens, Ga., 1988.

_____. *Virginia Soldiers in the United States Army, 1800–1815*. Athens, Ga., 1986.

Crofts, Daniel W. *Old Southampton: Politics and Society in a Virginia County, 1834–1869.* Charlottesville, 1992.

Davis, Richard Beale. *Intellectual Life in Jefferson's Virginia, 1790–1830.* Chapel Hill, 1964.

Dew, Charles B. *Bond of Iron: Master and Slave at Buffalo Forge.* New York, 1994.

Egerton, Douglas R. *Gabriel's Rebellion: The Virginia Slave Conspiracies of 1800 and 1802.* Chapel Hill, 1993.

Freehling, Alison Goodyear. *Drift Toward Dissolution: The Virginia Slavery Debate of 1831–1832.* Baton Rouge, 1982.

Goldfield, David R. *Urban Growth in the Age of Sectionalism:Virginia, 1847–1861.* Baton Rouge, 1977.

Jackson, Luther Porter. *Free Negro Labor and Property Holding in Virginia, 1830–1860.* 1942. Reprint. New York, 1971.

Jennings, John Melville. "Virginia's People in the Eighteenth and Nineteenth Centuries." In *Exploring Virginia's Human Resources*, edited by Roscoe D. Hughes and Henry Leidheiser Jr., 19–33. Charlottesville, 1965.

Jordan, Daniel P. *Political Leadership in Jefferson's Virginia.* Charlottesville, 1983.

Lane, Mills. *Architecture of the Old South: Virginia.* 1987. Reprint. New York, 1989.

Lebsock, Suzanne. *The Free Women of Petersburg: Status and Culture in a Southern Town, 1784–1860.* New York, 1984.

Lewis, Jan. *The Pursuit of Happiness: Family and Values in Jefferson's Virginia.* Cambridge, 1983.

Miller, F. Thornton. "The Richmond Junto: The Secret All-Powerful Club—or Myth." *Virginia Magazine of History and Biography* 99 (1991): 63–80.

Oates, Stephen B. *The Fires of Jubilee: Nat Turner's Fierce Rebellion.* New York, 1975.

Robert, Joseph Clarke. *The Road from Monticello: A Study of the Virginia Slavery Debate of 1832.* Durham, N.C., 1941.

———. *The Tobacco Kingdom: Plantation, Market, and Factory in Virginia and North Carolina, 1800–1860.* Durham, N.C., 1938.

Schwarz, Philip J. *Twice Condemned: Slaves and the Criminal Laws of Virginia, 1705–1865.* Baton Rouge, 1988.

Siegel, Frederick F. *The Roots of Southern Distinctiveness: Tobacco and Society in Danville, Virginia, 1780–1865.* Chapel Hill, 1987.

Simpson, Craig M. *A Good Southerner: The Life of Henry A. Wise of Virginia.* Chapel Hill, 1985.

_____ . "Political Compromise and the Protection of Slavery: Henry A. Wise and the Virginia Constitutional Convention of 1850–1851." *Virginia Magazine of History and Biography* 83 (1975): 387–405.

Stewart, Peter C. "Railroads and Urban Rivalries in Antebellum Eastern Virginia." *Virginia Magazine of History and Biography* 81 (1973): 3–22.

Savitt, Todd L. *Medicine and Slavery: The Diseases and Health Care of Blacks in Antebellum Virginia.* Urbana, Ill., 1978.

Shanks, Henry Thomas. *The Secession Movement in Virginia, 1847–1861.* Chapel Hill, 1934.

Civil War and Reconstruction

Brewer, James H. *The Confederate Negro: Virginia's Craftsmen and Military Laborers, 1861–1865.* Durham, N.C., 1969.

Dew, Charles B. *Ironmaker to the Confederacy: Joseph R. Anderson and the Tredegar Iron Works.* New Haven, 1966.

Freeman, Douglas Southall. *Lee's Lieutenants: A Study in Command.* 3 vols. New York, 1942–1944.

_____ . *R. E. Lee: A Biography.* 4 vols. New York, 1934–1935. A one-volume abridgement of this work, entitled *Lee* and prepared by Richard Harwell, was published in New York in 1961.

Hume, Richard L. "The Membership of the Virginia Constitutional Convention of 1867–1868: A Study of the Beginnings of Congressional Reconstruction in the Upper South." *Virginia Magazine of History and Biography* 86 (1978): 461–484.

Johnston, Angus J. *Virginia Railroads in the Civil War.* Chapel Hill, 1961.

Jordan, Ervin L., Jr. *Black Confederates and Afro-Yankees in Civil War Virginia.* Charlottesville, 1994.

Lowe, Richard. *Republicans and Reconstruction in Virginia, 1856–70.* Charlottesville, 1991.

Maddex, Jack P., Jr. *The Virginia Conservatives, 1867–1879: A Study in Reconstruction Politics.* Chapel Hill, 1970.

Mitchell, Betty L. *Edmund Ruffin: A Biography.* Bloomington, Ind., 1981.

Morgan, Lynda J. *Emancipation in Virginia's Tobacco Belt, 1850–1870*. Athens, Ga., 1992.

Noe, Kenneth W. *Southwest Virginia's Railroad: Modernization and the Sectional Crisis.* Urbana, Ill., 1994.

Robertson, James I., Jr. *Civil War Sites in Virginia: A Tour Guide*. Charlottesville, 1982.

_____ . *Civil War Virginia: Battleground for a Nation*. Charlottesville, 1991.

Thomas, Emory M. *The Confederate State of Richmond: A Biography of the Capital*. Austin, Tex., 1971.

Virginia Civil War Battles and Leaders Series. 42 vols. to date. Lynchburg, 1985– .

Virginia Regimental History Series. 88 vols. to date. Lynchburg, 1982– .

Wallace, Lee A., Jr. *A Guide to Virginia Military Organizations, 1861–1865*. 2d ed. Lynchburg, 1986.

The Victorian Era

Chesson, Michael B. *Richmond After the War*. Richmond, 1981.

Engs, Robert Francis. *Freedom's First Generation: Black Hampton, Virginia, 1861–1890.* Philadelphia, 1979.

Fraser, Walter J., Jr. "William Henry Ruffner and the Establishment of Virginia's Public School System, 1870–1874." *Virginia Magazine of History and Biography* 79 (1971): 259–279.

Lindgren, James M. *Preserving the Old Dominion: Historic Preservation and Virginia Traditionalism*. Charlottesville, 1993.

Link, William A. *A Hard Country and a Lonely Place: Schooling, Society, and Reform in Rural Virginia, 1870–1920*. Chapel Hill, 1986.

Moger, Allen W. *Virginia: Bourbonism to Byrd, 1870–1925*. Charlottesville, 1968.

Moore, James Tice. *Two Paths to the New South: The Virginia Debt Controversy, 1870–1883*. Lexington, Ky., 1974.

Pulley, Raymond H. *Old Virginia Restored: An Interpretation of the Progressive Impulse, 1870–1930*. Charlottesville, 1968.

Rachleff, Peter J. *Black Labor in the South: Richmond, Virginia, 1865–1890*. Philadelphia, 1984.

Shifflett, Crandall A. *Patronage and Poverty in the Tobacco South: Louisa County, Virginia, 1860–1900*. Knoxville, Tenn., 1982.

Wynes, Charles Eldridge. *Race Relations in Virginia, 1870–1902*. Charlottesville, 1961.

Twentieth-Century Virginia

Brown, Elsa Barkley. "Womanist Consciousness: Maggie Lena Walker and the Independent Order of Saint Luke." *Signs* 14 (1989): 610–633.

Buni, Andrew. *The Negro in Virginia Politics, 1902–1965*. Charlottesville, 1967.

Ely, James W., Jr. *The Crisis of Conservative Virginia: The Byrd Organization and the Politics of Massive Resistance*. Knoxville, Tenn., 1976.

Gates, Robbins L. *The Making of Massive Resistance: Virginia's Politics of Public School Desegregation, 1954–1956*. Chapel Hill, 1964.

Gottmann, Jean. *Virginia in Our Century*. 1955. Rev. ed. Charlottesville, 1969.

Heinemann, Ronald Lynton. *Depression and New Deal in Virginia: The Enduring Dominion*. Charlottesville, 1983.

_____. "Virginia in the Twentieth Century: Recent Interpretations." *Virginia Magazine of History and Biography* 94 (1986): 131–160.

Holt, Wythe W., Jr. "The Virginia Constitutional Convention of 1901–1902: A Reform Movement Which Lacked Substance." *Virginia Magazine of History and Biography* 76 (1968): 67–102.

Johnson, Brooks. *Mountaineers to Main Streets: The Old Dominion as Seen Through the Farm Security Administration Photographs*. Norfolk, 1985.

Lewis, Earl. *In Their Own Interests: Race, Class, and Power in Twentieth-Century Norfolk, Virginia*. Berkeley, Calif., 1991.

Link, Arthur S., ed. *Woodrow Wilson: A Profile*. New York, 1968.

Pratt, Robert A. *The Color of Their Skin: Education and Race in Richmond, Virginia, 1954–89*. Charlottesville, 1992.

Silver, Christopher. *Twentieth-Century Richmond: Planning, Politics, and Race*. Knoxville, Tenn., 1984.

Wertenbaker, Thomas Jefferson. *Norfolk, Historic Southern Port*. 2d ed. Edited by Marvin Wilson Schlegel. Durham, N.C., 1962.

Wilkinson, J. Harvie, III. *Harry Byrd and the Changing Face of Virginia Politics, 1945–1966*. Charlottesville, 1968.

INDEX

The Hornbook of Virginia History: A Ready-Reference Guide to the Old Dominion's People, Places, and Past was designed by Douglas W. Price and Paris Ashton-Bressler of the Virginia Department of General Services, Office of Graphic Communications. Page layout was produced by Paris Ashton-Bressler using Macintosh IIci and Quarkxpress 3.3. Text was composed in Palatino Roman and Italic. Printed on acid-free Lithofect Plus dull coated paper, 70-lb. text by Carter Printing Company, Richmond, Virginia.